12
25

THE
UNBOUNDED
FRAME

THE UNBOUNDED FRAME

FREEDOM AND COMMUNITY IN NINETEENTH CENTURY AMERICAN UTOPIANISM

Michael Fellman

CONTRIBUTIONS IN AMERICAN HISTORY

NUMBER 26

Greenwood Press, Inc.
WESTPORT, CONNECTICUT ● LONDON, ENGLAND

Library of Congress Cataloging in Publication Data

Fellman, Michael.
    The unbounded frame.

    (Contributions in American history, no. 26)
    Bibliography: p.
    1. Collective settlements—United States—History.
2. Utopias. I. Title.
HX653.F44   335'.9'73   72-797
ISBN 0-8371-6369-2

LIBRARY OF CONGRESS CATALOG CARD NUMBER: 72-797

ISBN: 0-8371-6369-2

FIRST PUBLISHED IN 1973

GREENWOOD PRESS, INC., PUBLISHING DIVISION

51 RIVERSIDE AVENUE, WESTPORT, CONNECTICUT 06880

MANUFACTURED IN THE UNITED STATES OF AMERICA

For Anita

Man, like these passive things,
Thy will unconsciously fulfilleth:
Like theirs, his age of endless peace,
    Which Time is fast maturing,
    Will swiftly, surely come;
And the unbounded frame which thou pervadest,
    Will be without a flaw
    Marring its perfect symmetry.
                    —Percy Bysshe Shelley, *Queen
                    Mab, A Philosophical Poem*

CONTENTS

ACKNOWLEDGMENTS

For permission to quote from their manuscript collections, I thank the Boston Public Library (Margaret Fuller Manuscripts and Horace Mann Letters); the Harvard College Library (Margaret Fuller, George William Curtis, and Edward Bellamy Manuscripts); the Illinois Historical Society (Albert Brisbane Manuscripts); the Massachusetts Historical Society (Horace Mann Manuscripts); and the Paulist Fathers Archives (Isaac Hecker, Letters to His Family and Early Diaries). Material excerpted from the Ignatius Donnelly Papers in the Minnesota Historical Society, St. Paul, is quoted by permission of the Society. For their material aid, I thank The Woodrow Wilson Fellowship Foundation, the History Department of Northwestern University, and the President's Research Fund Committee of Simon Fraser University. For interest, aid, comfort, and criticism, I especially thank Anita Clair Fellman, George H. Daniels, Ellen Dubois, Hugh Johnston, Don S. Kirschner, Stanley I. Kutler, Richard W. Leopold, Robert H. Wiebe, and Bertram Wyatt-Brown.

Vancouver, B.C.
February 28, 1972

INTRODUCTION

"Thus in the beginning all the world was America," John Locke poeticized in 1690, and for generations European rationalists would see America as an open place upon which to construct societies based on their clarifying abstractions. As late as the 1820s, Robert Owen, the English factory reformer, shared this vision of America as an essentially spatial and social void, the most unspoiled ground for his New Harmony settlement. Earlier, seventeenth-century English Puritans had come to this new and undefined space to build their city on a hill to serve as an exemplar to the Old World of a social and religious style which they hoped would prepare them for redemption. But the Puritans always believed that, even in their highest conception, their worldly projects were of limited intrinsic value: they were only part of the greater task of preparing a special people in this cleansed place for the saving grace of God in the next world. To aid their endeavor, the Puritans implanted as firmly as they could authoritarian social forms in the new land. Worldly life, like spiritual life, was controlled and demarcated rather than experimentally free.

America, conceived of by both Puritans and rationalists as a special place, apart and yet not separate from Europe, was thus inherently restricted as the place for the enactment of worldly social salvation. During the seventeenth and eighteenth centuries, and even after the American Revolution, Americans continued to see themselves in some European context, even while serving as agents of reform. Until at least 1815, in political, economic, and ideological senses, Americans could not forget the primacy of their connections with Europe and its intellectual and political influences. In

addition, Puritan certainty about the inadequacy of this life's potentialities endured with considerable tenacity despite Puritan adaptation to the more scientific, less fearful eighteenth- and early
nineteenth-century visions of possibilities in this world. American
life, however set apart from European, was limited as well by traditional lifestyles; farming, craftsmanship, and merchandising in
elementary local forms long continued to carry the weight of day-
to-day meanings for the average individual. The authority of the
church, the paternal rule of the successful and well-born on the
local level, and the centrality of the family as the basic social and
economic unit waned slowly. Life in the late eighteenth century
remained essentially localized, yet the authority shoring up these
customary forms was being undermined by technological and intellectual currents of change. The American Revolution unleashed the
possibilities for more egalitarian political methods and forms,
which even the counterthrust of the new Constitution could not
entirely restrain. The improvements in transportation methods,
coupled with the growth of a more complex interrelated economy,
though not fully rationalized for decades to come within national
or even regional institutions, disrupted the local sphere of life. Science increasingly seemed to explode old myths and superstitions
and destroyed traditional explanations of the meaning of life, which
had upheld the church's authority. At the same time, men of science could not provide generally accessible or satisfying ideas or
values to take their place. The forms remained, less altered than
their content.

With a peculiar suddenness, all tradition seemed to be evaporat-
ing and every question about the nature of man and society reopen-
ing in the intensely mobile America of the 1830s and 1840s. Both
the recent removal of active military threats from powerful European nations and the slow death of the political and social customs
of deference to the old authorities were consciously realized in a
burst of democratic liberation during this period. The removal of
an ominous Europe threw Americans into a truly independent
search for a democratic identity. Jacksonian politics, the usual
explanation for this liberation, was merely one symptom of the
sweeping social and intellectual reorientation of Americans at this
time. Jacksonian politicians destroyed some of the few national
political institutions, thus attacking what were for them some of

the central symbols of an archaic, hierarchical social structure. Jacksonians attacked what they perceived as the old elite in the bank war. President Jackson also vetoed bills for economic construction through federal bureaucracies, thus, perhaps unwittingly, supporting a rising new class of local economic entrepreneurs. As antitraditionalist, nationally negative politicians, Jacksonians could not design a centralizing political and institutional framework for the age. Moreover, there was little public demand or even understanding for such a social solution. Jacksonians could not replace an old authority with a new one as their limited politics was but part of a wider movement against traditional authority.

Other Americans, committed to social change, if not to Jackson, were out to destroy false authorities and to create new communities conceived in freedom and dedicated to democratic life, to the primacy of the individual, and to voluntary association. They expressed in these ideals a sensibility of their special individual and social mission. They were eager to bring about the worldly salvation that they felt was the final result of their spelling out of the underlying natural law. This affirmation of natural order and its successful and total application to society would be the only possible proof of their own state of moral superiority.

This feeling of freedom from traditional limitations was both frightening and exhilarating. The past apparently was dissolved, and the shape of the future would be determined by immediate efforts. Future orientation created great anxiety as well as great hope: aspiration met despair when the responsibilities for the future were so enormous and when the need for fundamental choices was so overwhelming. As Fred Somkin has argued, Americans had no intention of building just another traditional society: "Abandoning the doomed past to the Old World, Americans were convinced that they had preempted for themselves and for those who could muster the courage to follow their example the most valuable of all temporal categories, the future."[1]

If correct actions were not now discovered and asserted, evil social arrangements like those of the European-oriented world of the past would certainly be reestablished in America out of ignorance of social truths. The boundlessness that many Americans felt implied forthcoming limits, for although they had never known such a moment of apparent freedom, this time would pass and new structures would emerge. Now was the time for the implementation of moral truth. "This is the uniquely important point," Arthur E. Bestor, Jr., insists—"an organized effort to shape them would be effective only during the limited period of time that [American] institutions remained in embryo."[2] Even now new institutions were beginning to take shape, albeit unconsciously. Businesses changed form in the process of growing in size and complexity. The canal craze and land speculations were wildfire expressions of economic expansion and commercial optimism. Some churches were losing their loosely organized sectarian quality and taking shape as national denominations with increasingly complex bureaucracies and subordinate associations. Still primitive civic governments were appearing in the nascent cities. Educational institutions multiplied, even close to the frontier. And yet all this development was occurring in incipient, fragile forms lacking in basic authoritativeness; they were trials rather than establishments. Without the creation of credible explanations for new social forms, the old orthodoxies remained as intellectual and cultural hindrances. In addition, without serious efforts to develop a reformist ideology freedom from the past could only deteriorate into mindless, materialistic boomerism and expansionism, making a mockery of the possible positive meaning of a new American democracy.

Abstract systems, based on idealist concepts of the universe, carried a special potency in a nation whose old cultural and institutional modes were crumbling and whose new forms were yet ill defined. No traditional usages, authorities, or antiquities served to validate adequately central ideas and practices in time present. For many Americans, the dying forms were merely rickety obstructions; social and economic changes were as yet open to formulation. A cleansing internal morality, the origins of which lay in a state of natural purity within each heart, could be enacted fully and finally. Unorthodox religionists and reformers of many varieties shared this vision of the imminent perfectibility of man and his society. For such reformers, social fluidity was the perfect matrix for the creation of some new and total community in which to contain absolute freedom. So much more powerful and satisfying than the partially thought-out and implemented American social efforts then most common, moral truth could now be applied in some great reform, could be unloosed from any previously customary restraints of birth, position, or social limits, and could rush forth to cleanse the world. Discovered whole, not by rational processes but by transcendent human intuition, knowledge would spring spontaneously from its source of purified moral sensibility in some ultimate, organically unified form. From certain knowledge of morally informed absolute truth, correct actions would be deduced to resolve, immediately and entirely, all personal and social contradictions. Some newly created source of authority could be found to winnow the false from the finer elements of the social ties of the past. In this fragmented nation the search for wholeness and finality in thought and action took on an especially urgent meaning.

American society, perhaps uniquely in time and place, offered few obviously unbreachable barriers to this direct application of the inner moral law. In a fluid society, where absolute reform seemed so possible to so many, any proposed framework was potentially valid and could not be discounted automatically. Of course, not all, or even most, Americans held faith in this reform vision, but nobody had the authority to rule a fundamental reform proposal out of general consideration. At a time when many thoughtful people believed total reform could be enacted, in some sense every ideological position had to be considered and every plan of action opened to possible testing. Freedom seemed close, and some wished to extend its liberating effects without check; at the same time the possibility for a new, structured community to contain, limit, and define that freedom also was very approachable. A strong tension between freedom and community existed within American culture as a whole and within the divided visions of many reformers. A whole range of new forms—from moral authoritarianism to unstructured, anarchic libertarianism—was opened to trial. By twentieth-century standards at least, each man was allowed a wide latitude in seeking the central truth and in attempting to prove its validity through deductive demonstration. Reformers disagreed about the definition of the central problem and the method of its correction, but a great variety of reform movements in this nation of flux was grounded in this general intellectual style, this utopian sensibility.

Utopian communitarianism, the most explicit formulation of the utopian sense of potential for perfected life, was the attempt to enact the perfect vision of truth through small model communities. Once perfectly harmonious social forms were established and broadcast in a community based upon a true balance between authority and continued freedom, presumably those forms would be spontaneously accepted by all Americans, and then, as Bestor writes, "infinitely reduplicated" in communities across the waiting land.[3] Such communities were not conceived of as escape mechanisms from general society; they were intended to bring on the total reform of America by offering the perfect community where no alternative community existed in anything but embryonic form. Neither opposed to the current of American society nor alienated from it, utopian communitarianism was rather one expression, if an extreme one, of the possibilities for social reconstruction at that time. It carried argument through abstraction a very long way, but it was not different in kind from the moralistic, deductive manner with which many more Americans sought to achieve their agreed-upon task of perfecting their world. Utopian thinking, in other words, though especially clearly exemplified by utopian communitarians, was by no means limited to them in all respects. The correction of evil, the reshaping of the formless through the discovery and the implementation of some key truth enacted in a cleansed small locale characterizes the process of much of nineteenth-century reform.

Just because they used a relatively simple deductive reformist method, one should not conclude that the intellectual and emotional approaches of the utopianists were uncomplex or that their efforts to formulate appropriate lifestyles were less problematic than those who have followed them in time. Although they lived in a culture which may appear to us as quaint and plain, the personal and social choices they faced were hard and often frightening to them. They were committed to action but feared being unable to realize their goals. They wanted to be free, but they also desired to submit to true authority. The personal origins of their efforts, their struggles to bring their ideas to fruition, their satisfactions and frustrations were no less difficult, no less significant than those of later generations. Their actions grew out of their desire to find and apply some meaning in a chaotic world. Though these reformers can be seen to have shared a cultural sensibility in the broadest sense of the term, they each as well made personal sense of their self and their surroundings.

I have tried to enter the world of the utopianists both to exemplify their efforts to mold ante-bellum American society and to explore the general nature of the reform thought of that era. Through such communities, utopian reformers sought to conciliate their images of the unstructured freedom they sensed around (and often within) them with their need for formalism, for authority, for community to shape freedom. American utopianists sought their general ideas wherever they could find them, and they looked to European thought for models and ideals to incorporate into their vision of the proper framework for the new America. There is a danger, however, of too easily placing American utopianism within some European "construct" as part of a more general "romantic vision": these reformers used and discarded, accepted and altered ideas within their own cultural context.

Many reformers outside the strictly utopian communitarian persuasion—both those who were more interested in shoring up traditional values and those who, even more than the utopianists, were antiauthoritarian in their quest for freedom—worked within the same cultural context as the utopian communitarians. They conveyed much the same intellectual and emotional style. For different reasons, but with often parallel effects, traditionalists explored new forms (such as public schools) in order to recapture an older authority, while some extreme individualists saw all forms of association as using up energies needed on the path to continual self-culture. These other explorers illuminate, through their similarities and contrasts with the utopianists, the inner-world view of mid-nineteenth-century American utopianism.

Beginning in the 1850s, dramatically demonstrated and symbolized by the Civil War, the social and intellectual reference points for reformers slowly shifted from a spirit of boundless potentiality toward more circumscribed, consolidated forms.[4] The date of inception of this shift is less crucial than what proved to be its long-term, slowly changing cultural ramifications. Indeed, the never clearly worked-out experiment with national government as a centralizing, bureaucratic agency during the Civil War and Reconstruction was quickly disillusioning. It was mostly abandoned during the 1870s, 1880s, and 1890s and was not replaced at the time with any other well-articulated conceptual framework of nationwide organization. Yet national consolidation in some aspects of theory and social practice, the building of broader and more complicated methods and forms of human interaction, eroded the direct applicability of the simpler ante-bellum utopian communitarian model. Urbanism, business corporatism, bureaucratization, standardization, and the acceptance of at least the symbolic necessity of a national community simply were not related to the ideal of a small, model community, however perfect.

In the later nineteenth century, utopian communities continued to be built, especially along the West Coast, but these organizations did not hold the public eye as did the earlier utopian communities. Model communities no longer seemed a naturally plausible solution for social ailments. Finding any single key no longer appeared sufficient in a world of such obvious and often terrifying complexity of social and even personal arrangements. In a national setting characterized by larger and larger reference groups and by the development of bigger and bigger institutions, relationships became more formal and political, more intertwined and manipulative. Utopianism, expressed in forms such as communitarianism, seemed a less adequate way of coming to grips with social problems.

Many men with their origins in the earlier reform ethos tried to remain in contact with events by making their analysis and reform proposals more complex and by adapting to political methods. However, thoughtful men such as these did not suddenly abandon their old ways of thinking and believing for new methods and goals, especially as any foundations for new authority were so uncertain. They tried to reconcile and to adapt to the new ideas and situations that they sensed without losing what they had felt to be true, even as the applicability of the past beliefs seemed to be dissipating. It was no simple matter for them to find an adequate and satisfying replacement for the utopian reform style. Indeed, much of that spirit remained for decades, applied seriously in shifting settings and in different ways but not utterly altered. Striking changes in reform thought and styles should not lead us to obliterate a certain continuity of frame of mind. Much can be gained by examining later nineteenth-century reform in terms of its antebellum precedents.

The hesitant and troubled movement of utopian reformers toward a more national political point of view and the lessening and final disintegration of the faith that the nation could undergo any such total reform characterized the fading of the utopian vision toward the end of the nineteenth century. Little belief in a new construction of freedom and authority within the confines of a model community withstood the clearly nationwide and socially interrelated crises of the late 1880s and early 1890s. National strikes, international cartels, urban sprawls of poverty, mob violence, and corruption all were "discovered"; small communities were places to be vacated by the brightest of the young and never entered by the newer immigrants. The focus for some new authority, the structures to contain the new problems and freedoms, clearly required locales other than utopian communities. By 1900, the closing date for this study, utopianism was only a rapidly fading memory.

As the nineteenth century ended, progressivism took the place of utopianism with the same suddenness with which utopianism had first appeared.[5] Process-oriented, limited in its sense of final goals, and proudly believing in the organic nature of political power and of bureaucratic methods, this optimistic new group of progressive reformers was concerned with limited but well-defined action, with building efficient national institutions to respond to massive social problems. Although they continued to exude a certain air of moral certitude, in keeping with most American reformers, they dismissed utopia. In their view it was a worn-out, escapist fantasy. The idea of discoverable, essential truth was meaningless to them, and though the assumptions behind their new intellectual overview proved less certain than they originally believed, they brought a basically new and nonutopian vision into the center of American thought about a reformed culture.

Today we are witnessing a questioning and assault on that frame of reference as the inadequacy of progressive programs to deal with human needs through large-scale social engineering and ameliorative legislation is becoming clearer. Social ideals are crumbling faster than social forms, and utopianism, as one tentative means to find a new order in an anxiety-creating, chaotic world, is again on the rise.[6] The new utopia is developing this time as a counterculture, as a repudiation of the values of a society far more structured and confining than ante-bellum American society. The very basic questions of personal and collective goals, of moral values, of the nature and relationship of freedom and community, so long considered closed, in a society apparently so firmly set upwards on a progressive path, are being reopened and reconsidered. It is for this reason above all others that the history of utopianism must be reexamined not as an odd item of antiquarianism or as the mutant offshoot of an extremely distant time and place, but as an intrinsic part of American reform, of that deeply held, if sometimes buried, desire to frame a just American democratic life.

THE
UNBOUNDED
FRAME

1

THE SUBSTANCE AND BOUNDARIES OF

UTOPIAN COMMUNITARIANISM:

ALBERT BRISBANE AND JOSIAH WARREN

An ocean of Social Error flows over Humanity, but so mighty is Truth, that one drop cast into it will purify and give life to its dead waters. That drop, we believe is the principles discovered by Fourier.

>—Albert Brisbane, "Association,"
> *New York Tribune,*
> March 29, 1842

The next purpose was to form a model village, taking it for granted that principles so very simple, so unassailable, so capable of scientific demonstration, and so indispensibly necessary to order, peace, abundance, and "security," only needed to be seen in their beautiful and consistent symmetry to be at once approved and adopted.

>—Josiah Warren, *True Civilization*
> *an Immediate Necessity*

I

Belief preceded experiment for mid-nineteenth-century utopian communitarian planners; only the unity and order of a perfect image of the true life could breathe truth into an actual social trial. From moral certainty correct action would be deduced. At this especially fluid point in American history the discovery of truth and its projection into exemplary communities seemed to many to

3

be possible as never before. In a chaotic society apparently freed from all inextricable social and intellectual limits, the distance between an absolutely abstract utopian conception and the plausible enactment of that vision was quite insignificant to many. Moral analysis seemed wedded to social pioneering. In this chosen nation, at this correct moment, human artifice was to be directly applied to the moral certainty which had informed it so clearly.

Although all utopian experimental thought of this period can be viewed in this setting, the nature of the truth from which all else was to follow varied widely. The manner in which utopians discovered and applied "scientific," discoverable knowledge, their methods when proceeding into and beyond experiment, their sense of community and of its import for the wider American society, were all similar, even as their goals for that society differed. For example, Albert Brisbane, the American translator of Fourier, wanted to build a large, closely structured, authoritarian community, while Josiah Warren, an early American anarchist, desired to foster a totally unregulated and individualistic group, the members of which would live together completely voluntarily. Their similarities display the substance of experimental utopian thought; their differences show its range.

Both men believed that American society was in crisis: it would either soar to perfection or plunge into chaos in the foreseeable future. The sense of boundlessness thus bred deep anxiety as well as enormous hope for the future. For example, they feared a reenactment of ageless European decay in an American setting, the recurrence of a uniformly repressive past from which Americans, first by immigration and then through the Revolution, had tried to escape. To avoid this, all memory of Europe and all of its social reverberations had to be uprooted before the true virtues could dominate this new land. Warren wrote:

> Already have we in this country made an alarming progress in the road to national ruin; and unless some effort be made to prevent the accumulation of wealth in the country, in the hands of a few, we instead of setting to the world an example of Republican simplicity, of Peace and Liberty, shall soon add one more to the catalogue of Nations, whom Aristocracy has blasted, and whom

inequality of wealth has precipitated from a comparatively prosperous situation to the lowest grade of degradation and misery.[1]

Brisbane believed that America had been granted an almost accidental period of grace early in her national experience and that this incredible opportunity had to be systematically exploited in building the reformed society before the otherwise inevitable social collapse imposed itself on the new republic. "We are moving onward to the misery of the old World; our present prosperity is temporary, and the great object which we, as a People, should have in view, is to take advantage of our favorable position, and effect peacefully a Social Reform before we sink into the poverty and ignorance in which Europe is plunged."[2]

II

In order to rescue America and to set it on the upward path to purity, a task which both men approached with energetic optimism and a little trepidation, Brisbane and Warren each devoted his life to a single truth which they both had discovered when they were young. Throughout the vicissitudes of their careers, they held to the prophecy of these ideals with such fervor that in their own minds their own personal identities merged with their sense of absolute truth. The ideal, not the practical, was the center of their lives.

For Brisbane, the central principle was "attractive industry"—work made pleasurable through mutual assistance and governed according to correctly understood laws of human behavior. This one underlying law, correctly applied, would catapult man into a golden age of fulfillment by solving all social problems. "Attractive Industry is the first remedy to be applied to social evils; it would replace the present poverty and anxiety by riches and contentment, and relieve the mass from those harassing cares and physical wants, which deaden the intellect, and smother or pervert all the higher sympathies and feelings."[3] Complete insight and total moral reconstruction were possible for men because absolute laws governed the world and only awaited discovery to be applied. Revelation was certain as it came from a source infinitely greater than human rationality. "The system of Association which we propose to the world, is not the plan or scheme of . . . mere human reason. . . . It is deduced from and based upon universal Principles, and is the application to the social relations of Mankind of the Laws of Order and Unity, which govern the Universe."[4]

Brisbane suddenly and cataclysmically discovered this vision of truth when he was twenty-three years old. The pampered son of a wealthy upper New York State land speculator, who was nevertheless the child of a culture in flux, Brisbane had been traveling and studying in Europe for four years when the "word," as written by Charles Fourier, struck him in 1832. He had been only numbly aware of social problems previously. Now he not only comprehended the questions but envisioned the solutions as well. A friend had given him one of Fourier's works which he opened to the chapter "Attractive Industry." He later reported that "I sprang to my feet, threw down the book, and began pacing the floor in a tumult of emotion. I was carried away into a world of new conceptions."[5] In a flash of insight, Brisbane experienced what he later described as the secular equivalent of conversion to a complete faith. "That experience enabled me to conceive [of] the religious exaltations of the past, where a fervent faith had revealed the glories of the spiritual vision."[6] His first impulses after his sudden insight were mystical. He was "possessed with the strongest desire to get away from this world and to be able by some means to participate in that grand, Cosmic life."[7] Brisbane first conceived of utopia as an abstract and pure emotional and intellectual system not tied to earth, and its author, Fourier, as no mere mortal. Seen through his inspired book, Fourier appeared to be an almost disembodied intermediary between universal truth and men. "I swear to you," Brisbane responded to the friend who had passed him the divine work, "that I remain in the greatest astonishment and admiration toward this book. What a brain there must be in this man."[8]

After a brief interlude of such awe-struck contemplation, Brisbane plunged into his life's work: the application and propagation of Fourier's beliefs in America. Brisbane felt that he had just been purged of more than personal doubt; he had found the full basis for saving the still nascent American society from an otherwise impending social degradation:

> These views of Fourier produced a great revolution in my
> mind. The darkness which had rested on human destiny
> was dissipated; light began to shine in. In the application
> of law to the social organism I saw an invariable guide
> for the mind in the great work of social reconstruction;
> I saw a scientific certainty taking the place of all the
> blind, futile efforts of human reason.[9]

Brisbane planned to make the earthly trial of Fourier's theory
in America and wrote to the aging utopian in 1836 that he was
engaging in land speculation. "If all goes well, I will soon have
enough money for ten newspapers and to put fifty men to work.
I am determined to make the greatest efforts to earn enough in
order to work out in one trial Fourier's system."[10] It seemed to
Brisbane quite natural to proceed directly from an abstract utopian
theory to an experimental utopian community. Brisbane had discovered not a rationalist program of reform, but a completed blueprint for the creation of an immediately perfectible community.

For Josiah Warren as well, the discovery of the "first principle"
came in a sudden conversion experience. As a young mechanic,
he had left Boston for Cincinnati, and there he heard of English
reformer Robert Owen's forthcoming community at New Harmony,
Indiana. He spent two years (1825-1826) as a participant in this
first important secular utopian experiment set in America. As the
community disintegrated, Warren became convinced that the
rationalism and belief in ordered social structures that were at the
heart of New Harmony had caused its downfall:

> Many a time while in the midst of them did I say to
> myself, Oh! if the world could only assemble on these
> hills and look down upon us through all these experi-
> ences, what lessons they would learn!
> There would be no more French Revolutions. . . . no
> more organizations, no more constitution-making, law-
> making, nor human contrivances for the foundation of
> society. And what a world of disappointment and suffering
> this experience might save them![11]

Warren thought all formalized institutions were false grounds for hope. Owen had "resorted to contrivances instead of discovering laws."[12] Thus the whole purpose of utopian experiment had been aborted: the individual members had been burdened with new restrictions rather than freed from them. "They have overlaid and smothered the Individual in the multiplicity and the complexity of Institutions."[13] After brooding over this turn of events, Warren found the true path—"Disconnecting all interests, and allowing each to be absolute despot or sovereign over his own."[14] He would reverse the moral values presented by Owen. This revelation came suddenly and totally. "[A] sudden flash of light upon our past errors [showed] plainly the path to be pursued. But this led directly in the opposite direction to that which we had just traveled!"[15]

Individualism for Warren was as absolute a moral truth as was Fourier's blueprint for Brisbane. Since institutions would no longer maintain prescriptive powers over the individual, they thus would become "subordinate to our judgment and subject to our convenience; and the hitherto inverted pyramid of human affairs thus assumes its true position!"[16] All institutionalized relationships were to be demolished and replaced by completely voluntary cooperation. The search for the true community for Warren was the quest for a social arrangement where no behavior or belief was dictated by external force and where, consequently, every action corresponded with personal desire.

> The true business of us all is to invent modes by which all these connections and amalgamated interests can be Individualized, so that each can exercise his right of individuality at his own cost, without involving or counteracting others; then, that his cooperation must not be required in anything wherein his own inclinations do not concur or harmonize with the object in view.[17]

The center of Warren's program was "equitable commerce," the cooperative exchange of goods and services, which would eliminate not only profits but money as well. Price would thus be concrete, derived from cost added to time spent rather than an abstractly determined source of profit. Economic life would be rendered down to its simplest, face-to-face components, and social intercourse would become voluntary, simple, and self-evident. Warren thought he had reached the foundation of social relationships: "Combinations and all the institutions built upon them are the inventions of man; and consequently, partake of more or less of man's short-sightedness and other imperfections; while Equitable Commerce is a simple development of principles, which, although new to the public, are as old as creation, and will be as durable."[18]

III

"Science," Josiah Warren declared, "is simple and definite, and therefore easy to comprehend and uniform in its results."[19] The absolute nature of scientific knowledge and its direct applicability to human relations were standard beliefs of nearly all intellectuals of this period. If truthful religious doctrine was not the goal for Warren and Brisbane, a kind of God was still very involved in the discovery of knowledge; science partook of the nature of revelation. From one central certainty, through the correctly informed scientist, all meanings would be derived. As Brisbane put it: "The Duty of God is to compose a Social Code, and to reveal it to man. . . . The duty of man is to search for the Divine Code. . . . It is manifest that human reason has not fulfilled its task. This neglect being now repaired and [Fourier's] code discovered, it only remains to make an examination and a practical trial of it."[20]

Both Warren and Brisbane were fascinated by music and mathematics, intellectual forms where deduction seemed to follow set patterns from fixed first principles. Some divine inspiration, not human reason, created the first principles. Social order could be derived, both thought, by a similar process of unfolding true action from pure discovered truth. Applying a "store of simple truths," Warren wrote, is like using "the elements of arithmetic, we have only to improve our modes of presenting them, multiply examples, and supply the demand for them."[21] The order of music, Brisbane concluded, was analogous to the order given to human efforts by universal law: "The human mind acting in unity with the Cosmic Mind creates in its sphere as the Cosmic Mind creates throughout the Universe; and the manner in which man distributes sound to produce musical harmony does not differ from the manner in which the Mind of the Universe distributes worlds to produce planetary harmony."[22]

Brisbane often reflected Charles Fourier's passion for numerology. Fourier felt that emotional propensities could be named, classified, and then projected into social arrangements called "Groups," which would be orchestrated further into combinations of Groups named "Series."[23] Certain numbers held almost magical qualities in themselves in these social equations; Fourier wanted to specify absolutely a relationship between divine order and social behavior. Brisbane's desire was to make every element of the theory practical; with the proper quantity of combined elements he would enact Fourier's perfect vision. "An Association is a Phalanx or a Series of Series, as a piano-forte is a Series of Octaves; and we can no more have social Harmony without a sufficient number of Series, than we can have musical Harmony without a sufficient number of octaves."[24]

On a less abstract level, however, both men were willing to be tinkerers, inventors utilizing elements of the emerging Western technology. They were fascinated rather than frightened by tools and craftsmanship, and they both wanted to make money to support their social reform efforts. Brisbane worked for years on pneumatic tubes; Warren created and patented, among other inventions, an early cylinder press and stereotype printing processes.[25] Warren and Brisbane did not justify these inventions as goals in themselves, however, but merely as techniques for helping to effect man's moral revolution. The experimental method was useful only when informed by a set of general social values. For example, Warren believed that printing improvements would result in placing the power of propaganda in the hands of the previously mute and dispossessed common man who was the greatest potential source of reform:

> Public influence is the real government of the world. Printing makes the governing power: therefore, among the preparations for the general introduction of these [reform] subjects, are a simplification of printing apparatus which brings the mighty power to the fireside and within the capacities of almost any one. . . . Thus is this and every other subject of real reformation rendered independent of the [corrupt] common press.[26]

IV

Utopian communitarians believed that all social experiment would be the concrete demonstration of a complete moral theory. Even if each element of action were partial and came slowly, all made sense as parts of a movement toward a cosmic truth that was only temporarily veiled. In 1849, Warren summarized his own absolutely unchanging, long-term efforts: "The theory has been for twenty years kept in the background, while a silent but practical development has been going on in different departments of business and investigation. It only remains to put these parts together at some one place, so that the whole may constitute a practical demonstration."[27] Even the smallest community, Warren believed, if it were based on correct principles properly integrated, would lead naturally, peacefully, and swiftly to a new social order in America:

> How large a tiny thing may become! How often it has been that with twenty men or women taking the right positions and working from the true inspiration for those results which alone can come from true principles, could successfully begin the revolution which is so much needed, that the growth from that beginning would naturally extend and march indefinitely.[28]

All moral truths, which were universal in nature, could be reached within one communal structure and would then expand almost spontaneously to enfold the entire nation. Brisbane concurred with Warren on the ideal of the model community: "If we know how to build one house properly, we can, by erecting others, build a City; in the same manner, if we know how to organize one Township rightly, we can, by spreading those rightly organized Townships, cover a country with them, and establish a true Order of things."[29]

Implicit in such a vision of community were somewhat transmuted memories of the traditional limits and values of the village. Both men assumed that a pattern of close personal interrelationships would be at the root of self-fulfillment, and that, rather than extending the community into cold, formal, institutional arrangements as the new cities were threatening to do, new, small, tightly knit units would be formed. A perfected social form thus would put group life back into its "natural" channels and would assure warm, certain relationships, which were neither too severely fragmented nor too collectively impersonal. American expansion would be formulated in a comprehensible, orderly, and sociable manner; the best qualities of the fading family circle would be maintained in the order of the new communities. Warren wrote:

> One after another can be added to the circle till those living in its circumference are too remote from the boarding house, the schools, and the public business of different kinds; then another commencement has to be made, another nucleus has to be formed, and thus in a safe and natural manner may the new elements extend themselves toward the circumference of society.[30]

Quite obviously, utopian communitarians believed that traditional social forms had failed to bring about adequate and correctly informed institutions. Chaotic and aimless politics, which deeply frightened both Warren and Brisbane, had been a chief symbol of the destructive process which had created this collective failure and which still barred the way to true reform; the idea that politics could be purified and could become the vehicle for national reform appeared impossible. True reform was a process directly opposed to politics, to the manipulation of man through uses of power. Balance of power and limits on power were not sufficient checks. Political rationalism and its ugly products had to be discarded for intuitively revealed total reform. Jacksonian politics were, if anything, cruder and more destructive than earlier American politics. Brisbane queried: "Is our system of politics, with its intrigues, cabals, demagoguism and mock patriotism, party animosities, calumny, detraction, and general falseness and duplicity of action, Christian? If not, is not some reform necessary?"[31]

Far better means had to be found than the infamous political process to bring about reform, both Brisbane and Warren felt. Concerning implementation, however, the positions of the two men differed most widely. Warren wanted to build his individualist-oriented community through tolerance of all points of view, with the leadership remaining as passive as possible. Brisbane imagined a totalistic corporate structure led in every action by a correctly informed elite.

Although Brisbane, shaping his argument to fit what he felt to be American tastes, was a great deal less authoritarian than his teacher, Fourier, he nevertheless felt that correct societies had to be imposed by properly discerning leaders. Complete knowledge of Fourier's well-defined code of human relationships was needed before a community could be built upon it, Brisbane asserted: "The first practical experiment in Association should be directed by persons thoroughly acquainted with its mechanism, and perfectly convinced of the goodness of the passions and of the truth of Passional Attraction as a social guide."[32] The first association had to be a total, integrated structure, not a partial trial, Brisbane insisted. The apparent solidity of Fourier's vision, complete as it was with engravings of huge unitary palaces called "Phalanxes" and filled with 2,000 disciplined individuals enmeshed in attractively regulated units for work and play, was to be realized in one giant effort in America by Brisbane. Individuals were to be called together to be transformed by a perfect, moral community. Social salvation was to be immediate, peaceful, and complete.

> We must drag man out of this cramped sphere, out of civilization; we must found Association, we must build a Palace for a Phalanx of two thousand beings, in which human nature will be fully developed by the stimulants of social life, and by those which the Series will call into action; we must build a Palace in which all branches of industry, art and science can be combinedly prosecuted . . . Association will have its Architecture,—and it will be the architecture of Combination, Unity and Harmony . . . one vast and elegant Edifice [will] replace hundreds of the isolated and miserable of our civilized Societies.[33]

Only through this new community could mankind's brotherhood, under a secular God of moral truth, be reclaimed. Once more the pattern of life would become natural and whole as it must have been when the cosmic order first imposed itself: "This chain is

nowhere interrupted; the destiny of the individual is closely connected with that of the race; the destiny of the race with that of
the planet; and the destiny of the planet with that of the solar-
system."[34]

Warren on the other hand rejected the notion of comprehensive
institutions in traditional civilization and in new forms because he
felt that prescriptive communities would merely repeat ageless
social evils: "General organizations, for a multitude of undefined
purposes, to which consent is to be obtained or obedience
demanded after the organization is formed (like those of states or
nations), will be sure to proceed in confusion and contest, in violence and crime, and to end in disaster, defeat and disappointment."[35] Every decision in a just community was to be determined by each man for himself; involuntary relationships had to
be deracinated before tolerance and voluntary cooperation could
bloom in each man's heart: "With regard to mere difference of
opinion in taste, convenience, economy, equality, or even right and
wrong, good and bad, sanity and insanity,—all must be left to the
supreme decision of each individual . . . which he cannot do while
his interests or movements are united or combined with others."[36]

When the individual was freed from all subjugation to institutions
and to other men, mankind would discover the true life. Warren
knew that this vision was "rather negative than positive," but he
felt the role of the reformer was to show others that no chains
of tradition or inherent social order bound them together and that
they could be the complete masters of their own destinies. With
this truth understood, men would then join together voluntarily for
love and mutual sustenance rather than for the coercive exercise
of power over one another. Communal life, Warren wrote,

> consists more in Refraining from doing, than in doing,
> more in with-holding our artificial obstacles to the opera-
> tion of the government of consequences, rather than in
> disturbing the harmonious and beautiful laws of natural
> order by our short-sighted and presumptuous attempts to
> rectify and regulate the perfect.[37]

For Warren, the only clear role of the leader was to display the
true path for others to choose; he would have no function within

a group of the converted. In itself, the community would exist as a neutral place liberated from all external law. Men could develop at will, outsiders would derive a sense of the true life, and the natural order of things would arise from the ashes of social regulation.

V

To apply their visions, both Warren and Brisbane participated in utopian experiments throughout their lives. Yet just as the experiments were never as central to these men as were their theories, the broader meaning of the communities is perhaps less significant than the impetus behind them. Warren led three small communities in Ohio: "Equity" (1830-1831), "Tuscarawas" (1835-1837), and "Utopia" (1845-1851). Then he headed East and founded "Modern Times" (1850-1862) in Brentwood, Long Island. In these communities, Warren helped to facilitate the moneyless exchange of goods and services and gave frequent lectures, but he neither controlled nor directed any activities. To a great extent these obscure communities appear to have had no formal organization. Some degree of mutual aid and convenience alone kept them intact. In addition to community experiments, for short periods of time while he was still in the West, Warren organized "Time Stores," where he sold goods at cost, adding only an obligation of work from the customer equivalent to the amount of time he, as shopkeeper, had expended in making the sale. Once he had demonstrated to his satisfaction that the voluntary exchange of labor could practically and peacefully destroy the profit system, he closed the stores.[38]

Brisbane's participation in actual experiments was always ambivalent: "No uncertain prospects should exercise any influence," he wrote to George Ripley in 1845. "The means must be in hand before we make any decisive movement. . . ."[39] Brisbane was afraid to take risks before he was positive of his scientific insights and before he had in hand all the capital and persons so carefully specified in Fourier's tomes: "When a sufficient amount of capital and a thorough knowledge of the Associative Science are combined, Association will be demonstrated practically, and the world convinced of its truth. . . ."[40] In 1844, at the very height of American interest in Fourierist experiments, Brisbane returned to the hearth of the theory, France, to gain reassurance that he knew the theory so well that he could will it to work in practice. He could not willingly commit his increasingly purified theory to trial. He wrote from Paris:

> As we in the United States are now entering into the sphere of practical organization, which at the outset must, of course, be more or less experimental, all the knowledge that can be obtained calculated to make our course clear and easy, shall be concentrated; and I shall receive from the friends of the cause here the results of their studies, and their advice and counsel.[41]

Holding all these reservations about experimental utopianism, Brisbane still thought that trials were natural extensions of his theories and that his ideas presumed eventual concrete application. Throughout his life he helped to formulate Fourierist communities. In the 1840s, he was involved in Brook Farm near Boston and later helped to foster the North American Phalanx in New Jersey (1843-1853). In the 1850s, he aided in planning a community in Texas, and, in the late 1860s, he sponsored a Kansas group. Almost exclusively, Brisbane advised rather than led these groups; his own predilections were for propaganda rather than for administration. He held back from these attempts to put into practice his social theories, yet he never lost his hope that one such group would prove him to be true. There seemed to him to be no open alternative to a compact utopian community for testing and implementing the ideal society.[42]

VI

In 1875, when almost no one remembered him or his ideas, Brisbane reflected on his life and excoriated the failure of communitarian experimentation which had unfairly discredited Fourier's, and his own, theories in the minds of the American people. The theory, universal and certain, had never been given a fair chance because the impatient American populace had demanded premature and incoherent concrete trials. The theory had been dragged down to public ruin by breathlessly active advocates; Brisbane had been prevented from enacting the moral revolution through quiet, complete, and unitary theoretical elucidation: "I was influenced by a low practical ideal . . . little associations. . . . The grand idea was discredited. I should have preached the 'Divine Code,' the doctrine of the passions as a revelation of the human will; universal Association; the history of man as the Overseer of the globe. . . ." Brisbane no longer felt in the least capable of enacting utopia within a community; he now believed that his task was to make the theory even more clear and self-evident so that other men could place it into process. "What blow can I strike? I can't do much at propagation, no time for that. I must strike a pivotal blow. I must do something central and leave it to others to carry out my work. . . . I must give the world a Method of Study, and leave it to others to do the useful work."[43]

Methods for finding and propagating the true beliefs had not changed at all for Brisbane. "I acknowledge but one Mind on the earth—the great Fourier," he repeated in 1875.[44] His early conversion experience maintained its dominance over his mind as he again tried to proceed from revelation to properly deduced action. He went over and over the same ideas, trying to restate them in some new form which would revolutionize others as he had been changed so many years before. It was as if each new intellectual effort by Brisbane wiped out all past experimental attempts by proving that they were misunderstandings and misapplications of a thus really untried theory. In his last public message, *General Introduction to Social Sciences* (1876), he began:

> Fourier's theory is not in the least understood by the public in general—in fact it is radically misunderstood;
> . . . no practical trial of it has been made which in the remotest degree either proves or disproves the truth of its principles. Those interested in the subject will now be able to obtain a full and exact idea of what Fourier's theory really is.[45]

Brisbane was unable to comprehend or adapt to the emerging politically aware, more nationalist reformism of the America of the late nineteenth century. He feared that general and beautiful truths, central to his own faith in truly revolutionary moral reform, were now unappreciated: "These radicals are the weeds in reform, springing up and showing an ugly crop of ideas where flowers and fruits should grow with the perfume . . . of great truths."[46]

In his frustration at the disinterest of new reformers and of the post-Civil War public in his theories, Brisbane became increasingly authoritarian in his remote intellectual backwater. Sometimes he thought he must impose the truth upon others who were too disordered to accept it voluntarily. Within Association, men would be "overruled, restrained and silenced," he wrote in 1868. "If liberty were left to them they would soon destroy the organization. The 9/10 of men, in our incoherent civilization have no right to free will . . . there must be introduced a just and wise authority which may be absolute when necessary." A rigid code, derived from both Fourier and the simpler ideal of a "military regime," would govern all behavior. Then a true social application of theory, dictated by an inspired leader, would be bound to work. The followers would expunge their individuality and become integers in a grand system: "Everyone will know exactly what kind and degree of deference or courtesy are demanded from him, and will soon learn to conform to them."[47]

At other times as he grew old, Brisbane returned to his more characteristic vision of a peaceful utopian community. When he projected some small and quiet organization, he felt closer as well to the source of his theory: that special, suprageographical place, impossibly distant from the America in which he now lived, was to be built, ironically enough, back in Fourier's France. He desired, he wrote in 1887, "to buy a little domain in France—say between Paris and Tours, and on it organize a little Association of intelligent and refined persons, a large combined Home of production, self-supporting."[48]

"Having spent a long life in trying to find the roots of human miseries, and believing that I have succeeded," Josiah Warren lashed out in 1873, "I freely admit that I am very sensitive to the manner in which the results of a long life's labor are received."[49] As he grew old Warren felt that alien forces had prevented the enactment of his ideas, that even his pretended friends misunderstood him, and that he alone, by clinging to his moral insight, could survive the chaos of general social destruction in a haven of intellectual and emotional certainty.

Warren set himself apart from every other reformer. He refused all notions of class conflict and would not attack capitalists as younger anarchists urged. One professed disciple he denounced for linking him to the French anarchist Proudhon, another he attacked for watering down the concept of individualism and for flirting with corporatism. He alone had the correct insight.[50]

Warren sometimes identified the outside forces that plagued him as "subtle and (to general observation) the most incomprehensible obstacles," which were "cunningly contrived devices to set the public against [my theories]."[51] But the furies howling against him could only be clearly understood as a carefully coordinated "Popish" plot established to crush him: "My course now is to make the friends of [my theory] familiar with the designs and modes of action of the Jesuits, for I can account for what is passing . . . upon our ground in no other way than by admitting that we are already beset by them."[52] Foreign legions of destruction could discredit and erode the applications of righteous theory, but the core of belief would remain intact, even when finally Warren alone knew what was true.

2

UTOPIAN COMMUNITARIANISM,

FREEDOM, AND THE SEARCH

FOR EXTERNAL TRUTH:

ISAAC T. HECKER

> O man! were thy soul more pure, what a world would
> open to thy inner senses.
> —Isaac T. Hecker,
> Diary, May 16, 1843

I

Although he recoiled to a great extent from self-discovery and
searched for external structures to give his life a more secure basis,
Isaac T. Hecker never escaped the sense of personal crisis he most
deeply entered as a young man at the utopian community of Brook
Farm. That place symbolized for him escape from the traditional
forces that lay in his past, outside of his control. At Brook Farm
he gained what would prove an often illusive hope: that his growth,
rather than mere adaptability to externalities, would henceforth be
the core of his life. The search, for him, when he was at his strongest, overwhelmed the desire for form. He wrote while at Brook
Farm:

> The past is always the state of infancy. The present is
> an eternal youth, aspiring after manhood, hoping wist-
> fully, intensely desiring, listfully listening, dimly seeing
> the bright star of hope in the future, beckoning him to
> move rapidly on, while his strong heart beats with
> enthusiasm and glowing joy. The past is dead. Wish me

not the dead from the grave, for that would be death reenacted.[1]

The conflict between a process of continual personal growth and submission to some belief system larger than the self—so central to reformers in an age of cultural unease—is especially clearly posed in the anguished life of Isaac T. Hecker. Hecker revolted against a smotheringly conventional household which was placed in an unsettled general environment. His crisis led him first to Brook Farm and then into the Catholic priesthood. However, this was no teleological march to final personal resolution; within the church, as leader of a reformist, missionary American Catholic order, he remained doubting, striving to come to grips, through a close-knit, inspired community, with the developing nation around him. He sought to discover and then to impose authoritative intellectual and institutional forms to lend clear values to himself and to his whole culture, but he never could tie off the surges of free life that he felt within and around his person.

II

Isaac T. Hecker was born in 1819 in New York City, the youngest son in a middle-class German immigrant family. His father, a little-mentioned figure in Isaac's life, was evidently shiftless and unstable; his older brother John was the dominant man in the household. Isaac always remained attached to his mother, a devout Methodist, who was a firm yet fair disciplinarian. He was also close to his brother George. The warm family worked together harmoniously with the exception of the excluded father.

Isaac went to work at a young age in the Hecker family's new bakery. All the brothers devoted long, hard hours to develop this fledgling business, and Isaac had little time for formal education or for personal contacts outside of the family and business circle. As a group, the Heckers were interested in radical Democratic politics; they supported the Workingman's party and the Loco-Focos who followed. It was through this activity that the Heckers became acquainted with Orestes Brownson who at this time frequently lectured to radical groups in New York City. In these days Brownson was a "come-outer," an anti-institutional and anti-dogmatic Protestant preacher to the left of Unitarianism. Isaac's contacts with a broader world began as an offshoot of this family activity.

In 1841, for the first time, prompted by his new advisor Brownson, Isaac began to discover French and German idealism, probably in their distillations in Brownson's *Boston Quarterly Review*. He avidly and excitedly probed this new view of the world, and by the summer of 1842 he was deeply troubled and confused by his abrupt confrontation with new intellectual problems. He was frightened and suddenly alienated from his ordinary surroundings and work. This crisis deepened in the fall of 1842: Isaac felt he was retaining external control only with the greatest difficulty. Prompted by his feelings as well as by his concerned family, Isaac went to Boston to visit Brownson in December 1842. By now, Brownson was filling many of the paternal roles which Isaac's own father had failed to perform and which his elder brother could at best have partially filled. With Brownson's approbation and sponsorship, Isaac went on to the Brook Farm community in January 1843 for what was to prove an upsetting six-month stay. There, Isaac had the time, the will, and the active encouragement to explore his feelings. But while Brook Farm was a place conducive to personal exploration, it also heightened his tensions.

Externally Isaac appeared to the others at Brook Farm to be generally friendly and intelligent, although at times somber and moody. John Van Der Zee Sears, who then was a young boy at Brook Farm, wrote this general impression later: "He was a faithful and competent baker for several months; usually happy and cheerfully interested in all that was going on, but occasionally taking a day off for fasting and prayer."[2] Once, he gained an accidental view of one of the symptoms of Isaac's discontent when he was at play with another child. They were "on the far side of the pine woods," when they "came upon Mr. Hecker walking rapidly up and down in the secluded little dell that he used as a retreat. He was wringing his hands and sobbing so violently that we two scared children stole away, awed and mystified."[3] Publicly, Isaac never lost his self-control to such a degree.

George William Curtis, perhaps Isaac's closest friend at Brook Farm, understood more clearly Isaac's troubled existence: "He has certainly a great heart, more delicate in his character than I [had first] thought, with a constant force, nervous, not muscular strength."[4] Decades later, Curtis claimed that at this time he began to call Isaac "Earnest the Seeker."[5] He sensed Isaac's diffidence and realized, at least on later reflection, that what some felt to be Isaac's arrogance and remoteness was a necessary part of some very private search.[6]

On one level, Isaac considered Brook Farm a pleasant episode and a period of personal cultivation and warm friendships. At first he felt put off, an alien among a close, tight group: " 'Mr. Hecker' is pronounced in tones different from those in which they address others. I don't know but that I will be unable to become one of their Community. . . . Their life is different, and my speech is not understood or else misunderstood."[7] By the end of his stay, this had changed and Isaac did feel like a welcome member in many respects. He thought that his experiences in the community environment had broadened him and that he had undergone an extraordinary experience: "Much, very much has my character grown and been influenced in the period I have been here. . . . Many of my dreams and earnest aspirations have been met here. I do not ever anticipate such society and refining amusements again."[8] On the surface, Isaac thought that he had gained equilibrium and insight. His visible, happy adjustment, however, was strikingly split off from his continuing deepening sense of personal crisis.

Isaac at age twenty-three was groping toward maturity, and home and business—the regular expectations of a "normal" life as defined by his family and environment—suddenly all seemed empty. He had leaped far beyond their values: "I have grown out of the life which can be received through the accustomed channels of the circle that has surrounded me. I am subject to thoughts and feelings which those around me had no interest in—hence they could not be expressed. . . . I would be chilled to come back. . . ."[9] The outward definitions of the good life that he had always assumed now meant little to his sense of personal integrity. Beyond his rootlessness, he was enormously uncertain as to what he would become or what would be the basic dimensions of his identity. Nothing around him seemed real or concrete any longer; his capacity to assimilate what he experienced into an integrated whole had broken down. He was numbed and excited, powerless and questing, sad and thirsty for hope, alienated and longing for human contact:

> I feel that I am tossed about on a sea without a rudder of my own. What drives me onward or where I will be driven, is to me unknown. My past life is to my present like that of another person, and my present is like a dream. Where I am, I know not. I have no power over my present, and do not even know what my present is. And whom can I find like myself? And who can I speak to that will understand me? This makes me still, lonely and I can not wish myself out of this state. . . . All appears to me as seeming to be, nothing real, nothing that touches the life in me which is seeking for which I know not.[10]

Isaac felt compelled to rebel against the traditional social forms adhered to by his family, yet he regretted this haunting feeling with all his conscious might. Everything about this conventionally defined, materialistic, middle-class life he was expected to lead had become repulsive because it would block the search for personal growth that he now believed, and feared, was to be the only real path to truth. He felt forced to choose a morally absolute spiritual existence over the falsely insulated comfort of family and material goods.

> Two paths are apparently open to my view. . . . One road is to live in the world, in business, and make life as agreeable and as happy as possible, to accept all things with the least possible evil—a sort of computation of interest. The other road is to leave all, be self-denying, upturn all my former views of life, go into the blind world of chaos, of life, and live on.[11]

An enormous and terrifying gulf now separated him, seemingly irrevocably, from his past. He wrote to his family: "I would, if possible go back; but the impossibility of it I cannot express. . . . When I say my mind cannot be occupied now as formerly, do not attribute this to my wishes. This is my fear, which makes me almost despair—makes me feel that I would rather die than to live under such thoughts."[12]

If reviving the past were impossible, he had to confront the new, no matter what the consequences. Liberation from the past was neither joyful nor suddenly complete. A new way of living, utterly necessary for continuing the search, would not define the new man: the utopian setting would serve as a neutralized base for explorations. In comparison with Isaac's home, the community meant release from suppression and freedom to quest. His home now loomed in his mind as the antithesis of a place for self-discovery: "I cannot return to my old life, I do not see how I can [live] there; everything is so contrary to it."[13] Yet in terms of what he had been, Isaac felt further disassociated from life while at Brook Farm; no road was blocked, nothing was real externally, nothing was defined for him. Isaac sensed this both as he was about to enter the community and when he was established there.

> The life that was in me was consuming me. . . . It is a life in me which requires altogether different circumstances to live it. This is no dream. If it is, then I have never had such a reality.
>
> All is dark before me, impenetrable darkness. I appear to live in the centre. Nothing seems to take hold of my soul, or else it seeks nothing. Where it is I know not. I meet with no one else around me. I would that I could feel that some one lived in the same world that I now do. Something cloudy separates us. I cannot speak from my real being to others. There is no mutual recognition.[14]

With the sense of wholeness of a troubled young man, Isaac rejected all the values he associated with the old life. These values, which he categorized as debasingly worldly, stood absolutely opposite to his new search for ideal purity: "I would not take it upon myself to say that I have been 'born again', but I know that I have passed from death to life. Things below have no hold upon me further than lead to things above. . . ."[15] To return to even part of the old values became an impossible compromise of his unfolding new identity. In order to establish absolute, if temporarily unknown, new goals, he rejected what he felt to be the very core of the old. He penetrated to the nexus of the conventional family and business, and, with revulsion, despair, and also determination, he turned against heterosexual union.

> To keep company with females, which you know what I mean, I have no desire. In the sense of marrying, I have no thought. Company for such an end I feel an aversion for. In my whole life I have never felt less so. If my disposition ran that way, marrying might lead me back into my old life. But oh, that is impossible and to give up, as I have to do, a life which has often been my highest aim and hope, is done with a sense of responsibility I never imagined before. . . . It lies deeper than myself, and there is not the power in me to control it.[16]

During the months at Brook Farm, Isaac fluctuated between excitement and calm, revolt and longing to return to his old life. At one point, he had assured his family, "A little time; and, I hope, all will pass away."[17] Internally, Isaac was torn between a desire for concrete, even sexual union with others and a demand for etherealized individual purity. He tended to identify all sensual experience and all physical relationships with the world, but at the same time he longed for such contact, which he hoped would spring him from the prison of the self. He wanted to be absorbed in some absolute truth, utterly freeing himself from worldly compromise, yet he also feared the consequent loss of his membership in society. He was unsure which was the road to real freedom, to true union.

This conflict is most evident in Isaac's relationships with women. He interwove his vision of perfect beauty with his direct experience with women: his concept of woman as physical being was diffused and filled with idealized qualities. His uncertainty and extreme fluctuations in dealing with women when he lived at the utopian community demonstrate his attitude of looking back at the mundane society from which he was divorcing himself and forward to some better vision of life. Isaac was forced to confront this dichotomy while at Brook Farm, and his management of this question was symbolic of the tensions inherent in his desire to deal positively with the problem of freedom.

Isaac always adored his mother, even when in deepest crisis. While at Brook Farm he wrote to her telling her of his inexpressible gratitude, for the "tender care and loving discipline" he felt she had given him. He was positive "that there is nothing that can ever separate us. A bond which is as eternal as our immortality, our life, binds us together which cannot be broken."[18]

This idealization of his mother partially parallels a haunting dream that recurred frequently during the first phases of his crisis. A bisexual, diffuse, other-worldly, but nevertheless extremely exciting image of women welled up in this dream. This was a vision that contrasted sharply with any overt sexual confrontation that Isaac was likely to have had in his highly constricted youth. His tension and confusion were deepened by this dream. Isaac was aware that the implication of this vision took him away from the kind of relationships that eventually would have been demanded of him in his old life.

> I saw (I cannot say I dreamed; it was quite different from dreaming; I was seated on the side of my bed) a beautiful, angelic being, and myself standing alongside of her, feeling a most heavenly pure joy. It was as if our bodies were luminous and gave forth a moonlike light which sprung from the joy we experienced. I felt as if we had always lived together, and that our motions, actions, feelings and thoughts came from one centre. When I looked towards her I saw no bold outline of form but an angelic something I cannot describe, though angelic in shape and image. *It was this picture that has left such an indelible impression on my mind.* For some time afterward I continued to feel the same influence, and do now so often that the actual around me has lost its hold. *In my state previous to this vision I should have been married ere this, for there are those I have since seen who would have met the demands of my mind.* But now this vision continually hovers over me and prevents me, by its beauty, from accepting anyone else; for I am charmed by its influence, and conscious that, should I accept any other, I should lose the life which would be the only one wherein I could say I live.[19]

At Brook Farm, Isaac's most comfortable relationship was with pretty young Ora Sedgwick. Isaac was extremely fond of her, but in an entirely brotherly fashion. To as great an extent as possible, he defined her in terms of his dream: as an ideal of love rather than in any sense a potential love partner. Ora struck him as "one of the loveliest, most love-natured beings that has ever met any heart. There is more heart in her bosom, more heaven in her eyes than I have ever felt or seen in any other person. She is not lovely but love itself."[20] Isaac's crescendo of praise removed all physical qualities from Ora and turned her into a woman to be worshipped. Distance and unattainability increased love and allowed Isaac to bypass every concrete tie in favor of an idealized affection.

In sharp contrast, Isaac was confronted sexually by the reigning beauty of Brook Farm. The gorgeous and experienced Almira Barlow was in her early thirties, the mother of three children, and separated from her husband. (She was, Zoltan Haraszti suggests, perhaps the physical half of Hawthorne's raven-haired, earthy Zenobia.[21]) Almira, enormously attracted to Isaac, was not dissuaded by whatever reticence he may have shown toward her. One afternoon, as Isaac describes in an extremely confused entry in his diary, she came to his room, "and we entered a conversation, a—communion." Isaac tried to "keep myself at a certain distance, so that instead of being the motive, it is visa-versa [she advanced on him]. Instead of I *dissait aller* [*sic*] to her, she put forth her-what-love openly to me."[22] Whatever may have been the culmination of this meeting, it was certainly an overt confrontation. Almira represented the physical union which was half of Isaac's desire.

When they were apart for some time, Isaac offended Almira, perhaps purposefully, by the coldness of his letters. At the same time, he vaguely speculated on some clearer, more permanent relationship with her in the future.[23] He realized with pleasure that Almira had come closer to him than had anyone else, yet he consciously increased his sense of distance from her.[24] Isaac, deeply shaken, confessed to his diary that he was willing to break with Almira: "I would resign myself to it, not I confess without a deep struggle and considerable effort, but I could and would do it." Isaac tried to convert his memory of Almira into the comprehensible, ethereal images through which he had always been able to understand the sisterly Ora. He mused of his wish to "stamp her image deeper upon my heart and engrave . . . my memory" with a completed and thus beautiful idealization.[25] He could write openly of her only when their relationship was totally neutralized.[26] Even as they were first being tried, these fragile new ties with other people slipped from Isaac's grasp. Isaac rejected this sexual relationship and the kind of freedom from social regularity which it represented. Later he used the idealized image as the exclusive basis of his dealings with women.

The lack of inherent, formal demands in the utopian environment of Brook Farm allowed Isaac to experiment generally, as he had in his relationships with women. Before and after, Isaac was able to channel his confusion to a greater extent along paths which he felt were provided by his place in more recognizable social settings, but during his utopian experience, when he faced real alternatives, Isaac stalled off all important choices until he could again see himself as having decisions forced upon a more passive self. Isaac would never entirely eliminate confusion, but he would learn to confine it and would move as far as possible from the necessity for constantly choosing in a seemingly chaotic world.

After his severe test at the utopian community, and in part because of its impact upon him, Isaac focused, with as great a degree of exclusiveness as possible, upon personal purity as the right path. During the latter part of his stay at Brook Farm, he turned away from his fellows, though without renouncing them completely, and returned more completely to his lonely and prideful search. Increasingly he looked at his ties with other young community members as means to his personal development rather than as relationships with a special value of their own: "My life is not theirs; theirs is not mine, though they have been the means of giving me much light upon myself."[27] Isaac's relationships at Brook Farm had always been uncertain, but moving away from others there and into himself, he felt he was finding a somewhat clearer direction, a more consistent path with fewer obstructions to attaining pure insight.

It is impossible to chart with any accuracy the exact time at which Isaac abandoned the tentative relationships so tenuously opened during his utopian trials. He never fully thought out this movement away from personal experimentation toward ideological absolutism nor was he ever able to make this shift final. His change was not a complete choice between seemingly concrete things. Nevertheless profound changes did occur and Isaac the seeker became Father Hecker, the Catholic priest.

Isaac felt hesitant, even guilty, about the position he was so uncertainly assuming, yet he felt compelled to clarify his emotional status, to sort out more satisfactorily the elements of the world around him and put them into a more uniform and comprehensible ideology. He tried to transcend his sense of flux, of human limitations, of the need for experimentation: "This incessant activity of men is most devilish," Isaac wrote. "I would that all men should be made to stand motionless and still be men. All relations that we have are evil. And I would overcome death by not coming up to it. Let us go inwards instead of outwards. I will stop writing for this is foolish, and springs from a diseased irritation."[28] Isaac now wanted to become a still, almost nonexistent being, through whom truth could operate. He wished to be moved entirely by God rather than to move himself: "I want God's living work to do. My labor must be a sermon, every motion of my body a word, every act a sentence. My work must be devotional. I must feel that I am worshipping. . . . It must be Christ doing in me, and *not me.*"[29]

Even as Isaac was increasing his sense of self-denial, he continued to long for contact with others. He felt he still met others at Brook Farm only "by coming down into my body, of which it seems to me that I am now almost unconscious. . . ." At the same time that he was "filled to overflowing with love, and with desire for union," he sensed the increasing impossibility of worldly union given the asocial beliefs of which he now felt quite certain (despite his longings): "But there is no one to meet me where I am, and I cannot meet them where they are."[30]

In this estranged mood, Isaac visited Fruitlands, another Massachusetts community, where he made his final attempt at utopian living (July 11-26, 1843). Bronson Alcott's severe asceticism appealed to Isaac as he turned against the undefined experimentation of Brook Farm, which now appeared, as had his home earlier, too mundane to be of any further help to him: "I cannot accept this place," he wrote as he left Brook Farm; "it is not self-sacrificing enough for me; it does not attempt enough for me; it is too much like society."[31]

Now looking for some more external force to structure his quest for purification, Isaac had reached the limits of any utopian experiment. In actual practice, despite what was often their theoretical completeness, these communities were merely attempts at *creating* order by the members themselves; but Isaac could not believe that Brook Farm or Fruitlands represented order or were even well ordered. He was now certain that he needed an environment in which the form in no way depended upon his own creative efforts. At Fruitlands, he felt, a more constructive, positive definition of freedom existed than the one he had learned at Brook Farm: "They wish to purify the soul and body by the discipline of restraint and constraint. Instead of 'acting out thyself,' it is 'deny thyself.' Instead of liberty it is mutual dependence. Instead of the doctrine 'let alone,' it is 'help each other.' Instead of tolerance it is love. It is positive not negative."[32]

But Isaac's optimism was short-lived; he was soon completely disillusioned with Fruitlands. After all, these too were only men trying out ideas, men who could not assure him authoritatively of the truth of their concrete social forms. Isaac had already rejected their kind of approach: "They are too near me; they are not high enough to awaken in me a sense of their high superiority which would keep me here to be bettered, to be elevated."[33] With that realization Isaac was ready to leave Fruitlands, and after three more weeks at Brook Farm, to return to New York for a visit home. He never again returned to utopian attempts.

After these nine tumultuous months, Isaac went home still excited, yet more stable and self-assured. Still confused about the future, he was more certain of having found the right ways to begin. If he was not sure of the best course for a true life, he knew for certain that the old way was bankrupt for him. Isaac was positive before he went home that he had become a new person, unrecognizable to his family. He had led, he felt, a totally different life, one which had given him unique and enormous insights. He now existed, he trumpeted quite dramatically, on a much higher plane: "They expect what was to return home, their idea, their memory to be reproduced, but how they will be surprised to find a new being in place of the old. Alas! Isaac has gone, has fled. . . . They will clasp my hands with a cordial clasp and they will shrink as from the grasp of an electric rod."[34]

Though once again living at home and working in the family bakery, Isaac knew that he was only briefly postponing a new life based on his purified vision. He still had to determine his exact new role, but he felt prepared to enter an active, reformist life. This clear, though not fully worked out, realization kept Isaac from despair and made his return home only a visit, unrelated to his central quest.[35]

The following spring, April 1844, Isaac went to Concord to study the classics with his Brook Farm acquaintance, George Bradford, to prepare himself for the clerical life that he now felt was the best vocation for him. He lived with Henry Thoreau's mother, flirted with the idea of tramping in Europe with Henry,[36] paid several brief visits to Brook Farm, and tried to study between springtime, sylvan daydreams.[37] He felt submissive and therefore peaceful, "like a child full of joy and pliability," without the need of "externality." He felt quiet and full of faith, with "no more potency than a babe. . . ."[38]

Certain of his religious calling, urged by an old aesthetic attraction as well as by recent letters from Orestes Brownson, his mentor, who was also at the threshold of the church, Isaac calmly and easily turned to Catholicism. Converted to most aspects of the religious life during his stormy utopian experience, the last steps into the church were anything but cataclysmic. During the summer of 1844, in New York City, he undertook the formal process. The euphoric spring of 1844 was Isaac's happiest period. His outward conversion seemed a confirmation, at least for the moment, of having passed through the eye of his crisis, beyond trial, into personal purity. He felt that everything outside and inside was motionless, quiescent, perfect:

> I feel very cheerful and at ease and in perfect peace since
> I have consented to join the Catholic Church. Never have
> I felt the quietness, the immovableness and the permanent
> rest that I now feel. . . . No exterior realizations, events
> or objects can disturb the unreachable quietness, nor any
> event break the deep repose I am in. I feel centered,
> deeper than any kind of action can penetrate, feel or
> reach.[39]

In a paean to the Virgin, Isaac further expressed his spiritual communion. He felt completely enfolded in a unitary, purified, and
timeless future and lifted out of the implications of worldly existence: "Ah! so sweet, so harmonious, so delightful, like an angel,
like the bride of the pure and bright soul adorned for the nuptials,
do I see the future beckoning me with a clear, transparent smile
onward to her presence. . . . Ah! thou eternal, ever-blooming virgin, the Future shall I embrace thee?"[40]
Even on the edges of this ecstasy, however, Isaac realized that
his old doubts and fears were not to be quashed. If he had established a direction to follow, he had only coped with part of his
feeling; he had not banished the rest. As he chanted praise to the
"Virgin-Future," he saw that it was after all only he who was
singing and that his troubled, always tentative existence would continue: "But ah! my eyes, when turned upon myself, lose all sight
of thee, and meet nothing but my own spots and blemishes. How
canst thou love me?"[41] Isaac's haunting vision of an angel in his
bed, which he thought he had overcome, returned: "I feel that the
spirit world is near and glimmering all around me. The nervous
shocks I have been subject to, but which I have not experienced
for some time back, recurred this evening. I am known to spirits,
or else I apprehend them."[42] In the dreaded places not covered
by conversion, the old uncertainties again arose. Conversion to an
absolutistic faith added a further complexity as well as a shape to
Isaac's search for meaning. Conversion was not total; it did not
resolve the problems Isaac had confronted in the ambivalent utopian
setting.

III

In 1845 Isaac sailed to Europe to study for the priesthood with
the Redemptorist Fathers. He studied first in St. Trond, Belgium,
then in Wittem, Holland, and finally in Clapham, England, where
he was ordained a priest in 1849. He remained in England until
1851 when he returned to America—his permanent home.
These were years of confusion for Isaac. During his novitiate,
in which he was expected to fulfill certain formal learning require-
ments, he instead plunged into self-mortification. He was unable

to concentrate on studies, which seemed irrelevant to his inner quest. In 1848, he wrote of this period: "I was as it were inebriated with love so that I scarcely know what I said or did. . . . The end of my proper activity, I said to myself is its destruction. . . . My faculties were drawn and concentrated to such a degree towards the centre of my soul that I was as one bereft of his exterior senses and activities."[43] In no sense could Isaac rid himself, or even pretend that he could purge himself, of the inchoate confusion of his self-discovery. Although the forms of the priesthood might comfort him to a degree, they remained, to a large extent, just external forms.

When Father Hecker returned to the United States in 1851, he, with a small group of converted American Redemptorists, began English-language missionary tours. For the next six years, these priests, drawing from their American Protestant backgrounds, developed methods and arguments for appealing specifically to American audiences.[44] During these active years, Hecker developed the position that led in 1857 and 1858 to his break with the European-based Redemptorist Fathers, and to his founding, with the approval of the Pope, of the first American-based order of priests, the Paulist Fathers. Hecker believed that the Catholic church had a special mission—to make America a more unified community. Out of chaos, through the aegis of the Paulist Fathers, America would be purified and made whole. In order to fulfill this role, the church had to adapt to American surroundings with American leaders using American evangelical techniques. This new, independently developed American Catholicism would then, Puritan-like, rejuvenate the church in the Old World. Hecker's reformist technique was to work two ways: to fuse America with positive, binding tradition and to fill the old forms with a new, youthful spirit.

After Hecker and four others broke with the Redemptorists and formed their self-consciously small and tightly knit new community, they remained bound together more by their sense of special, immediate mission than by concrete institutionalized regulations.[45] Hecker wrote in 1862: "Seven priests who stand on their own feet are better than seven hundred who lean on each other—can accomplish more, *will* accomplish more. I feel as if we were nursing a young giant."[46] Hecker now had a deeper appreciation for the special role of a small innovative community than he had when he was at Brook Farm. He thought that this religious order could fulfill, for people like himself, the longings stirred but not settled by utopian experiments:

> What was attempted by those engaged in such movements as Brook Farm, Fruitlands, and other places of a similar character, the religious orders in the Catholic Church have always realized. . . . The inmost sentiments of our hearts, the lonely dreams of our youth, the demand of our manhood for self-sacrifice and heroism, are not only understood, but fully appreciated, and all the means to this fulfillment are offered to us in abundance.[47]

Closely sheltered and guided by the order, the firmly rooted individual priest could work actively and in concert with other like-minded men in changing the outside world.[48]

Cohesion within the missionary community was not, however, sufficient grounds for real success; the group also had to attune itself to the environment around it: "A new religious community, unless its activity is directed chiefly to supplying the special needs of its time, wears itself out at the expense of its true mission and will decline and fail."[49] The Paulist order was founded on the belief that the old Irish-dominated Catholic church in America had failed to communicate with native Americans and that Americans really would want the church if it were offered to them in ways which they could comprehend. Hecker was certain that the church could lend a community of faith to an otherwise shapeless and chaotic conglomeration of peoples: "The Catholic Church alone is able to give unity to such a people, composed of such conflicting elements as ours, and to form them into a great nation."[50]

The conditioning effect of American liberty left individuals so free to act, Hecker thought, that they could be led more easily to the church than could the citizens of a more tradition-bound society. American solitude had led to an extreme state of meditation and contemplation.[51] This introspective individualism bred insight and personal virtue, and virtuous men would be most likely to find the truth:

> The form of government of the United States is preferable to Catholicism above other forms. It is more favorable than others to the practice of those virtues which are the necessary conditions of the development of the religious life of men.
>
> This government leaves men a larger margin for liberty of action, and hence for cooperation with the guidance of the Holy Spirit, than any other government under the sun. With these popular institutions men enjoy greater liberty in working out their true destiny.[52]

Under these conditions a unified national Catholic community would arise spontaneously once the truth were made known. Hecker's own writings were bent on calm, thoughtful explanation to the broadest possible non-Catholic community. He began a mass publication society for books and pamphlets and started magazines for both children and adults.[53] Finding appropriate means to communicate the truth as he saw it was Hecker's central tactical problem. Once America was converted, this most youthful of Catholic nations would serve as a chosen community to rekindle active Catholicism throughout the world: "We must make Yankeedom the Rome of the modern world. . . ."[54]

If America and Rome were to be fused in the future, certain qualities of each would have to be subdued to create the mixture. Hecker confronted the conflict between community and individual freedom especially clearly in terms of the Paulist group, which he saw as a sort of microcosm of a potentially Catholic but still individualistic America: "The civil and political state of things of our age, particularly in the United States, fosters the individual life. But it should do so without weakening the community life: this is the true individualism. The problem is to make the synthesis. The joint product is the Paulist."[55]

In order to attract converts to Catholicism generally and to Paulist membership in particular, Hecker continually emphasized the importance of individualism within the church. The Paulist should retain his independence; he should fight all unreasonable demands which might compromise his integrity: "*Individuality is an integral and conspicuous element in the life of the Paulist.* This must be felt. One of the natural signs of the true Paulist is that he would prefer to suffer from the excesses of liberty rather than from the arbitrary actions of tyranny."[56] To ensure the spirit of voluntarism, the Paulists demanded as the basis for membership a kind of compact rather than formal, traditional vows. Whatever the difference in effect, the symbolic independence of American priests was fortified. Individualism, thus strongly stated, was to be countered in the individual priest by "a strong, nay, a very strong attrait for community life."[57] The sense of harmony within a Paulist should naturally lead him to yield—*not* sacrifice—to the common good. If necessary, final appeal could be made to the head of the order who would establish the truest possible relationships within the group: "At the head of affairs must be a true Paulist—that is to say, keenly sensitive of personal rights as well as appreciative of such as are common."[58] In 1868, writing in the *Atlantic Monthly,* James Parton, the non-Catholic journalist and popular historian, characterized Hecker's notions of individualism and community:

> Jefferson says, all men are equals. True says this American priest, because they are all brothers. . . . This Paulist community therefore is conducted on American principles: "the door opens both ways"; no man remains a moment longer than he chooses; and every inmate is as free in all his works and ways as the son is in the well-ordered house of a wise father.[59]

The developing structure of the Paulist community, in addition to conversion and priesthood, gave Hecker the greatest sense of stability and the most extended period of tranquility that he ever was to know. His need for guidance by an external force, his thirst for community, and his desire to bring reform to America were all satisfied in this Catholic order. Hecker did not feel that he had renounced his sense of experimentation as a Paulist. The struggle to establish and to propel forward a distinctly new community of priests put him in the vanguard of Catholicism. His faith gave him the feeling that, after his long personal struggle, he was now leading, reforming, shaping the whole nation through the Paulist community. In many respects he could feel that he was leading a new utopian experiment. This utopian feeling was limited by the degree to which Hecker felt submissive rather than active. So far as he

felt guided by an unseen truth, which expressed itself through eternal European institutions and was merely applied to the American
present by himself, Hecker was anything but the utopian experi-
menter. Finally then, Hecker had a problem of focus: should he
emphasize the activist, reformist element of his movement or
should he stress its place in an almost ageless tradition? Hecker's
happiness at this time was based on the feeling that the greater
tradition and his specific community were joint expressions of the
correct vision of the age and that his actions were the fruit of his
insights into history. His faith that history was turning his way
meshed his sense of experiment with his need for submission;
experimentation and the need for absolute faith met.

This balance did not last. Toward the end of 1871 Hecker began
to suffer from headaches, loss of appetite, "sleeplessness and
excitability of the nervous system."[60] He fell into a deep depres-
sion and by the following summer was totally unable to continue
his Paulist duties. He went south for the winter and then spent
two miserably lonely years traveling in Europe. In 1875, he
returned to New York, but still unable to function adequately, he
lived with his brother George for four years. From 1879 until his
death in 1888, Hecker resided with the Paulists once more.
Although he was able to write and talk with others, he never
regained a firm footing.

During this long breakdown, Hecker felt that his ability to act
in this world was meaningless and that he had to submit entirely
to God who was trying him. Somehow he had lost his nerve. He
felt, as he sometimes had in his younger years, utterly ridiculous
before others—a "big *fool*."[61] He was no longer able to say mass.
His attempt to do so in 1885 was described by one of his fellow
priests: "[Hecker] began to weep and cry in a very mournful way
and aloud . . . he blubbered out the words like a school-boy being
whipped . . . he was deeply affected and patted the floor with
his foot, sobbing aloud and acting like a child with an unendurable
toothache."[62] Hecker thought God was toying with his soul, that
he was utterly powerless, that all outward forms were empty in
comparison to his personal torment. Whereas in his early crisis he
had hoped for future, even worldly glory beyond his torment, now
he could see only death as the conclusion of this loveless trial.
Hecker wept to a friend in 1885, "God revealed to me in my

novitiate that at some future time I should suffer the crucifixion. I have always longed for it; but oh, now that it has come it is hard, oh, it is terrible.''[63]

Finally, then, all Hecker's feelings collapsed into a numb expectation of death. This disintegration is a credible comment on his earlier years only insofar as it shows the tensions under which he had continued to live. When he finally fell away completely from active participation in the world and when he lost his ability to deal with his always conflicting viewpoints, he could no longer function.[64]

IV

At no time in his life, not even during this final collapse, did Hecker turn against his experiences. He never renounced his utopian past as a total error; he never dismissed social and moral reform. Rather, he continued to deal with the problems he first fully confronted at the utopian community. He never completely buried his sense of freedom under the authority he sought. His life was a continual quest for the correct management of freedom within community; his sense of possibility was not overcome.

In contrast, Orestes A. Brownson, Hecker's early mentor and fellow convert to Catholicism, utterly renounced his reformist past. Brownson's denial of his own early life and Hecker's view of this renunciation offer another angle from which to look at the way Hecker dealt with freedom. From the outside, both men's paths, from reform to the church, appear quite similar, but internally their attitudes were very different.

Both in religion and in politics, from 1840 to 1844, Brownson repudiated all that he had stood for and rushed to the opposite extreme. He turned to political conservatism from, as he stated it, his former position of the "impracticable radical."[65] From his religious position to the left of Unitarianism, he shifted to the Catholic church. His new alignment was purposefully the negation of the old. Thus he concluded that "the condition of liberty is order, and that in the world we must seek, not equality, but justice. . . . Liberty is not in the absence of authority, but in being held to obey only just and legitimate authority. Evidently I had changed systems, and had entered another order of ideas."[66]

As freedom now meant authority for Brownson, so the old boundless concept of freedom was now totally wrong. As authority must be absolute to be true, it could be contained only in one way and by only one institution. Thus he urged Isaac into the church as he too was on the verge of joining in 1844: "If you enter the Church at all, it must be the Catholic. There is nothing else."[67] Conversion consummated the search for truth. Truth in the form of the church was to be completely accepted; this acceptance ruled out the process of further searching.[68] If the church were true, "then to refuse to accept it is to refuse to submit to God. . . . Our logic allows us no alternative between Catholicism and Come-outerism. But we have tried Come-outerism."[69] For Brownson, the intellectual trial was over.

Beneath this dichotomy between universal intellectual systems, Brownson believed that religion was the only true force running counter to lurking human irrationalism. In *The Spirit Rapper,* written in 1854, he turned viciously on reformers and, hence, on his own past. In this story, a spiritualist, who serves as the symbol for all reformers, casts a spell (as does, in other contexts, all irrational reform) over another man's wife, who is a deluded feminist, and lives with his victim in adultery. Reform thus is unnatural, a manifestation of the devil, the result of mere sensuality, an expression of the anti-Christ. Religion is a rationalistic method to counteract these evil forces. All thoughts straying from the one true path are flowers of evil. This evil surrounds us as well as welling up from within. Thus all subjective searching must be uprooted:

> You will never root out that superstition by denying the existence and influence of demons. The remedy is in religious faith, in cultivating a firm trust in God, in obedience to His commands,—and in the firm persuasion that all dealing with devils is unlawful, and that all regard paid to signs, dreams, and omens is superstitious and sinful. . . . No good can come from seeking knowledge by forbidden paths, and much evil is sure to come.[70]

Late in his life, Hecker wrote a series of articles on Brownson in which he disassociated himself from his teacher's renunciation of individual personality and social reform. Some of the depth of feeling in his critique might be attributed to Hecker's need to free himself from the intellectual and emotional sway of Brownson, this most paternal figure in his life. Hecker refused to turn against either the motivations of the reformers or the quality of their positive suggestions. He wrote: "We were guileless men absorbed in seeking a solution for the problems of life. Nor as social reformers at least were we given over to theories altogether wrong."[71] Hecker thought that Brownson was destroying his personal worth when he refused "to describe and develop and solve *subjective* difficulties." In arguing against personal probing, Hecker felt, Brownson destroyed his natural contact with contemporary American problems: "He should, in my opinion, have set to work to unravel the peculiar entanglements and minister to the moods of the New-Englanders of our day."[72]

Brownson's narrow way of logical argument and historical proof of truth, Hecker wrote, meant the destruction of the viability of Catholicism in America. A total rejection of experiment and the demand for absolute submission throughout one's life would lead Catholicism away from its developing ties to America. Hecker concluded that Brownson "had forgotten the bridge by which he himself had reached [the church], if, indeed, he had not actually turned about and broken it down."[73]

For Hecker, conversion did not mean destruction of his own past. Although he searched for absolutism, he could never renounce his special quality of questing. He endlessly juggled experimental freedom and obedience in a tortured manner, but he could never divorce himself from this tension necessary to maintain both his personality and his relevance to American society.

3

UTOPIAN COMMUNITARIANISM AND
THE ASSERTION
OF ABSOLUTE AUTHORITY:

JOHN HUMPHREY NOYES

I have begun to discover that I am fearfully and wonderfully made; that I am a glorious kingdom in myself. . . . When I have completely ascertained the limits, character and resources of this kingdom, quelled all the rebellions which waste it, and secured the revenue which is due to its king, I shall be prepared to assist other sovereigns in like enterprises.

—John Humphrey Noyes to His
Mother, September 9, 1835

I

One February day in 1834, twenty-three-year-old John Humphrey Noyes preached to a startled New Haven congregation that he who sinned was not a Christian and that some men could be Christian in this life, freed from sin. As have all creators of a church within a church, Noyes included himself in the elite; he declared himself purged of sin and thus perfected.

Immediately he began to convert others and to construct a sect based on this heretical doctrine of salvation in this life. Other New England religionists at this time still insisted that certain knowledge of salvation was beyond man's power to obtain and that new propensity to sin always lurked within each breast, but Noyes would build a new church based on absolute cognition of already obtained salvation. As steward of the cleansed morality, Noyes would usher his followers into a perfected community. He wrote that "the erection of a church, in which perfect and everlasting holiness shall reign at the center while believers at every stage of discipleship shall find in it a home, is a work which remains yet to be done . . . before the kingdom and dominion under the whole heaven can be given to the saints of the Most High."[1]

As well as being one of the most daring of nineteenth-century reformers, Noyes was one of the brightest, most logical, and most willful. The extraordinarily broad and dramatic rebellion that led him to his New Haven declaration and to the long-lived, well-constructed communal social structure in which he later manifested his vision forms the clearest example of authoritarian utopian communitarianism in America. The emotional and theological bases of his efforts for moral reconstruction, the means of social control used to maintain a following, the relationships of the saved elite to the wider world, and the tensions leading to the final disintegration of his efforts were all played out by Noyes with an unusually radical and dramatic clarity. Above all else, Noyes was a rule-breaker toward all social conventions and a rule-maker in relationship to his followers. He imposed on his community that which he knew, with towering positiveness, to be true, and he denounced, from his self-assuring utopian fortress, the iniquities of a damned society.

Although he was intensely intellectual and self-analytic, Noyes never called himself a rationalist. Most communitarians raised dangerous topics around which much of contemporary society built walls of repressive silence; Noyes went beyond the formulation of subversive questions and fully enacted his new views of social structure, the family, and sexuality. He was always outspoken in his criticisms of American norms of belief and behavior. Unlike the more abstract communitarian thinkers, Brisbane and Warren, Noyes felt that ideas were auxiliary to the actual construction of a complete social and personal life. In estimating human nature, though he valued the mind, he never used it to deny the nonrational impulses he felt. Nothing in men should be hidden, Noyes insisted: "I maintain that a really healthy man is omnivorous in the largest sense of the word. He has an eager desire for everything. . . ."[2] He valued all his feelings and was unafraid of his intuitions. The systems of thought and the communities that he founded were attempts to make concrete every element of his intellectual and his emotional life. Social mores that interfered with the process of realization were struck down. Noyes' efforts demonstrated both the powers and the limits of his insights, which, with his great abilities, he was more able than any other nineteenth-century reformer to cast into formal molds: "If you are governed by an instinct that comes from a power that is above you, then as a matter of course and necessity, you will do things that you do not understand yourself—your actions will be better than your thoughts; and an explanation of your doings will follow after."[3]

II

As he passed from youth to young manhood, Noyes stormed through an emotional and intellectual rebellion. Coming from backcountry New England where orthodox, revivalist religion remained the strongest system of thought, Noyes phrased both his personal and his ideological crisis in religious terms. He reshaped theological language and concepts at the same time that he disassembled and rebuilt his own life. He reconstituted all his relationships—with his parents, with mankind as a whole, and with God. From this youthful rebellion Noyes evolved a radically new emotional and religious position for himself, an ideology that he employed in founding a utopian community based almost exclusively on the resolutions of his own rebellion.

Noyes was born in 1811, the son of a modestly successful Vermont merchant and politician. After graduating from Dartmouth in 1830, he read law. Suddenly at a camp meeting he had attended only to please his mother, in September 1831, he was converted to a religious life.[4] (Such special pleading by a relative often led nineteenth-century converts to the revival scene.) Noyes left home in 1832 for Andover and then Yale Theological Seminary.

Noyes was stunned but unsatisfied by his conversion and his later religious training. Despite his great moment of revelation, his path through life seemed muddy. "My mind seemed to lose its faculty of self-control, and I was for several days at the mercy of my imagination," Noyes later wrote of this juncture.[5] His conversion left him unexpunged of skepticism. He wanted assurance of his salvation in an absolute, final manner. This was more knowledge than orthodoxy could provide: "I have been wishing today I could devise some new way of sanctification—some patent—some specific for sin, whereby the curse should be exterminated once for all."[6] Overwhelmed by a sense of doom, driven to escape the state of doubt, Noyes searched, within the customary religious language of his immediate environment, for a new intellectual framework to insure inner certainty. He wanted a second conversion: "The transition from the double-minded state to perfect holiness requires a radical conversion as really as the transition from impenitence to the double-minded state. Thus I learned to turn my back on my first conversion and press toward a second."[7] Soon, in February 1834, the second conversion came: "Three times in quick succession a stream of eternal love gushed through my heart, and rolled back again to its source. . . . I knew that my heart was clean, and that the Father and the Son had come and made it their abode."[8] The following day, Noyes made his New Haven declaration of freedom from sin. Denounced by his teachers, his license to preach revoked, he was driven from the confines of Yale in May 1834. His ouster mattered little to him for he had been born again, this time perfect and with a new ideology that swept aside all external structures and internal doubts: "And now my old conscience was gone. Its questioning no longer interfered with the dictates of my spiritual guide. [I attained] a feeling which a child may be supposed to have when it is fairly weaned from its mother."[9]

After his expulsion from Yale, Noyes' mother urged him to return home to Vermont, but he went instead to New York City to preach and to gather a congregation. In a further crisis, he freed himself from all fear of death: "From that time [on] I have acknowledged and felt no allegiance to death . . . I shall never die in fact or in form."[10] After a short period of hard work with Theodore Weld, Noyes began to wander around the city, eating and sleeping little, drinking, and visiting brothels, exalting in his newly discovered freedom from external authority and from what he called "the petty tyranny of fashionable morality." "Loosed . . . from my grave-clothes," he spent the next two years tramping through New England, begging for food and shelter.[11]

While he drifted, Noyes resisted all appeals to return home where he felt he would be compelled to submit to his mother's authority.

Uncertain of his own role, he was not about to be reduced to a mere dutiful son. He wrote home, November 12, 1834, "Am I a boy or a man? Am I sane or crazy? Am I a wretch or a servant of God? . . . I pray you believe by the help of God that I can best manage my own matters, and let your heart have peace." He threatened to exclude his family from his life if they challenged his vision in any way: "Family considerations have become with me subordinate to my relations to God, and, if there is any conflict between them, the first will be sacrificed without faltering." Finally, he demanded that his mother resign her domineering role over him: "Give me up, Mother, for the Lord's sake give me up! You must either learn the Amen or I cannot walk with you."[12]

Late in 1836, Noyes did return home, but on his own terms. He insisted, as his mother wrote of him, "that all who expected to attach themselves to him must take a subordinate place and have confidence in him as qualified by the special grace of God to take control both spiritual and temporal." In 1838, Noyes brought his bride Harriet Holton into the family home; she placed herself under his rule, as did one of his brothers and two of his sisters. Only Noyes' mother refused his absolute authority. She pleaded, "How could I, who had so long been the acknowledged head of the family, consent to give up the control with which I believed God had invested me? . . ." Noyes did not give equal validity or equal authority to his mother's version of God's word. Using his influence over his siblings and his wife, he battled his mother for power over the family and finally was able to ostracize her. "I was treated with decent civility," she later lamented, "but with a cold reserve that made my home anything but pleasant."[13] She refused to capitulate to her son and left home as the one holdout from his image of salvation. In 1839, however, she reversed her position publicly confessing, "the testimony that I now give to John H. Noyes as being to me a teacher and father in spiritual things."[14]

By careful and relentless pressure Noyes had reversed roles with his mother, breaking the traditional structure of parental rule and rebuilding authority on his own basis. Until her death in 1868, outcroppings of her resistance to him would sometimes reappear, but he repeatedly suppressed what he termed her "self-esteem" and her "haughtiness." He diagnosed her condition as a false belief in her own knowledge of divine truth which led her to attempt

to establish herself as an authority contradictory to him, and pre-
scribed a lobotomy of her will: "This delusion, which hinders her
from becoming a child and which embarrasses all our operations,
should be removed." Even before he was born, his mother had
discredited herself by marrying Noyes' father, whom Noyes felt
was "an ungodly man," who "taught us . . . to worship money
and to live for this world."[15] Noyes' father had become a hopeless
alcoholic, dominated by his wife. When Noyes forced his mother
to submit, he heaped ashes upon his despised father as well. After
a sleepless night in 1841, Noyes' mother came to him and told
him that he had faults as did every other mortal. But by this time
Noyes' self-possession was unchallengeable and he could easily
crush any value she placed in herself. "He soon convinced me,"
she wrote, "that my feelings were under the delusion of Satan
. . . he was answerable in these things to God alone, his maker
and employer."[16]

Many years later when his son Victor rebelled against his authority, Noyes committed him to an insane asylum. Noyes believed
only his own rebellion was permissible; self-discovery was for him
alone. His son, as his mother earlier, had to submit to his word
as law. Noyes refused to allow his son to become a man; he tried
to stop the progression of the generations. Noyes declared to his
son that if he insisted on continuing his rebellion he would be
imprisoned forever and that only if he gave back his will to his
father would he be released.

> You will have to be modest enough to acknowledge that
> you have been insane (which you have hardly done yet)
> and wipe out all notions that you have adopted during
> your insanity, and begin again as a little child. Till you
> do this, I do not believe you will escape confinement in
> some form, even if you should be discharged from the
> Asylum.[17]

In his theology the young Noyes rebelled against the traditional
epistemological limits imposed by his orthodox teachers and
insisted that he embodied absolute truth. The devil was as real for
Noyes as for all good Calvinists, but unlike them he was certain
that he had freed himself from sin and consequently could do holy

battle against Lucifer. Those who sin, he repeatedly insisted, are of the devil. The perfect are as visible as the damned and can be recognized by their absolute knowledge of salvation:

> The mind of Christ not only apprehends freely the mysteries of God, but detects readily the impostures of the devil; so that the spiritual man is firm and steady in the truth of the gospel. . . . They who are "tossed to and fro and carried about with every wind of doctrine," are babes, i.e. carnal believers. Spiritual believers are stable-minded.[18]

The possibility of spiritual certainty for others would be reestablished, Noyes believed, by a new "Primitive church," recreating the communalism of those early Christians who preceded the builders of the corrupt "church in Rome." The original congregations had been based on a covenant with God. As had God's first concord with the Hebrews, Noyes insisted, the second covenant had cleansed of unrighteousness all those who accepted it. God had purged not only present but all future sin as well and had granted the perfected group liberty from worldly law. The newly freed men were thus obliged to establish new rules; they could not passively follow traditional dictates. The saved were in Christ, "but not *under* the law of commandments or the law of sin or death."[19] The Primitive church had been redeemed, Noyes declared, by the bodily resurrection of Christ in about 70 A.D. Christ had kept his word as indicated several times in the Gospels and had come a second time within a generation. Thus the Primitive, redeemed church had not been related to the later, apostate Roman church, whose word had, for all these centuries, meant nothing. Noyes believed that history was cyclical and was about to repeat itself with another coming of Christ, and that a second Primitive church, modeled on the first, had to be prepared for the day of resurrection. The general structure was fixed but the precise date of the new coming was uncertain; Noyes could be apocalyptic while avoiding millenarian hysteria and could calmly but surely build a second Primitive church.

Noyes' absolute vision would provide the foundation for the new, perfect community. The saved, constituting a theocracy, would enact God's word. Democracy—each man controlling his own destiny—could not be trusted as the truth had been discovered only by special individuals:

> If our organization is from God, it is not liable to the objections which are justly urged against despotic governments. We can trust God to order our measures and appoint our officers, though we could not men. If no God is recognized, the next greatest source of authority is undoubtedly the people; but if a God is recognized, all officers must derive their authority from him.[20]

Solutions to current social evils, a process which Noyes would have called triumph over sin, could be established only within a disciplined community. Noyes was quite aware of the problems and potentialities of contemporary American society; his response, as it had been in his personal crisis, was couched in moralistic, religious terms, but it closely resembled the frameworks proposed by other utopian communitarians. He too felt that a small community could establish his vision of the true life, later to extend to the general public: "The sin-system, the marriage-system, the work-system, and the death-system, are all one, and must be abolished together. Holiness, free-love, association in labor, and immortality, constitute the chain of redemption, and must come together in their true order."[21].

III

Immediately after his return to Putney, Vermont, in 1836, Noyes began to gather a flock of believers. By 1840, he had started to lend formal, institutional shape to his following, a process which was solidified after the group was forced to leave Putney in 1847, and was reconstituted the following year in upstate New York as the Oneida Community. These communities were expressions of Noyes' ability both to break accepted taboos and to impose absolutely his views about social conduct upon his proselytes. He developed shrewd methods of regulating behavior, which, when added to what must have been his extraordinary charisma, kept the nearly five hundred members in tight rein. Because the community was so long-lived, lasting in Oneida until 1879, the relationship of the separated, redeemed group to the wider, unsaved society constantly perplexed Noyes and his followers. As Noyes knew, his views were heretical and in constant danger of censorship. Periods of withdrawal alternated with periods of missionary zeal, and hopes for establishing new communities vied with the need to exercise tight, centralized control over the one place Noyes was confident he could always master.

Noyes instructed that "afflatus," the communal spirit, orchestrated by a "medium," a strong leader, was the essential element of all successful utopian experiments. All assertions of individualism had to be subordinated to this collective spirit. Only the agreed-upon primacy of the group will could guarantee communal survival: "Our opinion . . . is, that the long quarrel between afflatus, and personality will be decided in favor of afflatus, and that personality will pass into the secondary position in ages to come." Thus securely based, the community should provide a total environment for the individual, replacing worn-out institutions with a complete and unified social structure: "The highest ideal of a successful Community requires that it should be a complete nursery of human beings, doing for them all that the old family-home has done and a great deal more."[22]

Those who entered Noyes' communities had to surrender all claims to self-governance and to submit to the discipline of the dictatorially led group. Noyes was intent on nothing less than the complete restructuring of personality, with the new forms based on his own certainties about life. Every element of the old life had to be pulverized before new men could be systematically constructed under his own direction. In order to evolve to perfection, each member was to deliver all worldly possessions to the group, to purge himself completely of his conceptions of his personality, and to swallow imposed regulations without challenge or even doubt:

> We want only those unalterably convinced, and who by religion are one with the Community not only in theory but in spirit. . . . Joining the Community cuts a person off from such worldly ties and connections as stand in the way of improvement, substituting spiritual relations

for merely natural ones. It calls persons to deliver their past lives for criticism. It implies the giving up of trivial personal habits and tastes for the general harmony. The freedom to go and come at will, irrespective of others, must be sacrificed. . . . The strong passions of ambitions, amativeness, and philoprogenitiveness must be yielded to a discipline which takes selfishness out of them and makes them obedient to science and to God. These things all come very near the center of life, and will appear, perhaps, to infringe the natural liberty we all love so much. Very well. Each one must judge for himself and choose his own platform.[23]

Developing techniques to achieve this discipline was Noyes' central tactical problem. Every element of individual and group life was open to systematic scrutiny and censorship. When necessary, Noyes asserted his personal power over recalcitrant members, but he relied generally on more impersonal, institutionalized means of social control. He preferred the role of humane, benevolent leader to that of punishing father, although he held the latter nature, of which everyone was aware, in ready reserve. The approved life pattern was well-known within the community; Noyes' implicit presence was the accepted basis for shaping social behavior. Oneida members struggled to achieve a proper fit within the group. Noyes' son Pierrepont reflected later that "conformity, as with many details of conduct, was enforced by public opinion or desire for the approval of Father Noyes."[24]

More formally, Noyes carefully regulated personal conduct and made all actions public. He abolished not only private property but also the legitimacy of private feelings. The much bruited about free love of the Oneida Community was in essence highly regulated sexuality. More than any other nineteenth-century reformer, Noyes understood, in a clear and uncondemnatory manner, the importance of sex. He guided sexual passion along lines that would both bring it to the fore and subject it to social control. "The desire of the sexes is a stream ever running," he wrote. "If it is dammed up, it will break out irregularly and destructively. The only way to make it safe and useful, is to give it a free natural channel."[25]

Free love was one implication of Noyes' self-assertion of freedom from sin and from external law, but for years, fearing social repercussions, he did not publicly affirm his belief in the doctrine. Indeed, in 1837, when his private letter supporting free love was published, he went to great lengths to disclaim his intention of enacting the idea. Only in 1846, after the Putney Community seemed to be securely established, did he encourage free love, and then only secretly for a small group within the community. He established his position on free love as a result of a critical personal episode. Walking one evening with Mary Cragin, the wife of a coworker, and "yielding to the impulse," he embraced her passionately, an action which she returned with ardor. Noyes would not permit sexual desire to be his exclusive guide. "The temptation to go further was tremendous. But . . . I said to myself, 'I will not steal.' After a moment we arose and went toward home." Noyes and Mary Cragin confronted his wife and her husband, who formally approved of their desire; thus they publicly constructed a new series of relationships: "The last part of the interview was as amicable and happy as a wedding, and the consequence was that we gave each other full liberty."[26]

As for his followers, the sexual impulse, like all other aspects of personality, was to be carefully controlled by Noyes. Soon after his self-initiation into free love, he told a married woman follower, when she asked his advice about the proper course to take with another man to whom she was attracted: "[Do not] allow him to feel free with you until he openly avows our principles and submits to my instructions."[27]

After the Oneida Community was established in 1848, Noyes made "complex marriage" an avowed institution for the entire group. Driven from Putney on charges of adultery as well as a result of some unsuccessful attempts at faith-healing, Noyes now clearly and openly enforced his will on the subject of free love.[28] The sexual sector of life could not remain private and exclusive. He wanted to extinguish all monopolies, on persons as well as on property, that led to anticommunal sentiments: "The abolishment of appropriation is involved in the nature of a true relation to Christ. Appropriation is a branch of egotism."[29] Furthermore, he now wrote that all kinds of love were beautiful both in themselves and as expressions of love for God and that it would be sinful to deny God's due: "Amativeness is in fact the first and most natural channel of religious love. This law must not be despised and ignored but must be investigated and provided for.''[30] Noyes believed that sexual passion was the well from which all art flowed and that to be creative one had first to uncover and understand one's own desires: "This subject is the vital center of society. It is the soul of the fine arts. It will be foolish for us to undertake to cultivate music or poetry or painting or sculpture, until we set the center and soul of them in its place.''[31] Sex should become the first of the arts, Noyes stated. Freed from morbid fears, "sexual intercourse [will] become a purely social affair, the same in kind with other modes of kindly interchange, differing only by its superior intensity and beauty.''[32] Love, beautiful and universal by its very nature, should not be artificially limited by restricting it to monogamous couples. Traditional marriage, which had systematically violated man's desires for a wide and open expression of his polymorphous passion, should be swept aside. Marriage should be expanded to be shared communally by all who love:

> Susceptibility to love is not burnt out by one honeymoon, or satisfied by one lover. On the contrary, the secret history of the human heart will bear out the assertion that it is capable of loving any number of times and any number of persons, and that the more it loves the more it can love. This is the law of nature, thrust out of sight, and condemned by common consent, and yet secretly known to all. . . . Variety is, in the nature of things, as beautiful and useful in love as in eating and drinking. The one-love theory is the exponent, not of simple experience in love, but of the "green-eyed monster," jealousy.[33]

At Oneida, Noyes established a social structure in which wide participation in sexuality was rewarded and tendencies to exclusiveness were punished; however, he bound his concept of free love, as he did all other aspects of community life, with careful restrictions in order to maintain discipline and authority. Couples were not permitted to maintain their marriage if they entered the community together. Young people were reprimanded if they devoted too much affection to "idolatrous" relationships. Rather than permitting the young to fend for themselves, older community members introduced them to sex.[34] Third parties were used extensively to encourage appropriate sexual partnerships and to maintain careful records of them.

Noyes insisted on birth control to limit the birth rate and to insure, it would seem, clear identity of paternity. As in the establishment of his other doctrines, Noyes arrived at the preferred method of birth control through personal experience. During the first eight years of their marriage, Noyes' wife had had five pregnancies, four of them ending in the death of prematurely born infants. He vowed never again to allow her to suffer from unwanted children and began practicing "male continence"—coitus ending short of ejaculation. He later formulated, "Men are entirely competent to choose in sexual intercourse whether they will stop at any point in the voluntary stages of it, and so make it simply an act of communion, or go through to the involuntary state, and make it an act of propagation."[35] Without "the horrors and the fear of involuntary propagation," Noyes claimed his own sexual experience and that of his wife had been enhanced.[36] Increasing both the possibilities for pleasure and the demands for self-discipline, birth control through male continence clearly fit Oneida free love.

The keystone to the pyramid of discipline and authority in the Oneida Community, controlling all other aspects of behavior, was what Noyes called "mutual criticism," a technique calling for each member to criticize repeatedly the causes of his behavior, under the broader public scrutiny of the group. Noyes allowed no relaxation into comfortable role playing at Oneida; every aspect of life was to be opened and corrected. He knew, with his extraordinary intuitive powers, that he had to disclose the past in order to reconstruct the future the way he wanted it: "Life, we say, is a ball, wound up with the threads of our passing experience; and whatever we have wound in the past, whether good or bad, is still there: it is vitally our own, and, in a very important sense, enters into our present character. We are, what our past lives have been." Any element of privacy, which might impede the community by protecting the individual, was to be crushed. "The time has come," Noyes concluded, "when the mere coverings of character are to be taken off, and when people will be forced to see things just as they really are."[37] Mutual criticism was in no way a form of group therapy among equals; the perfected, with Noyes at the head, would guide the meetings and would make the final pronouncements. Because everyone had to present himself for criticism, Noyes used this means above all others to direct, control, and rebuild the personalities of his followers. He incorporated within it a by now old-fashioned classical, autocratic political theory:

> [Mutual criticism] combines in itself all that is good in all other forms of Government. It is Theocratic, for in recognizing the Truth as King, it recognizes God who is the *source* of all Truth, and whose Spirit alone can give the power of genuine criticism. It is Aristocratic, in as much as the best critics have the most power. It is Democratic in as much as the privilege of criticism is distributed to all classes, and the highest attainments and skill in it are open to every one.[38]

"If my childhood was spent in surroundings totally unlike any other existing then or now," Noyes' son Pierrepont reflected years after the community had passed, "there was nothing tentative about that environment, either spiritual or physical."[39] Noyes had affixed a sense of institutional permanency to his ideas. If members accepted his discipline and became his loyal subordinates, they could feel that they had become enmeshed in a secure and truly communal home. From this redeemed status in this perfect place, many of them were positive they would eventually convert the outside world. One member reflected in 1866: "I believe that under God Mr. Noyes will drill the Community till we shall all feel that we do not belong to ourselves; and we shall gain the entire confidence of the world. We shall show them an organization that they can give themselves to, with perfect safety."[40]

As in all separatist communities, however, the relation of the enlightened elite to the ignorant but powerful outside world troubled the Oneida perfectionists. Carrying the word to nonmembers involved risks of rejection and perhaps even retaliation and destruction of the community. On the other hand, complete seclusion meant that the community, however stable and righteous in itself, would fail in its peculiar task as beacon of the true life to the world.

Corinna Ackley Noyes, his daughter, later recalled a dangerous incident in Grand Central Station in New York City, where one community institution, the wearing of bloomers, collided with general social customs:

> A few of our women, clad in the Community short dress, perhaps in an attempt to bring a message of deliverance to the fashion-bound women of the outside world, were held up to ridicule by an insensate public and had to be rescued by the police. After that, common sense was deemed the better part of valor, and worldly garments were provided for travelling females.[41]

Noyes himself was ambivalent about the relationship he felt the community should hold toward the outside world. Earlier, lack of caution had led to expulsion from Putney, and as Oneida flourished he always hesitated before risking the stakes he was building there. The apocalypse would come eventually of its own accord; Oneida had to be prepared carefully for leadership in that hazily timed future: "The spring in a lock moves along from day to day, without any violent demonstrations, but it is working all the time to uncoil itself. That is its natural propensity. So our clock keeps ticking—once in a while it strikes—and we shall be able to tell the world the time of day by and by."[42] If the world would never come around to perfectionism, Noyes sometimes felt, his community would form in itself a tiny island of certainty and beauty, safe from the enormous ocean of brutal despair. He wrote while still at Putney: "What if there is not another bright spot in the wide world, and what if this is a very small one? Turn your eye toward it when you are tired of looking into chaos, and you will catch a glimpse of a better world."[43] In his actions as well as in his thought, Noyes vacillated on the role the community should play in the world. He usually guarded the peculiar customs of Oneida from over-curious inquiry with a secrecy that prevented not only the outside from coming in but also the inside from going out. "The Association, in respect to practical innovations," he wrote in 1849, "limits itself to its own family circle, not invading society around it. . . ."[44] He eschewed discussion of national politics and legislation. At one point, in 1870, he barred all interviews with journalists, refusing ties with those outside who would sully the word of the perfected.[45]

Noyes, however, also yearned for a more active role in bringing about the great moral and social revolution. From 1850 to 1853, he lived in Brooklyn, New York, publishing the *Oneida Circular* there as a daily paper in an attempt to publicize his position. Periodically after his return to Oneida, he tried to be stridently outward looking. For example, he wrote in 1866, "We may as well make up our minds not to try to isolate ourselves from the world (for we cannot do it if we would), but to turn back upon it and conquer it. . . . Within the next ten years I want to shoot forth an organization that will reach clear into the very dens from whence the cholera issues."[46] Yet when he considered expansion, he profoundly feared not only outside contamination but loss of control over his followers as well. After 1870, the masthead of his newspaper declared that the Oneida Community was full and that no new members were wanted. Although he did establish a branch of the community at Wallingford, Connecticut, he was afraid of its potential independence and insisted on the complete need for unity and authority:

> Oneida Community . . . ought to go forth in omnipresence, *for the sake of unity.* Every new Community should be a *branch* of the *One* Oneida Community. . . . We should get above localisms in our spirits, and make the Oneida Community an omnipresent unit, ready to throw and even *hurl* the whole of its strength into every local point at the shortest notice.[47]

Ironically, the Oneida Community was preserved for so many decades by coming to terms with that most frightening of outside developments, industrialism. Canning and selling fruits and vegetables had only slowed the shrinkage of the considerable capital with which the community had begun. In the late 1850s, Sewell Newhouse, a somewhat primitive upstate New York trapper, was converted to the Oneida life and brought with him designs for efficient steel animal traps. Patents were secured, a factory was gradually built, and the Newhouse trap captured the national market; Oneida was financially secured.[48] To meet the demand for traps, Noyes was forced to hire outside labor and employ it with an eye to profits; the communist community ingested a capitalist factory.

Oddly, community eccentricities were rarely attacked by Oneida neighbors because of the employment and capital pumped into the region by the honestly managed trap industry. Noyes reconciled Oneida communism of property and services with his use of capitalism in an uncharacteristically disingenuous, if practical, manner:

> While the Community employs many persons for wages, it does not wholly approve of the hireling system, regarding it as one of the temporary institutions which will in time be displaced by the associative principle; but so long as men choose to work for wages the Community will do what it can toward furnishing them with remunerative employment.[49]

After producing traps for years, the community turned to silver plating, and manufactured what would later be advertized as the "silverware of brides."

IV

The second generation of Noyes' followers, who were the first to be born at Oneida, lacked the zeal of the original converts, their parents. Noyes had hoped that the faithfulness and fervor of the founders could be reimposed through disciplined education. He wrote, "The *habit of obedience* is instilled with greater care than any other, and is secured very early. The earlier a child learns to obey the more contented will be its disposition and the less severe discipline will be needed."[50] However, it was impossible to pass down the religious and social passions of the 1840s and 1850s to the following generation. In addition, Noyes and his chief lieutenants were aging. Once he even tried to demonstrate his continued virility to a group of young Oneida men by plunging nude into a pond that was covered with a thin layer of ice.[51] Noyes insisted that his hunger for life remained as great as ever and that he would never be overruled by the young. He would stop time. His appetites were "omnivorous," his desires "eager": "So you can judge what is your state of health by finding out what your appetites are. . . . As we lose our appetite for one thing after another, we grow old, and really lose our health. That is the very process by which we pass along toward death."[52]

In order to guarantee the continuity of young followers and to stave off the implications of the powerlessness of his old age, Noyes, in 1869, when he was fifty-eight, instituted a system of eugenics which he called "stirpiculture." Shored up by a perusal of Darwin and Galton, Noyes believed that inbreeding between carefully and scientifically selected couples would create a perfect race. His aim was nothing less than "to start a distinct family and keep its blood pure by separation from the mass of its own race. [Stirpiculture] is an attempt to create a new Adam and Eve, and separating them and their progeny from all previous races."[53] Thus Noyes wanted to use ablutions of semen to replace the fading word of truth. New science would spawn the techniques of social control to maintain the perfect community, superceding the religious methods that had become becalmed with passing time.

Inbreeding more than implied incest. Noyes believed that "first there must be, in the early stages, mating between very near relatives, as there was in Adam's family. . . ."[54] Quite obviously, Noyes himself broke that deepest of sexual taboos and had intercourse at least with his nieces and cousins if not with his daughters. More importantly, inasmuch as he was the general father of the community, all the young women with whom he now had children were his symbolic daughters. One final time Noyes obliterated generally accepted social norms and made his desires law. In 1869, he inaugurated the institution of stirpiculture by insisting that all the young women of the community formally pledge themselves as slaves to his orders:

> 1. That we do not belong to ourselves in any respect, but that we do belong first to God, and second to Mr. Noyes as God's true representative.
> 2. That we have no rights or personal feelings in regard to child-bearing which shall in the least degree oppose or embarrass him in his choice of scientific combinations.
> 3. That we will put aside all envy, childishness and

self-seeking, and rejoin with those who are chosen can-
didates; that we will, if necessary, become martyrs to science, and cheerfully resign all desire to become mothers,
if for any reason Mr. Noyes deem us unfit material for
propagation. Above all, we offer ourselves "living sac-
rifices" to God and true Communism.[55]

At least nine of the fifty-eight children born under this system
during the following ten years were sired by Noyes.[56] Although
he attempted to soften the impact of stirpiculture by permitting all
men who so desired to father one child, all births beyond that were
in effect dictated by a committee of elders, which Noyes controlled.[57]

After years of smoldering resentment, the young men in the community finally opened a rebellion against Noyes and the other aging
first fathers of Oneida. Noyes had refused to transfer any control
to them; he had enchained them in every imaginable way. By the
mid-1870s, the community had developed a deep generation gap;
the young felt their only recourse was to eliminate completely the
uncompromising Noyes and all his radicalism in order to reclaim
their own manhood. Previously, secrecy and business success had
kept the outside world at bay, but now the Young Turks threatened
to bring the law to bear against Noyes' inbreeding methods, to
invite in comstockery in order to discredit Noyes and destroy
Oneida.[58] Instead of permitting himself to be humiliated publicly,
Noyes fled to Canada in 1879.[59]

Not only stirpiculture, but complex marriage and communism
of property—in short all the basic and distinctive Oneida institutions—were eliminated within the next eighteen months. A rash
of marriages in the worldly mode followed. Private property
became something of a fetish after the capital of the community
was distributed. Quite unintentionally, Noyes himself had established what was by now a guarantee of continued economic sol-
vency for former members in the steel works. The Oneida factory
was simply rechartered as Oneida Ltd., a corporation which still
exists.

Noyes established residence with a few of the faithful founders
in the "Stone Cottage" overlooking the roaring Canadian portion
of Niagara Falls.[60] Long before his death in 1886, he had become

quite deaf and could not raise his voice above a ghostly whisper. Alone in his front bedroom he would rock gently in a chair for hours with a rug on his lap, talking to no one, staring at the immense Horseshoe Falls.

4

A TRADITIONALIST ANALOGUE TO

UTOPIAN COMMUNITARIANISM:

HORACE MANN AND THE COMMON SCHOOL

The human soul, immortal, invulnerable, invincible, has at last unmanacled and emancipated itself. It has triumphed; here, in our age and in our land, it is now rising up before us, gigantic, majestical, lofty as an archangel, and, like an archangel, to be saved or lost by its obedience or its transgressions. Amongst ourselves it is, that this spirit is now walking forth, full of its new-found life, wantoning in freshly-discovered energies, surrounded by all the objects which can inflame its boundless appetite, and, as yet, too purblind, from the long darkness of its prison-house, to discern clearly between its blessing and its bane.

—Horace Mann,
Lectures on Education

I

Utopian communitarians were not just wild offshoots from the assumptions and hopes held generally in ante-bellum America; they were only further and thus clearer articulators of commonly held intellectual positions in that era of what to many seemed limitless democratic potentiality. Much of their analysis of the plasticity of American society and of the need for its immediate and basic reform, as well as their fervent belief in the discoverability of moral truth, was shared even by contemporary traditionalists who also wanted to create new model institutions in which properly bounded men would be recreated. In this context, a traditionalist was one who wished to reestablish what he felt was the correct old social and moral order upon some new footing in order to stave off what he found to be the frightening possibilities of democratic social revolution, who wished to explore new forms not for the revolution they would bring or as ends in themselves but simply as means to regain ground that was now slipping. American life had to be made calm and certain once more, but as the old methods had failed, new means to social safety were demanded. Many participants in legal and penal reform, in societies for temperance and for better treatment of the insane, and in educational reform movements, viewed themselves as such upholders of tradition. One educational reform leader, Horace Mann, can serve as a particularly clear model of a traditionalist whose analyses and activities, though derived from a different purpose, were often strikingly analogous to those of the communitarian reformers.

Horace Mann, born in 1796, an upwardly mobile Massachusetts lawyer and politician, was named first Secretary to the Massachusetts Board of Education, where he served from 1837 to 1849. From there he took John Quincy Adams' seat in Congress upon Adams' death and filled it until 1852. Then he became the founding president of Antioch College, where he remained until his death in 1859. His most effective years were those spent as the leading pioneer in American public school education. As Secretary, and real head, of the Massachusetts Board of Education, he tried to establish a new institution to lead American society through the maelstroms of her disintegrating old social structures and her unauthoritative new ones into a place of bounded instincts, general civic-mindedness, and safe democracy.

Mann was both excited and frightened by the apparently inevitable growth of democracy in America. He did not hail its coming but girded himself for the new society and sought to reinforce the old moral certainties through new forms. Contemplating the future filled him with both deep anxieties about social destruction and hopes for human perfectibility. The traditional institutions, with their accompanying ideals of rank, authority, and deference, Mann was sure, had passed. At this unique moment in our national life, he felt, new social structures were needed to uplift the suddenly liberated American and to save him from the immediate threat of a return to savagery that his freedom implied. Either salvation or cataclysm was just around the corner:

> Even the last generation in this country,—the generation that molded our institutions into their present forms, —were born and educated under other institutions, and they brought into active life strong hereditary and traditional feelings of respect for established authority, merely because it was established,—of veneration for law simply because it was law,—and of deference both to secular and ecclesiastical rank, because they had been accustomed to revere rank. But scarcely any vestige of this reverence for the past now remains. The momentum of hereditary opinion is spent. The generation of men now entering upon the stage of life,—the generation which is to occupy that stage for the next forty years,—will act out their desires more fully, more effectively, than any generation of men that has ever existed. Already the tramp of this innumerable host is sounding in our ears. They are the men who will take counsel of their desires, and make it law. The condition of society is to be only an embodiment of their mighty will; and if greater care be not taken than has heretofore been taken, to inform and regulate that will, it will inscribe its laws all over the face of society in such broad and terrific character, that, not only whoever runs may read, but whoever reads will run.[1]

Mann feared that the lower classes, gaining the power to enact into law their raging and uneducated will, would destroy the better classes, who remained the repository of true values. He wrote to a supporter in 1843: "I wish our wealthy men could realize what conditions they and theirs will be in, with the power in the hands of the people, and that people partly ignorant and partly wicked . . . for ignorance and wickedness will be the mitre and sulphers to blow them up."[2] Mann held an abiding fear of humanity in its natural state. He could not trust men if they were not bound by careful social censorship. Yet he was no reactionary prophet of despair; he searched for new institutions that could be built for men to enter even as they left the old. Furthermore, these new forms could maintain what had always been and always would remain the best of human nature: "I ask, with the deepest anxiety, what institutions exist amongst us, which at once possess the power and are administered with the efficiency requisite to save us from the dangers that spring up in our own bosoms?"[3]

In order to "furnish defence or barrier" against our dangerous "propensities," Mann felt *"it must be mainly done during the docile and teachable years of childhood."*[4] The common schools, controlled by upright men, if fully cultivated, could become the single strongest force to reach democratic man and direct him along the paths of the traditional virtues. Each man could be guided properly as he grew up, and as learning would surely overmaster ignorance, proper social training would stem the tide of anarchic individualism:

> Common Schools derive their value from the fact that they are an instrument more extensively applicable to the whole mass of the children than any other instrument yet devised. They are an instrument by which the good men in society can send redeeming influences to those children who suffer under the calamity of vicious parentage and evil domestic association. . . . The institution of Common Schools is the off-spring of an advanced state of civilization, and is incapable of coexisting with barbarian life, because, should barbarism prevail, it would destroy the schools; should the schools prevail, they would destroy barbarism.[5]

Through this one institution, the social dilemma, conceived thus simply, would be solved. Mann shared the clear, universal moral insights and the sense of the deductive nature of social alternatives from these truths with his more radical reformist contemporaries. Once the first right steps were made, the rest of the stages to salvation would follow automatically.

In Mann's case, the corrected society was not an especially shining vision. All men would be made more alike and, with social divisions blurred, life would become less dangerous.

> It does better than to disarm the poor of their hostility towards the rich: it prevents being poor. . . . The spread of education, by enlarging the cultivated class or caste, will open a wider area over which the social feelings will expand; and, if this education should be universal and complete, it would do more than all things else to obliterate factitious distinctions in society.[6]

Most importantly, men would be saved from the evil in their natures, and the ageless glories of civilization would be maintained within the new egalitarian framework. America would prove the example to the rest of the world of the sobriety and fruitfulness of democracy. Morality would be made universal through morally rigorous education for all.

II

From childhood, Mann had been drilled in morality, duty, and orthodox religion. Fulfillment for him could only come through service to mankind, not through personal development. He demonstrated his acceptance of this lesson in a letter which he wrote at age eighteen to his family: "I believe there is no one so happy as he who does his duty. There is a self-satisfaction, above all estimation, which he alone enjoys, who is conscious of having fulfilled his part well."[7] Just after he arrived at Brown University in 1816, as a poor and painfully ambitious young man, he echoed his youthful seriousness and sense of purpose. "I have been so fortunate as to enter a class," he wrote to his parents, "the major part of which are remarkable for their steadiness and sobriety, which you must know is very consonant to my feelings."[8] Whether he always lived up to this ideal of good behavior (and there is evidence that he took part in some elaborate school pranks), this credo would always remain his model. Later, as secretary to the board of education, he would put in fourteen to eighteen hours a day in devotion to his principle of correct action. His moral commitment to duty was more important than his health. He wrote to a supporter in 1844, "I hardly get any sleep; and the absence of sleep is not so far from insanity. Still, I am willing to be insane, or suffer anything else, would I see the thing [education] prosper."[9]

Mann believed that his devotion through work to moral truth was the opposite of lighthearted social play, which at any rate made him uncomfortable. Human intercourse, transient at best, was dispensable; life was a resolute commitment to goals. Effort was precious and was to be stored up and spent only for distant, final attainments. He wrote to the wife of his Brahmin friend, Josiah Quincy, Jr.:

> You have bantered me not very infrequently on my want of appreciation for elegance, and adornments; and I readily confess that I have as often spoken disparagingly of those things that perish with the using compared with those treasures, of which heaven consents to be the banker. But I think you never heard me disparage *Idealty*, if Benevolence and Veneration and Conscientiousness were enthroned above it. . . . Surely I have no objection to any one's enjoying this world's goods, provided they do not withdraw himself from the world's duties.[10]

Concomitant to his rejection of material possessions and worldly pleasures in favor of obligation to duty, Mann sought to repudiate all fantasy in order to pursue single-mindedly logic and science. When he was at college he wrote to his family that fiction should not be read as it "induces an indolent, desultory habit of reading."[11] Later, in shaping public-school curricula, Mann would order an injunction against the reading of fiction to prevent children from exploring ideas that might divert them from social duty. It would be unrealistic and immoral, Mann felt, to carry on internal explorations that are ungoverned by the hand of moral law. Men must live in a world where universal, final judgment ordains correctly obedient behavior:

> [Knowledge of fiction is] one of the standing causes of insanity. . . . [It] is about as fit a preparation, as a knowledge of all the "castles in the air," ever built by vis-

ionaries and dreamers. . . . And the reason is, that, in the region of fiction, the imagination can have everything in its own way; it can arrange the course of events as it pleases, and still bring out the desired results. But in actual life, where the law of cause and effect pervades all, links all, determines all, the appropriate consequences of good and evil follow from their antecedents with inevitable certainty. The premises of sound or false judgments, of right or wrong actions, being given, the course of Nature and Providence predestines the conclusions of happiness or misery, from which we cannot escape.[12]

Mann's path, so straight and narrow, shut out any access to emotional self-exploration. Just as the common school was to discipline children ceaselessly to the right, so his whole life was an endless struggle to prove his obedience to absolute moral convention. He had to attempt to uproot the lurking, inchoate, evil emotionalism that threatened to throw him off the long highway to judgment into the swamp of self, from duty into despair.

Uncertainty gnawed at Mann's ideas of a proper personal lifestyle. In his relationships with his two wives, first Charlotte Messer, and then Mary Peabody, one can sense his difficulty in establishing close human ties. When Charlotte Messer married Mann in 1830, she was twenty-one, thirteen years his junior. She was the sweet but sickly daughter of Asa Messer, the president of Brown University, Mann's alma mater.[13] Her parents zealously guarding her health, kept her in Providence against Mann's anguished but respectfully muted desires for most of their brief marriage. When she died in 1832, probably of tuberculosis, Mann was crushed, as much by not having established a real home with Charlotte as by her physical suffering.

To assuage his grief, Mann's friends induced him to move from Dedham to Boston. There he met Mary Peabody to whom he poured out his sorrow. As shown in their correspondence, she provided warmth and a lighter touch for Mann, while always guarding against jostling the widower's memories. Mann was in the process of beatifying his image of Charlotte, turning her into a symbol of absolute perfection, which he, of course, had been too base to approach. He wrote of Charlotte to Mary: "Within her there could be no contest with sordid passions or degrading appetites, for she sent a divine and overmastering strength into every generous sentiment, which I cannot describe. She purified my conceptions of purity and beautified the ideal of every excellence.''[14] In this fashion Mann put beauty in the next world, insurmountably distant from his own attempts at human bonds.

On every anniversary of her death, Mann poured out his ritualistic incantations of suffering in a journal begun in 1837. As he canonized Charlotte, he interred himself emotionally. Since he was fearful of openly attacking an omnipotent God who had failed him, he turned inward and attempted to bury his desire to love life in Charlotte's grave: "I feel as one would, who had life and consciousness in a tomb. . . . How like this has been my existence for years. When, Oh when, will it cease?''[15] In order to remain true to Charlotte's memory, thus elaborated, Mann felt compelled to ward off any new human bonds. But at the same time that he feared changing and marring his unhappiness, Mann felt new stirrings of longing for others: "How many lonesome feelings have thronged around me today. I want inward life. I have no bosom friends, with whom to sympathize, or who can sympathize with me.''[16]

While he privately wrote of his divorce from life, Mann constantly visited and corresponded with Mary Peabody. Although he probably thought that he was maintaining a proper aloofness, she was responsive to him and tried to draw him into a more calm and cheerful disposition. "You must not live apart from human beings while you can make them so happy by a smile," she gently urged. She wanted a more open relationship with him and was "sometimes tempted to tell you the story of my life." She was put off by his composure and distance at the same time that she was interested by him. "I am a little afraid of your logic sometimes, but it is a logic that often enlightens me much.''[17] For a decade, Mann continued both his grief over Charlotte and his friendship with Mary.

Suddenly, in the final entry in his journal in 1843, Mann declared his imminent marriage to Mary on the eve of his departure for a long trip to Europe. He had made no prior suggestion in his journal of this plan: "[Mary] had long since won my admiration and love. *Circumstances have hitherto rendered it improper that*

I should avow my secret affection for her, but certain affairs in my life are approaching at such a crisis, that it could not, will not be delayed much longer without being smothered forever.''[18] Mann had felt so bound to the traditions of mourning that he had not been able to confide his feelings for Mary in his secret diary. His self-denial had carried with it self-deception. His grief was not disingenuous; rather, he placed a higher value on the trials of his sufferings than on the search for release into joy. Behavior according to form had squelched introspection. It would also prevent any very emotionally satisfactory relationship with Mary during their marriage.

Mann sometimes discussed his sense of emotional limits in terms of his Calvinist rearing. As an adolescent, he had revolted against all formal ties with a church based on such an unrelentingly angry God. Later he would write, "My nature revolts at the idea of belonging to a universe in which there is to be never-ending anguish.''[19] His rebellion turned him into a militant secularist in public education and drove him to seek a scientific view of life, where God would become unnecessary. Yet on a less conscious level he felt, as he grew older, that he had been so trapped during childhood in the fears induced by Calvin's God that he would never be able to escape emotionally. Mann realized to some extent that he could not find any meaningful approach to the peace and fulfillment he wanted and needed. In 1856, in what was an unusual emotional outburst, he looked back over his whole life to his youth and wrote to a young friend about his feeling of abiding emotional thirst:

> I feel constantly, and more and more deeply what an unspeakable calamity a Calvinist education is;—what a dreadful thing it was to me.—If it did not succeed in making me that horrible thing, a Calvinist, it did succeed in depriving me of that filial love for God, that tenderness, that sweetness, that intimacy, that . . . nestling love which I say is the very nature of the child. . . . [But the] old Calvinist spectre thrusts itself before me. I am as a frightened child, whose age, knowledge, experience, belief even are not sufficient to obliterate the image which an early fright burned into my soul. . . . I would not

part with one idea, one conviction, on the other side of
my moral life; but I feel as tho' I should be a better man
and a vastly happier man, if I could add your side to
mine.[20]

Austin Craig, on whom Mann showered this passionate history
of deprivation, was a young preacher whom Mann hoped to attract
permanently to Antioch. Mann was deeply attracted to Craig, who
seemed to have all the ease in forming intimate relationships that
he lacked. In a letter written in 1854, Mann pleaded for Craig's
aid and companionship, in rhetoric atypical for him, if common-
place in his culture: "I sat down this time to make love to you!
Do not be alarmed. I am serious and literal! I must woo you; and
nobody could woo you who did not hope to win."[21] Craig, after
a long holdout from Mann's request,[22] did go to Antioch for two
short periods, but left for good before Mann's death in 1859.[23]
He could not provide, or Mann could not find in him, any respite
from his great loneliness.

By the end of his life, Mann often felt that he was pursuing
a duty empty of all meaning and that he was repeatedly rehearsing
correct action for no particular end. He wrote to Charles Sumner
in 1856: "I am like an old stage-horse that remembers the crack
of the whip long after being put out to pasture."[24] He took pride
in his service to mankind and he had helped create new institutions
with which to reinforce American life while working through his
sense of duty, but the demands that led him to social achievements
also led him away from himself. He could never break out of his
conservative Calvinist chrysalis and could never temper it with personal experimentation. To a large extent, he was bound to repeat
his past in whatever he created.

III

Theodore Parker, that shrewd New England theologian, reflected
shortly after Mann's death that Mann, "bred in the worst form
of Calvinism," never overcame "the dreadful smooch" that it
made on his personality. Parker felt that Mann, in his public life,
saw motivation in others with a special clarity that wiped out any
ambivalence in his judgments of them and rendered them into stock

idealizations of good and evil. Thus political life became gladiatorial moral warfare, with Mann in the angelic camp. The fearful spirit of Calvinism rephrased in secular terms, Parker believed, remained at the heart of Mann's reformist position:

> He loved strongly and idealized the objects of his affections, making them quite other than they were; but he also hated terribly, and never, I think, forgave a public or a private foe. His hatred idealized men downwards, and he could see no good in them, or, if any, it was deformed by the evil motive which he saw (or fancied he saw), prompting and controlling it all. . . . He had not great confidence in the moral and still less in the religious instincts of mankind; so after he had broken with the substance of the [orthodox] theology . . . he yet clung to the hollow form, and used the language of theology, not as figures of speech, but as symbols of a fact.[25]

His preacherlike dispensation of moral judgments debased the motives of others; he was possessed by the idea of expunging error and resecuring men. Yet in the same pamphlet wars in which he was so hard on his opponents, he promoted a warm, humane view of education.[26] His greatest foes were always the orthodox, who assumed that man's fall was the inextricable foundation of human nature. Mann, in attempting to reach a more pleasantly ameliorative position where evil was not inherent and where love and not authority was to control men, hated his foes as one can only hate sinners and denounced them as inferiors. This denunciatory quality does not destroy the value of a positive approach to education, which Mann stressed. He was groping his way from an orthodox background toward a freer and more beautiful vision of human nature.

In 1844, a group of orthodox Boston teachers, reacting to what they felt was Mann's softness toward children, excoriated him publicly. For them, fear and not suasion was at the root of social order, for men were stained by original sin. Institutions had to be imposed on men whose natural impulses were anarchic. Only obedience to authority, drilled into the pliant, weak young, could lead to the continuation of law and order. The schoolmasters exhorted: "Since,

then, fear is most predominant in childhood, being the natural concomitant of weakness and dependence, we should take advantage
of it, and make it subservient to good ends." Force, not willing
acceptance, they claimed, would finally enforce social mores:
"True obedience is a hearty response to acknowledged authority.
It does not voluntarily comply with a request, but implicitly yields
to a command." The wrappings of paternal patience and kindness
should never fully disguise the real basis of the relationships of
subjects to ruler: "Physical coercion is but the final application
of moral suasion. . . . Indeed, all government must end, if need
be, in a resort to physical force."[27]

Mann scorned this position, which he felt was archaic despotism,
both because it was irrelevant to the emerging American democracy
and because in itself it was repugnantly brutal. He damned the
character of these teachers who would follow such a terrorizing
course. "My accusers," he replied, in "concocting their libels
against me," were filled with "execrable hypocrisy" and "a cul-
pable indifference to the truth." Although their attack was only
an "air-blown vesicle," it was evident that Boston school children
were in constant danger of "moral mutilations."[28] The teachers'
dependence on terror would undermine, not reinforce, social order:
"Physical power can make subjects, it is true, but moral power
makes allies;—and how much better is an ally than a captive."
Furthermore, the naked use of power implied that men were not
redeemable and that education could not be a morally sound process. Schools would be reduced to training grounds for the use
of force: "What a damning sentence does a teacher pronounce upon
himself, when he affirms that he has no resources in his own attainments, his own deportment, his own skill, his own character; but
only in the cowhide and the birch, and in the strong arm that wields
them!"[29]

Although he believed in discipline, Mann said it should only be
self-taught and could not be imposed by external authority.
Teachers were to demonstrate rather than demand, suggest rather
than prohibit. At his most optimistic Mann believed that human
nature was at least neutral if not good, and, as moral law certainly
existed, men could be both free and freely obedient to law.
Teachers could accept children as morally unformed rather than
inherently evil and still turn them, with their cooperation, to the

right way. The tradition of law would remain, sprung from the custom of force and shaped in new molds. "Forms may be revolutionized or abolished," Mann insisted, "but the substance is indestructible and lasting as eternity."[30]

That an underlying substance, a natural law, existed, Mann never fully doubted. The sole reason for educational reform was to clear the overgrown path to the omnipresent truth. Then, once again, would properly educated men fit voluntarily within the embracing order of law: "The process of education is the orderly and symmetrical development and strengthening of all our powers, and the acquisition and cultivation of such a knowledge and purpose as will enable us to adapt ourselves to the benign and wonderful laws of the system in which we are placed."[31] Freedom in this context meant correct adaptation to fixed law; rebellion would be immoral disobedience. Therefore, discovery of one's true place was the correct reformist process. We might not, Mann wrote, "disobey the laws of our nature, or exempt ourselves from their penalties when broken." We could only use our reason "in attempting to discover . . . laws, and [use] our own free will in obeying them; and thus to perform the conditions under which alone a rational and free being can fulfill his destiny."[32] The need for social experiment can be seen only very dimly through this rigorously restricted traditionalist demand for obedience. Mann wanted no gratuitous law breaking; instead, he wished to find a methodology for securing certainty.

Phrenology, Mann believed, was the scientific method through which he could uncover the laws of behavior to be applied to children through correctly informed educational methods. To some extent, phrenology, before it was taken over by county-fair fakirs, was a crude sort of learning theory that taught that an absolute set of rules for character training could be derived from an analysis of the effects of behavior on the mind. Although this may strike us as more circular than scientific, it shored up Mann as it reinforced his belief that various moral qualities within individuals could be shaped, enlarged, or shrunken through willed effort. Education would be the means of restructuring humanity when the scientifically trained educator could reach malleable youth. Thus a new and blessedly scientific method, exercised in the controlled environment of the school, would train men in the ageless values.

Or, as Merle Curti puts it, "Were character training resorted to in accordance with the principles of phrenology, the old-time New England virtues of honesty, frugality and uprightness would prevail even in a changing and unfriendly world."[33]

At his most self-assured, and writing privately, Mann was certain that the oncoming discovery of laws would enable man to perfect himself. As did John Humphrey Noyes, Mann sometimes felt that all suffering, disease, and (by implication) death could be banished through full knowledge of nature's code. He wrote to Bayard Taylor in 1855: "When His laws are discovered and obeyed, these privations and torments of the body will cease to be; in fine; . . . as a man who never violates God's moral laws will never feel remorse, so a race which never violates the laws of the body will never know physical pain."[34]

If such laws were discoverable and if he could possess some of the keys to unlock them, Mann's role would be clear and exalted. Discord and doubt would be banished. He would be the heroic builder of the first true institution, a missionary to the future and savior of the past. Truth, through education, would be salvaged, and humanity would be made whole once more. "I know it is the greatest of earthly causes," wrote Mann. "It is a part of my religion to believe that it must prevail. The pioneer in it [education] may get scratched, perhaps shot, but his services will, at some time produce their effect. This sustains me thro' all these conflicts."[35]

The correct method to find true morality, rather than the explication of a system of intellectual knowledge, would be Mann's discovery. He had no real interest in dogmatic codes of belief, but he felt sure of finding a moral law that would guide correct behavior. Men would find and adopt a sense of the right rather than obeying authoritarian positive law. Unbreakable and unbending personal conscience would be the goal. Schools would "bend their energies to secure, not uniformity of a supposed good creed, but universality of known good morals. Conscience has a higher function than intellect; the love of truth is better than the love of logic."[36]

Immorality, not irrationality, was the central opposing force to Mann's sense of truth. Finally, he was not a rationalist but a moralist, and sin rather than illogic was his fear. Each man's moral sense, served by his reason, would conquer his tendencies toward evil. The "depravity" which shaped the past threatened anew to "pour out its agonies and its atrocities." The danger of immorality lurked inside each bosom. Man's raw emotional nature was always the enemy to his love of truth as his "propensities have no affinity with reason or conscience."[37] For men as social beings in the emerging democratic age, true morality had to be ingrained by the school or else the horrid inner passions would conquer all: "If the multitude, who have the power, are not fitted to exercise it, society will be like the herding together of wolves."[38] For Mann, there was no resolution between what he wanted humanity to become and what he feared men might be. The wolves always howled, just out of sight.

5

THE INDIVIDUALIST SEEKS FREEDOM:

MARGARET FULLER

Happy are all who reach that shore,
　　And bathe in heavenly day,
Happiest are those who high the banner bore,
　　To marshal others on the way;
Or waited for them, fainting and way-worn,
　　By burdens overborne.

　　　　　　　　　　　　　—Margaret Fuller,
　　　　　　　　　　　　　"Sub Rosa Crux"

I

Thomas Carlyle wrote to Emerson that Margaret Fuller wanted to swallow the world whole. No doubt Emerson clucked his tongue in slight distaste, but Fuller would have been pleased that Carlyle, of all men, had cast her in Byronic proportions. She did not believe in partial social constructs or goals but wanted to sense and experience everything for herself. American women, whom she wanted to serve as torch-bearer, had been even more tightly constricted by social conventions than had any other group of white Americans; now they too were free to taste, experiment, and look for a new life. Boundless, if undefined, and sometimes frightening, freedom dawned for her and for them:

No traditions chain them, and few conventionalities, compared with what must be met in other nations. There is no reason why they should not discover that the secrets of nature are open, the revelations of the spirit waiting,

77

> for whoever will seek them. When the mind is once
> awakened to this consciousness, it will not be restrained
> by the habits of the past, but fly to seek the seeds of
> a heavenly future.[1]

The seeds of human consummation lay in each breast, not in some
collective soul. Even if the explorations of one person could imply
meaning for every other person, each individual had to seek his
destiny by directly confronting the cosmos. No formalized sets of
relationships carried positive meaning for Fuller as they did for
other utopians and moral reformers. Association, she wrote, playing on the Fourierist concept, could be found only in similar
destinies, not in joint work: "Each one, by acting out his own,
casts light upon a mutual destiny, and illustrates the thought of
a master mind. It is a constellation, not a phalanx, to which I would
belong."[2]

In her search for absolute individual freedom, Margaret Fuller
reflected upon utopian communitarians and upon the general society
which all serious thinkers of the age hoped to lead toward a new
day. She both criticized and applauded the communitarians. She
held the same belief in revolutionary possibilities for human reconstruction, and, if her social analyses were more oblique than theirs,
nevertheless she too commented on the way the new world should
proceed and ached to apply her sense of cosmic moral truth to the
mundane world. In her highly individualistic fashion, Fuller tried
to build a new approach, a new lifestyle, a new emotional sensibility with which to face a rapidly opening world. As a pioneer in
creating a new role for liberated, artistic women, she had few
usable precedents upon which to draw and little help or understanding from society. Leaving conventional society, going out of any
present or future communitarian ideal or form, she was in constant
danger of becoming isolated and stranded.

Although she had been involved in the original planning of
Brook Farm, Fuller never lived there. She visited her many friends
there several times but always remained skeptical of such specific
social cures for humanity's malaise. She thought that men were
not wise enough to build model communities and that ideal men
might perfect social forms but that average men could not be essentially transformed by institutions. Individual liberation had to pre-

cede any social reconstruction. She did not believe that the environment could be a positive factor on the human will. She stated to William Henry Channing, "I will not write to you of these Conventions and Communities unless they bear better fruit. . . . I feel and find great want of wisdom in myself and the others: we are not ripe to reconstruct society yet."[3]

Any social scheme, Fuller felt, would be a "mere experiment" and could not produce immediate results.[4] Discovery had to be at the same time on a universal and on an individual level, and for each person the process had to be founded on unstructured, spontaneous, and continually shifting vantage points and goals. "Our lives should be considered as a tendency, an approximation only," she wrote.[5] Fuller's real anxiety about utopian communities was their tendency to become dogmatic and rigid even though they were reactions against those same qualities in the world outside. Any system of belief, however enlightened at its inception, could be transformed into an uncompromising code that would destroy the very freedom it was meant to foster: "Exclusive or excessive devotion, even to the worthiest objects, brings with it the evils of idolatry. What was intended to make the stair for man to rise to Heaven becomes a wall and a roof to shut him out from Heaven."[6]

Self-cultivation, not social adjustment, was always Fuller's central concern: "Very early I knew that the only object in life was to grow."[7] A timeless, perfected place would be an impossibility: A utopian community, however great its inspiration, could only be an unrealized experiment.[8] Nevertheless, as an experiment, communities could be worthwhile and should be attempted. No conceivable stone in the path to self-knowledge should remain unturned. Unlike her utopian contemporaries, she could not trust discovery through community, but she applauded them insofar as they conceived of themselves as experimenters in universal enlightenment. She viewed communitarians as her brethren while she had little faith in their projects: "Utopia it is impossible to build up. . . . Yet every noble scheme, every poetic manifestation, prophesies to man his eventual destiny."[9]

During the late 1840s, while in revolutionary Rome, Fuller moved to a more unqualified public affirmation of utopian socialism although she never became an essentially social and political thinker. In 1847, she found the European Fourierists wed to placid system and "terribly worrisome," and yet she felt that the emerging society would be theirs and that she had to try to conform her thought to theirs: "They serve this great future which I shall not live to see. I must be born again."[10] During her involvement with Mazzini's Roman Republicans, she absorbed something of their socialist spirit, at the very least as an intellectually meaningful alternative to the horrors of war and poverty that she observed around her. After the republic fell, she wanted to maintain her belief in the imminent advent of the socialist world community. She wrote to friends in 1849, "I have become an enthusiastic socialist. Elsewhere is no comfort, no solution for the problems of the times."[11] Yet in her heart, as she confided to her journal, also in 1849, she felt that any systematic social solution was just as distant as it had always been and that her utopian friends, however well intentioned, continued to see only a distorted part of the universe. "I take an interest in some plans, *our* socialism, for instance, for it has become mine too, but the interest is as shallow as the plans. They are needed, they are even good, but man will still blunder and weep, as he has done for so many thousand years."[12]

II

Margaret Fuller was permanently torn between serving truth—someone or something or some place greater than her and worthy of her worship—and acting out her own impulses without pattern or limits. At times, hers was a vision of ultimately being entrapped by fate, with the process of life an unfolding, unchallengeable inevitability; at other times, she felt that life was utterly free of any objective limits and that she could create whatever she willed. Fuller always longed for some deep, surging sense of fulfillment, and through this need she was driven into a process of renewed seeking, even as the goal of the quest would have been the resolution of the search.

Until she was thirty-five, in 1845, when she finally left New England for New York City and then Europe, Fuller remained in a highly constraining environment, which magnified her sense of incompleteness. She stayed at home most of that time, caring for her invalid mother and her younger sisters and brothers. Even her famous transcendentalist friends treated her with an extreme reserve that she longed to bypass for a deeper contact. She felt bound within a social pattern that gave her little room for personal experimentation and growth toward some heaven richer and warmer than the lean and cool one of the transcendentalists.

From her childhood, Fuller carried feelings of deep personal inadequacy. She felt that her father both overtrained her intellectually and starved her emotionally, thus sharpening her ability to analyze without giving her an adequate center of peaceful wholeness around which to build her ideas. She later reflected that his drills "finally produced a state of being both too active and too intense," which "wasted" her body and turned her into a freakishly divided self—by day a "youthful prodigy" and by night "a victim of spectral illusions, nightmares and somnambulism."[13] While her father was alive, she believed that she was unworthy of him and unable to give him anything of value; she thought that her only role was to sit mute, worshipping at his feet. She wrote to him in 1825: "I cannot make myself interesting to you; to your strictures on my conduct and manners—however valuable to me, I can return nothing but thanks."[14]

Even when the child Margaret was at her happiest, walking alone in the springtime in the family garden, she felt she was too base to be alive among the newborn flowers. Nature was fresh and lovely; she was homely and in unhappy confusion, far beneath nature's purity. Just to conceive of nature's perfection, far above her meager potentiality, made her feel lowly and earthbound. "When all things are blossoming," she lamented one May in her journal, "it seems so strange not to blossom too; that the quick thought within it cannot remould its tenement. . . . I am such a shabby plant, of such coarse tissue. I hate not to be beautiful, when all around is so."[15]

If the ideal resided in nature's springtime, Fuller wanted to be as pure as the flowers: "An ambition swelled in my heart to be as beautiful, as perfect as they."[16] Later when she more actively pursued a specific location in which to find fulfillment, the simplicity of nature and the importance of a direct relationship between it and herself remained in the back of her mind. She needed to

be alone in her earliest remembered place, her garden, but somehow filled with a greater peacefulness. She wrote to William Henry
Channing in 1843: "I must be gone, I feel, but whither? I know
not: if I cannot make this plot of ground yield corn and roses,
famine must be my lot forever and forever, surely."[17]

Far from feeling fruitful, Fuller sensed that the building of possible approaches to fulfillment had been prevented by circumstances.
She was burdened, especially after her father's death in 1835, with
the care of her impoverished family and with living much of the
time in places remote from the quicker pulse of Cambridge and
Boston. She was cut off from those friends who might meet her
on a high plane. Inwardly, she was constantly sick, as were so
many nineteenth-century ladies, driven by terrible headaches to take
refuge in her bed nearly every afternoon, there to write passionate
letters to her distant female friends and more awkward and proper
ones to men. Enervating illness and physical remoteness kept her
away from nature, from people, from much hope for her future.
She lived for any possible glimmer of self-transcendence: "I dreamt
that my body was a dungeon, and a beautiful angel escaped at the
head."[18]

Ralph Waldo Emerson seemed to offer Fuller, when they were
together, something of the relationship she wanted. He took her
very seriously. From about 1836 to 1842, they carried on a friendship with an accompanying correspondence which Perry Miller has
aptly called a "sexual duel."[19] As close as they came and as much
as she admired him, she was alienated and finally repelled by his
steely old New England reserve and sense of propriety. She wanted
to flow and he made her freeze. He was very puzzled by her as
well. "There is a difference in our constitution," he wrote her.
"We use a different rhetoric. It seems as if we had been born and
bred in different nations."[20] With Emerson, as with her father,
Fuller did not know what she could do or how she should act.
Her desires divided, she wanted both to attract him by her passion
and to conform with greater passivity to his constrained personality.

> The genial flow of my desire may be checked for the
> moment, but it cannot long. I shall always burst out soon
> and burn up all the rubbish between you and me, and
> I shall always find you there true to yourself and deeply

rooted as ever. My impatience is but the bubble on the stream; you know I want to be alone myself;—It is all right.[21]

Finally, Fuller felt that allowing Emerson to control their relationship by enforcing his sense of proper distance would lead her only to destructive self-denial. Even *his* approval was not worth the violation of her pursuit of open, passionate friendships—a betrayal which she grew to believe his nature demanded. With Emerson, she came to realize that she would always be on the outside looking in, and she was, by 1844, rebellious enough to blame him for this condition: "But Waldo, how can you expect the Muse *to come to you*? She hovers near. . . . Sometimes she looks in at your study windows when she can get a chance, for they are almost always shut."[22]

Fuller felt that both her father and Emerson, the two most significant men in her life, had rejected or at best only tolerated her as an emotional being; they had not attempted to find her inner nature. If she could not captivate them with what she thought were her very best qualities, to whom could she turn for acceptance? She must have felt like the passionate native princess crushed by the deacon of social rectitude whom she described in a book review written in 1846:

[Pocahontas] alone among strangers, rushes to [Captain Smith], calls him *father*, secure of a kind welcome to his heart. He, entrenched in cold conventional restraints, takes her hand, and leads her to a chair, addresses her as Miss or Madame, and freezes back at once the warm gushing stream of her affections with the ice of civic life.[23]

Since the central men in Margaret Fuller's life failed to meet her needs, she increasingly questioned the whole accepted ideal of finding answers in a man, in marriage. She wondered if she needed any guide to give her life direction, or if, instead, she could find her way alone. These were uncharted seas in her era and place. There were no exalted alternatives open to a woman outside of the home. Freedom in the simple sense of refusing to remain subor-

dinate to convention implied self-destruction. Merely to leave the
hearth meant being alone in the most frightening sense: it meant
going where no one had been before. Fuller long hesitated before
making her choices and continued, at times, to want to retreat into
a customary marriage. At the same time, she realized that she had
to go on, impelled by the idea of finding a role true to herself,
no matter how difficult. She confided in a reminiscence:

> My mind often burns with thoughts . . . which I long
> to pour out to some person of superior calmness and
> strength, and fortunate in more concrete knowledge. I
> should feel such a quieting reaction. But generally it
> seems best that I should go through these conflicts alone.
> The process will be slower, more irksome, more distress-
> ing, but the results will be my own and I shall feel greater
> confidence in them.[24]

During one of those moments when her loneliness overcame her
pride, Fuller wrote that she "should be a pilgrim and sojourner
on earth, and that the birds and the foxes would be surer of a place
to lay the head than I."[25]

No man she had known could give her real guidance: she needed
an ideal of the individual, a genius of universal proportions and
superhuman insight: "Such a man would suddenly dilate into a
form of 'Pride, Power, and Glory,'—a centre, round which asking,
aimless hearts might rally,—a man fitted to act as interpreter to
the one tale of many-languaged eyes."[26]

This genius was no mortal male; he was the exemplar of human
perfection toward which Fuller herself could strive. Only a magnificent model could call for that ultimate demand upon her own
actions which would lend full justification to her life. Thus she
was expressing more than sexual confusion when she wrote to William H. Channing: "I wish I were a man, and then there would
be *one*. I weary in this play-ground of boys, proud and happy in
their balls and marbles. Give me heroes, poets, lawgivers, Men."[27]
She had to aim for the pantheon herself, to be the genius for her
age.

She knew, of course, that she could not turn herself into a man,
and so, as a woman, the manner of climbing the stairway

to greatness was undefined. She did not know how to go about reconciling the conditions and values imposed on womanhood in her day, many of which she did not want to reject, with the demands of a life of artistry and genius. The problems of alienation from the general American society, which all members of the newly emerging cult of art were experiencing, were in her case magnified by the dilemma of being a pioneer woman emancipationist. She concluded:

> I want force to be either a genius or a character. One should either be private or public. I love best to be a woman; but womanhood is at present too straitly-bounded to give me scope. At hours, I live truly as a woman; at others, I should stifle; as, on the other hand, I should Palsy, when I would play the artist.[28]

III

After drifting beyond youth in which she correctly performed her roles of daughter and elder sister within the home, taught a little, wrote for and helped to edit the pretentious *Dial*, and held conversations with proper Boston ladies, Margaret Fuller at age thirty-five took her destiny fully in her hands and leaped toward a freer life. Transcendental contemplation inside old New England cottages, even with their lovely gardens, was insufficient. Henceforth her life was to be her art. "I cannot endure that the beautiful in feeling should not be manifested by the high *in action* rather than in that inward life which to many of the highest, seems to suffice."[29] Never in life having had "the happy feeling of really doing anything," she was ready "really to feel the glow of action!"[30] She went to New York in 1845, to work on Horace Greeley's *Tribune* as the first professional woman journalist in America. Two years later, she departed for Europe where she was to find a life of greater intensity and, finally, tragedy.

While Fuller was in America, her image of Europe had been dominated by the ghosts of Goethe and Beethoven, illuminated by George Sand, so free in her Paris salon, and prepared by an emerging generation of liberal romanticists for the great forthcoming revolution of hope. Here was fertile ground for the flowering of genius; this would certainly be her true homeland as well. She went to Europe, as would many later generations of young Americans, to reclaim her proper birthright in the lands of America's parentage. She was certain, after her first tour through the continent, that she had found her stage for true action, and only regretted having waited so long for her voyage of discovery. In addition, Fuller was immersed in her first sexual affair with Giovanni Ossoli, a somewhat simple but nevertheless handsome Italian count who was ten years her junior. She wrote to Emerson from Rome in December 1847:

> I find how true was the lure that always drew me towards Europe. It was no false instinct that said I might here find an atmosphere to develop me in ways I need. Had I only come ten years earlier! Now my life must be a failure, so much strength has been wasted on abstractions which only came because I grew not in the right soil. However . . . Heaven has room enough, and good chances in store, and I can live a great deal in the years that remain.[31]

Then, in early 1848, she discovered that she was pregnant. Refusing Ossoli's offer of marriage, she went into the hills near Rome to await childbirth. Her son Angelo was born on September 5, 1848.

Giuseppe Mazzini proved to be a renewing messenger to Margaret Fuller's hopes for heroic life. In February 1849, his supporters created the Roman republican rebellion into which she was swept. Putting aside her personal difficulties, she returned to Rome and plunged into the battle, nursing wounded soldiers, encouraging Mazzini and his young aides, enjoying a deep and active revolutionary involvement in what seemed at the moment the first wave of an oncoming flood of European democratic liberation.

By July 1849, the Roman Republic was encircled and slowly crushed by French troops, and Fuller fully realized that her personal quest for a new lifestyle had failed as well. The hopes of the year before seemed dashed, reversed. Nothing had worked out as she had hoped and planned. Europe, first an idealized projection of her hopes and then the vessel for her activism, had been trans-

formed into the shattered hull of despair: "The world seems to
go so strangely wrong! The bad side triumphs; the blood and tears
of the generous flow in vain. . . . Eternity is with us, but there
is much darkness and bitterness in this portion of it."[32] On all
levels of her perception, life on the heightened plane of newly liberated, daring participation had been overwhelmingly defeated; only
a spark of stoicism kept her at all sanguine about the future.
"Private hopes of mine are fallen with the hopes of Italy," she
wrote to her brother Richard. "I have played for a new stake and
lost it. Life looks too difficult. But, for the present, I shall try
to waive all thoughts of self, and renew my strength."[33]

Blind fate, Margaret Fuller now was positive, had always possessed her; she could will nothing. All the events in her life were
merely symbols or signs imprinted by some omniscient force. She
had not willfully created a heroic style of existence by challenging
a destructive society; rather, her life had been an unfolding series
of metaphors, directed in every instance by some unknowable and
ravaging fate. "It does not seem to be my fault, this destiny. I
do not court these things,—they come. I am a poor magnet, with
power to be wounded by the bodies I attract."[34] Fuller was sure
that the gods would now destroy her, as they had already ruined
her quest for consummation, and that no actions of hers could prevent her demise: "My life proceeds as regularly as the fates of
a Greek tragedy, and I can but accept the pages as they turn."[35]

With the Roman rebellion so brutally repressed, the politically
suspect Fuller was no longer welcome in Italy. She had to find
a new home. The thought of returning to America without money,
without prospects, and without youth to buoy her dreams of the
future depressed her deeply. As proud and independent as she was,
she still was full of anxiety about the reactions of her New England
friends, for she felt she had broken all their taboos on marriage,
family, and sexual decorum—rules that remained very real even
though she had thrown herself against them. "I have acted with
great carelessness, but do, if you can, excuse," she begged one
friend.[36] She was defensive to the point of shame about her son
and about Ossoli, whom she finally married in Florence in September 1849, for his youth, his exotic background and his lack
of intellect and learning. He was a distant shadow of the "heroes,
poets and lawgivers" she had once demanded. Yet she loved in

him that which she feared others would mock and reject—his "simple, childlike piety."[37] Ossoli would not fit in her serious-minded New England circle. Her often cold brother Richard, she wished, would take her faunlike husband under uncritical charge: "For a good while you may not be able to talk with him, but you will like showing him some of your favorite haunts: he is so happy in nature, in sweet tranquil places."[38] Knowing that she was preceded across the Atlantic by "a cloud of false rumors and impressions," she girded herself for the voyage:[39] "I go home prepared to expect all that is painful and difficult."[40]

In the end, Margaret Fuller Ossoli was without a place to go. Genuinely homeless, with nothing in the cultures of Europe or America to console her, without even the comfort of other sufferers in her situation, she was truly lost. There was no remaining community or projection of desires in which she could place her faith.

On July 18, 1850, as the Ossolis approached New York, a terrible storm broke up their ship. Although some of the other passengers were able to reach shore during lulls in the high winds, Fuller remained on board with her family until the vessel was utterly torn apart and they were thrown into the sea and drowned.[41] The final scene in the drama of her life was written. Instead of persevering into increasingly painful and humiliating wanderings in her homeland, her life had been tragically resolved. Ironically, she had been able, to some degree, to choose a beautiful death.[42] Making no move to go ashore was a negative yet willful action; by waiting on board she helped fate.

6

FROM UTOPIA TOWARD POLITICS:

GEORGE WILLIAM CURTIS AND

CIVIL SERVICE REFORM

The active sentiment of nationality is a growth, and a growth so gradual and unconscious that its force, in our own case, was ascertained only by the severest test. The old ideal of a cluster of small, individually powerless communities, leagued against a possible common enemy, vanishes under certain conditions as surely as dew dries when the sun rises. Community of race, of language, of religion, of tradition; immediate neighborhood, and constant and necessary mingling of people, combination of interests and purposes, and the welding together of remoter parts by steam, the telegraph, and space-annihilating inventions and enterprises; and over all the instinctive knowledge that cohesion is life, and that separation is death—these make a nation of such neighbors, and a nation that can not be disintegrated.

—George William Curtis, "The Easy Chair," *Harper's Monthly* (May 1881)

I

As did dozens of reformers, George William Curtis rallied loyally to the nation during the Civil War. Experimental communities designing future perfection had to be thrown to the winds of memory while the question of social survival remained central. The demands of the individual and the special interests of small groups of men meant nothing in the face of a war made holy by sacrifice. The experience of the Civil War led many reformers to begin to redefine what were the natural means and ends of social action. For Curtis, the demands of the war took freedom away from the individual and the fragmented local communities in order to guarantee the unity that was essential to the maintenance of national liberty.

> War is totally inconsistent with the unrestricted enjoyment of personal and political rights. However consecrated, however inevitable, war secures its ends by brute force. It must have unity of sentiment or, that being impossible, it must disembarrass itself of criticism which would be armed opposition if it dared. When, therefore, battle begins, debate ends, because then words are things. . . . Therefore when war is unavoidable and as holy as ours is, we must embrace it wholly and heartily for the sake of peace. You can not carry the olive-branch and the sword together, for the olive will hide the sword, or the sword the olive. . . . War willingly accepted is the willing renunciation of rights for a certain time and for a particular purpose.[1]

Doubt would have undermined the national morale. It would be unthinkable to permit active opposition to the war. "Now to oppose the war, under whatever pretext, is to favor the rebellion, and compass the overthrow of the Government. Is then, encouragement to the rebellion a legitimate constitutional opposition?"[2] Curtis repressed his own anxieties about the conduct of the national leaders, suspending judgment because he believed they were carrying out the national will. "They know the actual details which must control action, and as long as I know that and do not doubt their loyalty, I can stand waiting to understand their course."[3] After the war, his hard-learned subordination of criticism to the demands of national loyalty would remain to circumscribe forever the previously far less limited range of social thought which had made the enactment of utopia seem plausible to him.

A new American arose from the war, purged of the contamination of false compromises, purified by the blood of his martyred brothers. Curtis had written as the war began: "Do not suppose that the suffering of the few heroes who fall in maintaining principles which shall make all mankind happier, and finally spare their blood, is a worse thing than the canker of a false peace, which corrodes caution into cowardice, and for patriotism gives us pusillanimity."[4] Even more important than this birth of the heroic citizen was the emergence of a belief in the nation as an imperishable, solid entity. Localism and self-serving individualism had been burned down, and a national consciousness had grown, overriding and enveloping all the other conflicting sentiments held by Americans. "Every man who has been proud of his country hitherto has now profounder cause for pride," Curtis wrote at the time of Appomattox. "Our system has been tried in every way; it rises purified from the fire. No one man is essential to her, however deeply beloved, however greatly trusted."[5] It now remained to embody permanently that consciousness within new social forms.

The Civil War was a symbolic watershed for George William Curtis. Before the war, he was a dreamy individualist at Brook Farm and a mystical travel writer about the Orient; his temperament contained nothing of the lockstep order which he imbued during the war. With the approach of the conflict, his faith in internal exploration began to diminish as his commitment to abolitionism increasingly inclined him toward what he considered appropriate social realism and nationalism. His considerable Unionist propaganda efforts as editor of *Harper's Weekly* and *Harper's Monthly* sealed for the rest of his life his frame of reference. After the war, as leader of the civil service reform movement, he remained in the national political field of battle despite his growing disillusionment with the corrupt national politics. A fastidious Brahmin, he never enjoyed the conflict of the late nineteenth century, yet he stayed in the swirling mainstream of events. Guiding his continued efforts was a vision of an ideal political process cleansed of intruding spoilsmen, returned to the pristine clarity of the Founding Fathers' vision. His movement was an elitist effort to show the way of public virtue to the nation through the aegis of an efficient and positive national government. Although he was playing a different game, responding to a far different world from that of the ante-bellum utopian communitarians, much of their spirit of social resurrection remained with Curtis' memory. The distance between utopia and feasible social reform had vastly increased, but Curtis could not have maintained his reformist stance without some hope of a culmination for society brought on by a specially informed group.

II

Brook Farm had been a gentle, pastoral, undefined experience for Curtis. Decades later, he remembered it as a perfect conclusion to childhood, an Eden where some men had found a cleansing community of love: "It lingers in the generous faith which no disappointment can finally chill, in the unsullied friendships, in the inextinguishable hope of humanity, which are doing their work elsewhere, and to which Brook Farm is but a beautiful and long-vanished mirage of the morning."[6] He had gone there in 1842, as a handsome, well-bred, and dreamy young man and had left the following year for a further period of drifting. Brook Farm reassured him of the value of independence and wandering; he gained neither great insight into society's problems nor a belief in their resolution through a perfected community. Upon entering Brook Farm, he had held a vague hope that, in scaling down life to simpler bucolic forms, men could escape a growing social degeneracy and recapture a natural artistry; but while he was there he came to believe that only the individual could find this pathway, that the potentialities for self-discovery had not been blocked by existing institutional forces, and that no general reform of society was needed. In 1844, he wrote:

> When I went [to Brook Farm], it seemed as if . . . the return to simplicity and beauty lay through the woods and fields, and was to be a march of men whose very habits and personal appearance should wear a sign of coming grace. The longer I stayed, the more surely that thought vanished. . . . Now I feel that no new order is demanded, but that the universe is plastic to the pious hand.[7]

The Fourierist systematization that the Brook Farmers attempted to adopt in the later stages of the community appalled the now-departed Curtis. Social amelioration would be brought about by each man's inner reform, Curtis wrote, rejecting the notion of progress through material redistribution; environmental shifts could be genuine only if they flowed from change in heart. "Leave to Albert Brisbane, and *id omne genus*, these practical etchings and phalansteries; but let us serve the Gods without bell or candle. Have these men, with all their faith and love, not yet full confidence in love? Is that not strong enough to sway all institutions that are, and cause them to overflow with life?"[8] In addition to rejecting environmentalism, Curtis discarded the idea that a man's basic identity was to be found in his membership in a definable community. At this time, reform meant for him, as it did for Margaret Fuller, continual self-culture individualism, not saving mankind by establishing the absolutely correct means of social action. Social relationships would be secondary and subsequent outgrowths of self-knowledge.

> What we call union seems to me only a name for a phase of individual action. I live only for myself; and in proportion to my own growth, so I benefit others. . . . Fourier seems to me to have postponed his life, in finding out how to live. . . . Reform is purification, forming anew, not forming again. Love, like genius, uses the means that are, and the opportunities of to-day.[9]

The possibilities of an individual's life, as Curtis sensed them, were boundless. Men could impose no final framework upon the world without constricting the movement of each man through ceaselessly shifting life. Clear individual identity, traditional relationships, permanent institutions, Curtis felt, were obstacles to man's ability to know his universe. "Is there any law at last? Nature seems so general and yet so intensely individual. . . . At bottom no things are similar. Harmony is only union, not identity."[10]

"Your nature leads you to general action upon the many," Curtis wrote to his fellow Brook Farm alumnus, Isaac T. Hecker; "mine sends me home that I may build a finer house and entertain nobly what ghosts may come."[11] Curtis left the community to find himself from the inside out. Nothing outside of him seemed valid, defined by law. Even his closest friends seemed so unreal in comparison to the swirling torrents of reactions they triggered within him, that he had trouble pursuing relationships. "My dreams do sometimes so surpass the waking reality that the charm of the suggesting person, if not lost, is indefinitely subdued and postponed."[12] Waking was a less vivid state than dreaming; worldly pursuits were only dim shadows cast by the inner light. In a poem, "Destiny," Curtis wrote:

> That dream was life, but waking came,
> Dead silence after living speech,
> Cold darkness after golden flame,
> And now in vain I seek to reach
> In thought that radiant delight
> Which girt me with a splendid night.[13]

Curtis pursued this fantasy beyond rationality when he traveled to "Araby."[14] He wanted, at least in part, to escape from the rigorous Western definitions of time and of history. "The Howadji . . . [travelers] . . . seek Cathay. In the morning, with widewinged sails, we shall fly beyond our history. Listen! How like a Pedler-Poet of Cairo chanting his wares, moans Time through the Eternity."[15] Timeless and boundless movement and color would be the properties of the place that would allow him to turn inward most freely. "No region is so purely the property of the imagination as the East."[16] In such a land of dreams, Curtis might transcend all traces of his former identity. "Once in Egypt, you are so far removed from things familiar, that you wish to unsphere yourself entirely, to lose all trace of your own nationality and to separate yourself from the past."[17] Such freedom implied limitlessness. Every emotion was expressed in every element of the life which moved around the perceiver, constantly calling on a welter of reactions.

> The East, like the natures which it symbolizes, is a splendid excess. There is no measure, no moderation in its richness and beauty, or in its squalor and woe. . . . Western beauty is intellectual, but intellect has no share in this oriental charm. . . . Men of profoundly passionate

natures, instinctively crave the East, or must surround themselves with an Eastern atmosphere and influence.[18]

As the Howadji, Curtis came to the verge of merging with this exotic rhythm, to the edge of sensual mysticism. He later described his strong reactions to two Egyptian belly dancers. The erotic bluntness of their "solid, substantial spasms" quite naturally aroused him. Theirs was "the most voluptuous motion—not the lithe wooing of languid passion, but the soul of passion starting through every sense, and quivering in every limb. It was the very intensity of motion, concentrated and constant."[19] At this point, Curtis withdrew from the final implications of his desire to blend into the East. With an unintentionally ironic wistfulness, he refused to conclude what he had started and turned from experience into memory. To the dancing girls he replied, "Addio, still-eyed dove! Almost thou persuadest me to pleasure. O Wall-street, Wall-street! because you are virtuous, shall there be no more cakes and ale?"[20]

The more he reflected, the more Curtis returned to the Western frame of mind. In his memory of the eyes of another Arab girl, he saw things he knew he could not have if he were to retain his old identity: "Gazelle-eyes, perhaps, the poets would have called them, not so much because the eyes of gazelles are intrinsically very beautiful, but because every association with the animal is so graceful and delicate, so wild and unattainable."[21] Progress and success were foreign to this place where individuals lost their distinctiveness. Nothing could be formulated intellectually so nothing could be changed. "Thus oriental life is an echo and a ghost. . . . You are pursued by the phantoms of unachieved success; you stumble along among ruined opportunities; it is a sphere unoccupied, a body unformed."[22] Curtis stopped looking for those ghosts he had been pursuing. He gently rejected mystical wandering and began to adapt to a sense of self, of time, of place, which he felt the traditional Western culture demanded of him. "The dream passes as the day dies, and to the same stars which heard your morning shout of desert praise, you whisper as you close the tent-door at evening: 'Better fifty years of Europe than a cycle of Cathay.' "[23]

Back in America, all of Curtis' images of utopia receded. They lived, if no longer reverberating in the center of his soul, then twinkling along its far edge. He wrote in 1857, "Utopia, Arcadia and the moon, are mirages in the very next field to youth; but they vaguely glimmer upon the distant horizon of age."[24] He now interpreted his earlier wandering as only a passing phase, as the merest unreal state of mind. "Bohemia is a fairy land upon the hard earth. . . . How many a youth on the verge of college and of manhood looks wistfully into Bohemia! How alluring it hangs before him!"[25] By 1856, Curtis had married, embarked on his life-long literary career, and entered politics as an abolitionist-Republican. As these commitments grew deeper, Curtis buried his earlier rootless feelings as Margaret Fuller never did.

By the time the Civil War began, he had long departed from the boundless search for self. His nationalist patriotism during the war confirmed his sense of increasing personal belonging in a set-ting of consolidation and continuity. He wrote to his wife in 1860, on the occasion of his thirty-sixth birthday, "I am no longer a waif, floating along Time like a leaf upon a stream, but in you and Frank and all my duties, I am so bound up and content, that I no more have those vague, restless yearnings, which were so sweet, yet so sad and disheartening."[26]

III

When the war was over Curtis remained a firm nationalist and loyal Republican, but he also searched for a means to purify the Union that was so firmly established as an ideal. If problems were now national in scope and relationships between large groups more political than moral, the goal of absolute social salvation remained from the ante-bellum utopian communitarian program. Reform of the civil service, a cause which he led from the war's conclusion until his death in 1893, was designed to cleanse national leadership of encroaching corruption and to return the Union to the unques-tionably high values of its origins. One group of vigilant men would use a single means to lead the citizenry to victory over evil. As had the ante-bellum utopian communitarians, Curtis placed central emphasis on the leadership of an enlightened elite, but he conceived of this special community as a pressure group within a national political context. Curtis accepted evolving American consolidation as natural and inevitable, but he hoped to shape it on the basis of timeless principles. He would remain a Republican for most of his life, but he would place the ideal of the nation above the party. He expressed both his hopes for salvation and his fears of a possibly ruinous future for America in an ambivalence toward his own political participation and in a certain aristocratic wariness about democracy, yet whatever his own preferred tastes, he never pulled himself out of an active role in the confusion of political life in the second half of the nineteenth century. Because it expressed both his participation and his alienation as a nationalist reformer in postwar American life, the civil service crusade was, for Curtis, the reform for the age.

The patronage system was to him the fulcrum of self-interested partisan power which threatened to capture all political positions and to use them corruptly, thus blocking any expression of the true will of the people in new governmental forms. Combatting this spreading evil would be another test of national virtue.

> The huge ogre of patronage, gnawing at the character, the honor, and the life of the country, grimly sneers that the people can not help themselves and that nothing can be done. But much greater things have been done. . . . If the spoils system, a monster only less threatening than slavery, be unconquerable, it is because the country has lost its convictions, its courage and its common-sense. . . . I know that patronage is strong, but I believe that the American people are very much stronger.[27]

Spoilsmen were a particularly dangerous group of ticklike men who were everywhere actively burrowing themselves into the flesh of the nation and drinking its blood. Curtis saw a "rapidly increasing range of patronage and a highly organized army of party stipendiaries distributed about the country and supported by the public treasury."[28] The emplacement of these men "fosters personal and official corruption, it paralyzes legislative honor and vigilance, it poisons the spring of moral action, and so, vitiating the very character of the people, it endangers the permanence of the nation."[29]

The portrayal of corruption was sharp and clear, the danger

imminent; men of virtue had to continue to rally against the forces of darkness: "The time has come when the people of this country must grapple with the trading politicians, the men who trade in politics for their own advantage, the vampires who suck the moral life-blood of the nation."[30]

If such a greedy group maintained itself in power, the people would be demoralized and would then turn against true principles. As early as 1860, Curtis had warned that "the leaders first debauch, flatter, and incite the ignorant masses, and then they fear them."[31] In this statement, Curtis betrayed an anxiety deeper than a fear of a small group of despoiling leaders. The people as a whole worried him. He found it difficult to trust a nation that would allow spoilsmen to arrogate power in the first place. The counterattack could not flow naturally from such a populace; it would come only from the educated, natural American elite, who instinctively knew virtue because they were virtuous. Curtis had long believed that men of character were foolishly shortsighted in their refusal to accept their political responsibilities. "How soon are politics likely to become cleaner in the hands of dirty men? Do you know what makes them so unclean now? It is not the beastiality of the groggery that does it—it is the indifference of the parlors."[32] It behooved the polite class within the parlors of decency to arouse itself in order to fight strangling public corruption, which would otherwise destroy it along with the rest of the nation. "If we would cleanse the foul chamber let us throw the windows wide open, and the sweet summer air will sweep all impurity away and fill our lungs with fresher life."[33]

Curtis operated on the unstated assumption that a clear moral issue would banish his own doubts about contradictions in the national character and direction. Publicly and consciously, he believed that an open conflict would mobilize the best men and clarify the lines between good and evil. The nation would morally reconstitute itself once more through a holy battle. Memories of his Civil War experience must have resounded in his head. "It was the fanaticism of abolitionism that has saved this country from the fanaticism of slavery," he had orated in 1864. "It was fire fighting fire. And the fire of Heaven is prevailing over that of hell."[34]

Curtis understood that national political parties were now permanent, if still not fully defined and consolidated, institutions and that he and all other reformers would have to operate in relationship to them. Yet this did not imply to him that he would have to swallow what he considered to be the degenerate morality of politics. "Undoubtedly party is the effective agency of progress, and organization is essential to party. But it does not follow that any kind of organization, used in any way and for any purpose, is indispensable or tolerable."[35] He always was conscious of a goal; he feared that politics tended to become a self-defining and self-justifying game, with no sense of ultimate values and hence with no moral direction. "The first object of concerted political action is the highest welfare of the country. But the conditions of party association are such that the means are constantly and easily substituted for the end. The sophistry is subtle and seductive."[36]

To counter the lowest common denominator version of partisanship, Curtis argued for the rule of the truly informed: "A crowd is not wiser than the wisest man in it."[37] America had been formed, he argued, by an elite of well-placed men, who had brought national aspirations up to their level. Such a class expressing purified values would always remain the conscience of the nation, the steward of timeless republican values to be protected against the dangers of democracy.

> It was not a mob, an ignorant multitude swayed by a mysterious impulse; it was a body of educated men, wise and heroic because they were educated, who lifted this country to independence and laid deep and strong the foundations of the Republic. . . . As educated America was the constructive power, so it is still the true conservative force of the Republic. . . . [This class] teaches patience in politics and strengthens the conscience of the individual citizen by showing that servility to a majority is as degrading as servility to a Sultan.[38]

Within the political system of his time, Curtis tried to maintain his vision of the true leader as a man of absolute principle. Only devotion to a truthful goal could validate participation in the political process. In his eulogy of Charles Sumner in 1874, he defined his version of the ideal politician:

> He was essentially an orator and a moral reformer, and
> with unsurpassed earnestness of appeal, emphasized from
> first to last by the incalculable weight of his commanding
> character, his work was to rouse and kindle and inspire
> the public opinion of the country. [He] fanned the flame
> of a holy hatred of the intolerable and audacious wrong.[39]

But how could such a soaring figure descend into the murky
battlefields of late nineteenth-century politics? Curtis knew that he
represented a despised minority. Yet he was sure that his class,
with its superior ethical gifts, could destroy the real forces of darkness and win a love from the people equal to that awarded to the
Founding Fathers: "It is educated citizenship, the wisdom and
energy of men who are classed as prigs, pedants, and impractic-
ables, which is first and most efficient in breaking the machine
and releasing the majority."[40] Only cleansed politics could create
a meritorious democracy. Curtis feared pulling himself down
through political participation into the filth of sordid actualities as
much as he believed that only through political activity could he
bring America up to that ideal republic which he visualized so
clearly. "If democracy means dirt and coarseness and ill-feeling
and bad manners, the less we have of it the better. If refinement
of manners is inconsistent with democracy, then democracy is
inconsistent with the highest civilization."[41] He felt that his natural
home was on that higher plane, aloof from entangling politics, but
that his duty demanded that he swallow his disgust and involve
himself. This ambivalence always lent a hesitant quality to his
political participation. In 1877, he wrote to Charles Eliot Norton
from his summer retreat in the Berkshires, "Oh dear! how much
I prefer these quiet hills, and how I am driven out on the stormy
seas."[42]

Despite all this intellectual and emotional distance from political
machinations, Curtis stayed in New York Republican politics
throughout the roughhouse era of Roscoe Conkling and fought the
machine with considerable insight and vigor. In national circles,
in 1871, he was named chairman of the Civil Service Commission
by President Grant, but in 1873, when that unfortunate man undermined his own agency due to senatorial pressure, Curtis resigned.

After 1876, as a leading anti-Conklingite, Curtis had a strong influence in the Hayes presidency and was offered the ministry to England, which he refused. He made his way among the feuding factions of his party better than many of the more professional politicians he so despised. Curtis was not without personal political ambitions. In 1869, when he refused the party's nomination for secretary of state of New York, he realized, with only partially concealed regret, that now he would never win the Republican bid for governor. His gentlemanly code prevented him, however, from openly acknowledging a desire that might conflict with higher principle. He wrote to Norton:

> Of course the party, as a party, must be vexed with me.
> . . . It spoils, probably, my political career, in the ordinary sense. . . . But at the bottom of my heart, I don't want to be [governor]. I couldn't enter upon public, official life, and devote myself to a political career of that kind with so much pleasure to myself or profit to the country or to the Cause, as in other ways. So what seems the loss of a great opportunity, to many of my friends, and to all politicians, is not a loss to me but a gain.[43]

Such irregularity kept Curtis out of power and out of favor with the managers of power. They resented Curtis' debasing portrait of them and could not believe that, as the author of haughty attacks upon them, he was motivated solely by principle. In a classic attack on gentlemen-intellectuals in politics, Roscoe Conkling denounced Curtis to the New York Republican convention of 1876 as the leader of the "man-milliners, the dilletanti and carpet knights of politics." To Conkling, men like Curtis "forget that parties are not built up by deportment, or by ladies' magazines, or gush. . . . Their vocation and ministry is to lament the sins of other people. Their stock in trade is rancid, canting self-righteousness. They are wolves in sheep's clothing. Their real object is office and plunder."[44] During this tirade Curtis sat calmly in the audience and quietly responded, according to Chauncy Depew, " 'Remarkable!' 'Extraordinary!' 'What an Exhibition!' 'Bad Temper!' 'Very Bad Temper!' "[45]

Of course Curtis' reactions against sullied partisanship ran a great deal deeper than that, and when the Republicans nominated James G. Blaine for President in 1884, Curtis was a leader of the Republican Mugwump decampment in favor of the Democrat Grover Cleveland, who promised greater decency and more civil service reform. At the Chicago convention of 1884, he had refused to bind himself to the Republican nominee. "A Republican and a free man I came to this convention," he declared, "and by the grace of God, a Republican and a free man I will go out of it."[46] As a free man, Curtis refused to place party loyalty above his private judgment of the worth of a candidate. In the acid test, principle triumphed. He renounced Blaine and the party that he loved: "I cannot urge anybody to support for the presidency a man who has trafficked in his official place for his private gain, and still less upon the ground that the party that nominated him is a better party than the other."[47]

The withdrawing purism of the Mugwump grew within Curtis during his later years, and he slowly started to sour on the direction of American change. He began to fear that continued immigration would destroy national patriotism and solidity. In 1888, he orated, "Let us beware, then, how we recklessly water our life-blood. [We should not] be imperilled by the ignorant, lawless, idle, and dangerous overflow of all other countries."[48] Although he was able to sympathize somewhat with workers when their means of protest were peaceful, if striking unionists employed violence, Curtis' deepest emotional propensities were repressive.[49] Immediately after the Haymarket Riot of 1886, he applauded "the heroic fidelity and bravery of the police of Chicago in the late street battle with brutal ruffians, all of whom seem to have been foreigners." There was no ambivalence in Curtis' alignment with the police: "It was an outburst of anarchy; the deliberate crime of men who openly advocate massacre and the overthrow of intelligent and orderly society."[50] The forces leading to national decay seemed out of hand. Discouraged about the effect of the partial reforms of the civil service, alienated from his party, unable to adjust to the apparent disintegration of the national will, by 1892, Curtis felt that American democracy had become a mockery. He praised the memory of Alexander Hamilton "and his scorn of spurious Democracy which is always found in all American parties."[51] Curtis felt only very remote hopes for the national future which he would not live to see. America had begun to consolidate, not only in corrupt national frameworks, but around the wrong values as well. Possibilities for national purification seemed as distant as the memories of Brook Farm and the Orient.

7

THE EVOLUTION OF ORDER:

EDWARD BELLAMY'S

NATIONALIST UTOPIA

> With a tear for the dark past, turn we then to the dazzling
> future, and, veiling our eyes, press forward. The long
> and weary winter of the race is ended. Its summer has
> begun. Humanity has burst the chrysalis. The heavens are
> before it.
>
> —Edward Bellamy, *Looking
> Backward, 2000-1887*

I

"Evolution, not revolution," Edward Bellamy declared in 1889, "orderly and progressive development, not precipitate and hazardous experiment, is our true policy."[1] For Bellamy, reform was a natural developmental process, not a sudden and total imposition of truth. The growing industrialism and social consolidation of his era could be coupled with correct moral values through minimal human effort. The mushrooming network of industrialism was not necessarily evil—it could be directed toward the public welfare. A nationally owned and managed economy would soon arise, binding the whole populace into one enormous community.

> The combinations, trusts and syndicates of which the
> people at present complain, demonstrate the practicality
> of our basic principles of association. We merely seek

to push this principle a little further and have all
industries operated in the interest of all by the nation—the
people organized—the organic unity of the whole
people.[2]

Organic totality would mark the end of social process. Once society
had burst the shell of its limitations, evolution would have finished
its task; order, having arrived, would be absolutely complete, and
history would be both finished and fulfilled.

Laurence Gronlund, Bellamy's intellectual associate, clearly
demarcated the line that he felt existed between earlier deductive
utopianism and Bellamy's inductive progressivism, when he wrote
of Saint-Simon and Fourier: "These primitive Socialists were true
'Utopists': they invented Systems; we are intent on discovering the
laws of development. They formed universal precepts; we ascertain
universal sequences."[3]

Bellamy was quite willing to envision himself as an heir of utopian communitarianism, albeit in a changed society which made
different demands. The ante-bellum abolitionist crusade, he felt,
had supplanted and redirected earlier associationist efforts, thus
breaking the direct chain tying him to past collectivist movements:

In a broad sense of the word the Nationalist movement
did arise fifty years ago, for in spirit if not in form it
may be said to date back to the forties. Those who are
not familiar with the history of the extraordinary wave
of socialist enthusiasm which swept over the United
States at that period and led to the Brook Farm Colony
and a score of phalansteries for communistic experiments,
have missed one of the most significant as well as most
picturesque chapters of American history. . . . Horace
Greeley would very possibly have devoted himself to
some line of socialistic agitation, had not the slavery
struggle come on, . . . and in this respect he was representative of a large group of strong and earnest spirits.
But slavery had to be done away with before talk of a
closer, kinder brotherhood of men was in order or,
indeed, anything but a mockery. So it was that presently
these humane enthusiasts, these precursors of National-

ism, were drawn into the overmastering current of the anti-slavery agitation.[4]

When some of his followers proposed the formation of new utopian communities, suggestions which demonstrated the tenacity of the communitarian model, Bellamy dismissed the idea as risky and at best anachronistic. The recourse to a perfectible community no longer seemed natural to him. All men, deeply tied together as they were by social conditions, now shared a mutual fate. A colony would provide escape only for the few; it would not serve, as antebellum communitarian theorists had believed, as the inevitable, institutional basis for imminent chain-reaction salvation. "We nationalists are not trying to work out our individual salvation, but the weal of all, and no man is a true nationalist who even wishes to be saved unless all the rest are. A slight amendment in the condition of the mass of men is preferable to elysium attained by the few."[5]

For Bellamy, national resurrection was the natural focus. Yet in wishing to achieve control and integration of the entire social organism, he aimed for a resolved and tranquil collective unit, a goal similar in spirit to that of earlier communitarian reformers. Inexorably proceeding, evolution would achieve a result as timeless and sufficient as the earlier collectivists would have built by deductive human fiat. The parallels should not be overdrawn; Bellamy grew to consciousness and made reformist efforts in what he felt to be a more complex environment than that of ante-bellum America. His uses of symbols and his vision of the size and the methods of organization of the completed society differed from the earlier communitarians. But the notion of replacing the chaos of history with a concrete, final, and truly moral image of the future, the desire to perfect men through environmental change, and the central question of proceeding from here to there remained central problems for Bellamy.

II

Sickly from early childhood (b. 1850), Edward Bellamy always maintained an invalid's voyeurist disposition. Expansive action was generally so remote from his very middle-class bedroom that he

tended to view life as a passive onlooker far from personal involvement. In his notebooks he once sketched out a "story based on
view from a mountain top of country round and oversight of the
doings of men. Narrated in first person by an invalid. . . . A big
telescope his only recreation."[6] For the confined Bellamy, contact
with others was most often built through an abstract imaginative
process, employing only one-sided observation. He plotted a story
of a "sly old bachelor who falls in love with a girl by watching
her through a telescope."[7] Bellamy was aware of the danger of
antisocial, antiexperiential self-absorption that could result from an
invalid's living so far from others: "[He conceived of a] case of
a man who loves a woman in his dreams who does not exist out
of them, and because he experiences deeper, keener, more voluptuous passion for this dream creature than he ever felt for a live
woman, he surrenders himself to the passion. How it affects and
wears him out."[8]

Bellamy both longed to enter emotion-filled relationships and
feared the consequent loss of self-control which such ties implied.
Concerning sexual passions, he felt dual tendencies within himself—comfortable conformity to a decorous external code and personal rebellion against expected modes of behavior. He confided
to his journal:

> To love a woman, to lose one's self in the intensity of
> passion, must be a fine thing, but the experience is said
> to be thorny. I fear I am too thoroughly self-conscious,
> a little too well-acquainted with the mechanism of my
> emotions to be capable of losing myself, except very tem-
> porarily, and then with a perfect knowledge of what I
> am doing, in any enthusiasm whatever.[9]

In all matters, Bellamy considered himself to be essentially a conservative. "I have a deep-seated aversion to change," he once
wrote. Yet he declared in the next sentence that he wanted to smash
stifling conventions and forge an active life that would contain its
own individualist ethic of activism: "There are times when a man's
vagabond instincts, all his longing for a wide, free life, rise in
terrible insurrection against all the stable, conservative habits and
assumptions of his life which . . . weigh him down."[10] This rebell-

ion through passive withdrawal rather than confrontation gave Bellamy the feeling of anticonventionalism at the same time that it fortified his sense of remoteness from life. He could both dramatize his continued retreat and bring select others into the circle of his more fervent, and thus redeemed, seclusion.

In the early 1870s, as he embarked on a career as a writer of fiction, Bellamy wanted above all else to break through the crust of convention and show men as they truly functioned beneath their social exteriors. Cultural repression, he believed, had only permitted the literary expression of surfaces; the more important, passionate insides of men had been covered by civilization's prudery.

> In Anglo-Saxon days when morality and tight-lacedness
> rule the roost there is no such thing as expression for
> the one half of human thought. The body in these latter
> straight cut days is covered to the chin and only the seven
> by nine patch of real skin called the face is left visible.
> So it is with the soul, so it is in literature. Only a conven-
> tional scope of ideas finds utterance. The rest are ignored.
> The great seething, storming, lusting, blaspheming soul
> of man is turned back on itself, and scarcely a foam fleck
> tosses over into the polite and proper world. It is as if
> the good folks thought that by refusing to see the ugly
> side of themselves, it would pine for lack of notice and
> after a while cease to exist. . . . For God's sake off with
> these interminable veils and petticoats wherewith ages of
> prudes have covered the antique strength and ruggedness
> of man's true nature. Let us for God's sake get at the
> truth, and have done with our ahs and ohs and qualms
> and queries.[11]

Despite this bold declaration of unbared naturalism and of a manhood he wanted to achieve, when he set his pen to work on stories Bellamy found directness in emotional, sensual expression hard to realize. He was very disheartened that he could not recreate in art the passions he felt welling within him and that the distance between awareness and expression remained so great. Through one of his characters, a female painter, he analyzed this anxiety: "What she most regretted was that she could not indicate in her sketch the swelling breasts of the knolls on the farm, for she had gone quite daft on the beauty of the curves of the hills, the secret of strength they seemed to hold.''[12]

For several years Bellamy mulled over the tensions he felt between action and observation, conventionalism and rebellion. In ''Eliot Carson,'' a story which he never could complete, the protagonist, instead of raising a family and entering the newspaper business as had Bellamy by this time, fled conventional life and resided Thoreau-like in the woods. Eliot rejected the definitions of time and work as contemporary American society so formally and rigorously established them. Business and the professions, the natural courses for respectable middle-class men, Eliot mused, ''all alike are states of involuntary servitude; all alike involve the cessation of anything like sustained mental culture or a life of thought at the threshold of manhood. Intellectual development thenceforth, though acute and brilliant, is limited to bread making expedients.''[13] In his sylvan hermitage, Eliot hoped to recapture the open searching of adolescence, the unstructured life possible in what had been the frontier and what was becoming bohemia. His rebellion, by its own dynamics, would lead him into a state of almost passive purity, into the perfection lying beyond the contradictory strivings of the will. ''I don't intend to do anything, but I hope to be something.''[14]

To show the distance between unconventional emotionalism and standard marriage, Bellamy cast two dissimilar women opposite Eliot in different versions of the story. One was the sweet preacher's daughter, Nelly Dona, who had offered to Eliot the kind of marriage Edward Bellamy probably felt he himself had entered. Early in this sketch, Eliot declared to Nelly that only her love had kept him on the narrow path of proper behavior: ''If you had refused me, I should have done the next best thing which would have been to adopt a lonely, loveless life of culture. Your love, my darling, redeems the life of physical labor from its grossness and its tedium, but without your love I would not live it.''[15] Eventually Nelly sensed the self-deceiving nature of this statement and realized that Eliot wanted his freedom, a state of nature to which she could not allow herself to descend. She gave him up to the true life, unleashing him from ''the load on your back which broke your wings, bound you to the ground.''[16]

The other woman, Edna Damon, had been as much a convention breaker as Eliot: she had renounced her faith publicly in her church, causing a scandal that forced her out of her community. Searching for a means to formulate her liberation from traditional faith and place, she literally stumbled into Eliot's special arcadian glade. Though Edna's presence offered Eliot everything the Nellies of the world could not, Bellamy balked at allowing consummation of such an obviously illicit relationship. Instead of giving himself entirely to her, Eliot gave her only his ideas. "She had fallen almost in a daze to the attitude of a learner at his feet. . . . He had broken the vault that had closed like trees over her and given her an infinite outlook and flight."[17] Eliot could approach closer to Edna only after convincing her of his intellectual beatitude and only when she had fallen asleep. Even at this juncture, it was she who had to bridge the final gap, and he never committed himself to sexual intercourse. The story was discontinued at this critical and, for Bellamy, unresolvable juncture.

> To make her regard him as a prophet and priest, worshipping him with an adoration too fine to be touched with love, or to admit of coquetery, until, when she comes to his hermitage, and he kisses her while he thinks her unconscious. Her blood takes fire at this caress as also his and their mutual passion dates from that hour. She then begins to try to captivate him.[18]

Even though incomplete, this story presented ground too dangerous for Bellamy to tread. He forced himself to retreat away from rule-breaking experimentation into more traditionally sanctioned relationships with men as they functioned in the society of which he felt a part. In the only story on the hermit theme which Bellamy published, a quite unthreatening lady who was bitten by a snake in the woods was rescued by a seemingly dangerous hermit who turned out to be a gentleman in disguise.[19] As with Marie Antoinette in her Versailles milk parlor, civilization was firmly and properly entrenched below the very thin veneer of a strangely primitive encounter.

Too ambivalent to pursue his internal longings for absolute and unbridled personal expression, Bellamy instead buried his passions and turned toward the outside world. Duty would replace self-analysis as his focus. One of his unpublished stories first placed a young minister on the brink of suicide—the final gasp of intro-spection—and then pulled him back from self-destruction at cliff's edge and into a life of service. "An hour afterwards I was on the midnight train bound for New York where six months of the hardest mission work among the poor and sick gave me health and strength again. After being so long a prey to a mania born of morbid subjec-tivity, I felt a tremendous urge toward objectivity."[20]

Subjectivity could be calmed by placing oneself within some lar-ger community of fellow men. Self-control and satisfaction would be obtained only through the subordination of individual personality to an enveloping social ideal. This discovery of salvation through social bonds, Bellamy called, in 1874, his religion of solidarity. "The instinct of universal solidarity, of the identity of our lives with all life, is the centripetal force which binds together in certain orbits all order of beings. In fine, the instinct of solidarity in the moral universe correlates with the attraction of gravitation in the material world."[21] In this concept Bellamy found an apparently naturalistic explanation for his membership in spiritual community. This affiliation, based on a belief in a positive moral structure lar-ger than the individual, reassured him that his new efforts were part of some cosmic scheme. "The genius is never self-conscious while the afflatus is upon him. He is beside himself and thus delivers his oracle of the universal, himself a priest of the infinite."[22] Presumably the cosmic order could evolve among men with the now tightly reined Bellamy as its prophet. By discovering external truths, he could quell his own doubts; when he forced him-self into duty, he found potential social laws. There would be, at the end of some heretofore unexplored process, a framework which would answer the needs of each man as part of humanity.

In his fiction of the late 1870s and the 1880s, Bellamy searched for some key to unlock the mysteries of change, some central insight to gain control over life. He sought to clarify both the shape of his own ongoing duty and the goals toward which society was progressing. Within the confines of fiction, one way to gain greater certainty would be to abolish the cyclic pattern of time and the vicissitudes of human existence within this uncontrollable con-tinuum and to create pure future by abolishing past and present.

To accomplish this ideal, in several of his stories Bellamy explored the current spiritualist idea of mind-reading and extended it to gaining foresight in life. "We write of the past when it is still in the future, and of course in the future tense," wrote a clairvoyant Marsman to a voyager from Earth in "The Blindman's World."[23] Absolute knowledge of the future would stop the flow of history. Contradiction would be ended within one-dimensional time; Adamic perfection would be regained. After his trip, the enlightened Earthling mused:

> The spectacle of a race doomed to walk backward, beholding what has gone by, assured only of what is past and dead, comes over me from time to time with a sadly fantastical effect which I cannot describe. . . . The people of that happy sphere [seem to] represent the ideal and normal type of our race, as perhaps it once was, as perhaps it may yet be again.[24]

Men would gain and maintain such a utopia only if they remained absolutely passive and allowed history to work on them. But unlike the earlier "Eliot Carson," this was a collective, not an individualist purity. As with time, man's physical and emotional nature would be fused and stilled. In a story similar in its theme of foresight to "The Blindman's World," Bellamy wrote of a clairvoyant race: "The absolute openness of their minds and hearts to one another makes their happiness far more dependent on the moral and mental qualities of their companions than upon their physical."[25]

Doctor Heidenhoff's Process, an early Bellamy novel, employed a magical electrochemical machine to destroy the evil memories belonging to a girl possessed by her past sins. She could not maintain a divided sense of self, and the good doctor promised a mechanical means to end one half of her dual nature, freeing the rest for pure love.[26] In *Miss Ludington's Sister*, a young spiritualist brought the past into the present for an old woman by bringing her long dead daughter back to life. All that had transpired since that death was abolished, and time was stopped in the past.[27]

In all these stories, Bellamy separated the narrator—and thus himself—from the process that seemingly had abolished contradiction. He proclaimed that he believed in reality and that his creations had been either hoaxes or mere fantasies of the characters within the stories. Through his declaration of distance from his creations, he tried to retain the conventional gulf between the imaginative and the actual. His stories, however, built rather than reduced an active, intertwining tension between these spheres of sensibility and led the reader to question what, at least for Bellamy, was illusion and what was "true reality." Furthermore the mysterious links between the sets of meaning, the seemingly hidden, but absolutely central, means of squaring realized life with potential life was diffused, not clarified or dismissed, in these stories. Bellamy muddied accepted definitions of man's limits of knowledge, his place in the world, and the nature of his universe as a whole. He implied absolute discovery and final control as mankind's destiny, but the method of evolution and the shape of the final order remained uncertain. Bellamy's self-imposed duty to the human community was to find the way.

III

It was by probing the fantastic as a means of obtaining final objectivity that Bellamy wrote his utopian masterpiece, *Looking Backward*, in 1888. He fell into his first political novel quite by accident. "I had, at the outset no idea of attempting a serious contribution to the literature of social reform. The idea was of a mere literary fantasy, a fairy tale of social felicity . . . a cloud palace for an ideal humanity," he reflected in 1890, during the novel's enormous vogue.[28] In the novel, he analyzed the social ills around him and proposed a cure for them, one key for turning seeming chaos into positive pattern. He achieved what he had felt was his duty, and by showing the combined evolution of industrialization and nationalization, pointed the way to a final, completely regulated, and consolidated society. He called both the evolutionary process and the goal "nationalism": "It takes the place of all other reforms not because it excludes any but because it includes all."[29]

In *Looking Backward*, set in Boston in the year 2000, the new society was complete and perfect. As opposed to the conflict-filled Boston of 1888, which Bellamy discussed in the novel at length, this was a place without tensions where men were freed from all

social and personal problems. Wise organization of the environment
had led men into the golden age.

In 1888, society had been divided by growing class acrimony,
with an emerging aristocracy forcing workingmen into permanent
proletarianization and draining the middle classes of their security.
The future had been bleak apparently for a society which resembled

> a prodigious coach which the masses of humanity were
> harnessed to and dragged toilsomely along a very hilly
> and sandy road. The driver was hunger, and permitted
> no lagging, though the pace was necessarily very slow.
> Despite the difficulty of drawing the coach at all along
> so hard a road, the top was covered with passengers who
> never got down, even at the steepest ascents. These seats
> on top were very breezy and comfortable. [Yet] the seats
> were very insecure, and at every jolt of the coach persons
> were slipping out of them and falling to the ground,
> where they were instantly compelled to take hold of the
> rope and help to drag the coach on which they had before
> ridden so pleasantly.[30]

These social divisions were, however, false surface appearances
obscuring far more hopeful underlying developments. The men of
1888 had had only to recognize an inevitably progressing societal
movement to escape their gloom.

> It was not necessary for society to solve the [labor] riddle
> at all. It may be said to have solved itself. The solution
> came as a result of industrial evolution which could not
> have terminated otherwise. All that society had to do was
> to recognize and cooperate with that evolution when its
> tendency had become unmistakable.[31]

Looking Backward was Bellamy's demonstration of this grand tendency. To him all indexes pointed through industrial development
to one final human consolidation: "The nation . . . organized as
the one great business corporation in which all other corporations
were absorbed . . . became . . . the Great Trust."[32]

The all-absorbing trust of *Looking Backward* had arrived shortly after 1888, when men reworked their frame of thought away from individualism toward collectivism.

> The movement toward the conduct of business by larger and larger aggregations of capital, the tendency toward monopolies, which had been so desperately and vainly resisted, was recognized at last, in its true significance, as a process which only needed to complete its logical evolution to open a golden future to humanity.[33]

This mass awareness apparently had been arrived at voluntarily when some unspecified forces—novels perhaps—caused Americans to see the truth. Conflict and violence withered in the face of real insight. "There was absolutely no violence. The change had been long foreseen. Public opinion had become fully ripe for it, and the whole mass of people was behind it."[34] Later, Bellamy compared this momentous shift to an enormous surge of religious conversion—which was as close as he got to explaining the social change which incorporated his optimistic progressivism: "The Great Revival . . . was the general awakening of the people of America . . . to the profoundly ethical and truly religious character and claims of the movement for an industrial system which should guarantee the economic equality of all the people."[35]

The central organization of the new society Bellamy called the Industrial Army. This was, he felt, merely the formalization in a sophisticated nation of the natural ties between all men—"a complex mutual dependence," Bellamy called it, which became "the universal rule." "Every man, however solitary may seem his occupation," Bellamy continued, rejecting outmoded individualism, "is a member of a vast industrial partnership, as large as the nation, as large as humanity."[36]

As a youth, only his weak health had prevented Bellamy from entering West Point, and his continued admiration for the supposed orderliness and efficiency of military rule was a repeated theme in the organization of the new society he imagined in *Looking Backward*. For Bellamy, enlightened authoritarian direction was the

natural response to the wasteful diffusion of power and wealth that
he saw around him.

> The effectiveness of the working force of a nation, under
> the myriad-headed leadership of private capital . . . as
> compared with that which it attains under a single head,
> may be likened to the military efficiency of a mob, or
> a horde of barbarians with a thousand petty chiefs, as
> compared with that of a disciplined army under one
> general.[37]

Lines of command and responsibility, the structure of power, were
cast into a concrete, pyramidal elite in Bellamy's vision. This was
a completed, permanent society, with the order-giving agencies
absolutely constructed and the mobility of the agents of power and
the relationships between them clearly understood. There was a
place for each man and each man was to be put in his place.

> The line of promotion for the meritorious lies through
> three grades to the officer's grade, and thence up through
> the lieutenancies to the captaincy, or foremanship, and
> superintendency or colonel's rank. Next, with an inter-
> vening grade in some of the larger trades, comes the
> general of the guild. [He] holds a splendid position, and
> one which amply satisfies the ambition of most men, but
> above his rank, which may be compared—to follow the
> military analogies familiar to you—to that of a general
> of division or major-general, is that of the chiefs of the
> ten great departments, or groups of allied trades. The
> chiefs of these ten great divisions of the industrial army
> may be compared to your commanders of army corps,
> or lieutenant-generals, each having from a dozen to a
> score of generals of separate guilds reporting to him.
> Above these ten great officers, who form his council, is
> the general-in-chief, who is the President of the United
> States.[38]

Further social restructuring was unnecessary; the new society, by
building order, had eliminated destructive variation. Perfected

institutions had guaranteed the permanent fulfillment of society, ending the need for politics to provide for further change. "We have nothing to make laws about. The fundamental principles on which our society is founded settle for all times the strifes and misunderstandings which in your day called for legislation."[39]

The rebuilt environment had perfected man's nature, Bellamy projected. "You will find . . . not only a physical, but a mental and moral improvement."[40] Bellamy's chronology of man's perfection was somewhat unclear at different points in the novel—mankind's moral revolution seemed both to have brought on the social revolution and to have followed from it. Bellamy clouded his analyses of the relationship between morality and social forces and that concerning the genesis and the continuing nature of change. What was certain was the final perfection of both man and his environment. Social and personal disorganization and, with it, all aberrant social behavior was ended: "the world has outgrown lying."[41]

Bellamy could not quite come to grips with potential slackers, nonconformists within his new nation. In one solution to the problem, he was willing to resort to coercion if men refused their obligations as members in the unitary society: "A man able to do duty, and persistently refusing, is sentenced to solitary imprisonment on bread and water till he consents."[42] This authoritarian statement, however, must be squared with Bellamy's belief that man's nature would have been changed and that the mass of people, now made "normal," would need no prodding. Antisocial or nonsocial behavior clearly would be a rare mental illness, Bellamy believed: "the new society proceeded to deal with all vicious and criminal persons as morally insane." Such persons were to be segregated in pleasant but remote places "and absolutely prevented from continuing their kind." Thus the gene pool would be washed clean, and the potential contamination of others by the unredeemable would be eliminated. Following this line of reasoning Bellamy ended contradiction within his envisioned society through humanely applied antiseptics, not through violence. He wrote several years after *Looking Backward*, "By this means the race, in the first generation after the Revolution, was able to leave behind itself forever a load of inherited depravity and base congenital instincts, and so ever since it has gone on from generation to generation, purging itself of its uncleanness."[43]

As with the shadowy process of transition into the perfected society and the clouded manner of the moral shift to man's better nature in Bellamy's vision, so the techniques of the novel itself unfocused the levels of apparent reality on which he was working. Bellamy used as his narrator Julian West, a nineteenth-century Boston aristocrat who was transported into the twentieth-century utopia. Nearly an invalid due to his insomnia, West slept in a hermetically sealed underground chamber, encapsulated far from the noise of his surrounding world. In addition, he often used sleeping potions and employed a hypnotist to put him into a trancelike sleep. The trance worked too well, however, and sleeping unscathed through a fire that destroyed his house above his chamber, West awakened one morning in the year 2000, whisked unchanged through the decades in a state of suspended animation. Thus, the transportation between the two worlds was accomplished through fantasy, but West remained materially "real," alive in his own skin, with all his faculties intact and unaltered.

As West tried to adjust to his new surroundings, he at first felt schizoid: "The idea that I was two persons, that my identity was double, began to fascinate me with its simple solution of my experience."[44] West feared that there was such a strong division between his perceptions in the new world and his memories of the old that he would no longer be able to retain an integrated sense of self: "The mental image of the old city was so fresh and strong that it did not yield to the impression of the actual city, but contended with it, so that it was first one and then the other which seemed the more unreal."[45] After an emotional crisis, West was redeemed, in the best nineteenth-century fashion, by a woman's love. But she was, as it happened, the direct descendant of West's fiancée in the old life; the long time sequence through which West and, through him, his society passed into salvation was magically collapsed rather than naturalistically broken apart into chaotic segments. Later West had a nightmare that returned him to 1888 and thus changed his frame of reference from the new world in which he had been living into the old one of time past, transforming realized perfection to mere hopeful fantasy. Though Bellamy awakened his hero in the Boston of the year 2000, the relationship of dreaming to waking and the lines between reality and fantasy in the texture of the novel as a whole were even more deeply blurred.

Sequential and spatial relationships between events in *Looking Backward* did not form a simple linear progression to a goal. The places and times and relationships and transitions between Bellamy, West, the characters of the new society, and the readers in the old all seem partly concrete, partly ethereal. The ideal society was on the one hand a culmination of a realistic depiction of history and on the other a timeless, suprahistorical reality above the chaos of the mundane and false world of transitory events. The role of human effort was consequently uncertain: men seemed to be asked both to strive together toward socially comprehensible, external goals and to seek the essence of truth through a strictly internal, individualistic conversion.

As did thousands of the readers of *Looking Backward*, Bellamy desired to institute his social vision immediately in America. Yet no method of enactment could be imposed which would incorporate at once the totality of that vision, and the fulfilling wholeness of the new society was its central attraction. Continuing illness as well as uncertainty about his proper role kept Bellamy from an activist stance, as perhaps did some deep fear of spoiling the clarity of the product of his imagination through the application of his worldly will. In addition, he had little self-assurance that he and his potential allies could manipulate America's vicious political system. Instead, he predicted that, in the tangible future, these evil processes would disintegrate, creating a vacuum to be filled spontaneously by honorable men using far different and purer methods. Thus, the same vagueness that characterized the social transition within *Looking Backward* reappeared in Bellamy's attempts to translate his fictionalized vision into political action. He wrote to a supporter in 1894:

> I've seen great things ahead. . . . I think the significant thing now is the break-up of parties in Congress. There is going to be right away a complete smash-up of party politics, and for many years there will be nothing but confusion. Then nationalism will crystallize; that, however, is not yet by a number of years.[46]

Without any guidance from Bellamy, "Nationalist Clubs" sprang up all over the country after 1888. The clubs spawned *The Nationalist* journal (1889-1891), and Bellamy later edited *The New Nation* (1891-1894), a monthly which replaced the earlier one which he did not publish. He was pleased that there was no centralized organization to these discussion and propaganda groups; their uncontrolled, evolutionary growth seemed to forecast the kind of political revolution he hoped for:

> There never was, perhaps, a reform movement that got along with less management than that of the Nationalists. There has never been any central organization of the clubs. . . . While these clubs have been and are of the greatest use, and have accomplished remarkable results in leavening entire communities with Nationalism there has never been any special effort to multiply them or otherwise to gather the whole body of believers into one band.

The clubs were but one result of "forces long in operation," which were working "consciously or unconsciously towards the same inevitable result."[47] To connect the "inevitable result" with current social dilemmas, Nationalists generally supported municipal gas and water socialism. On the national scale, Bellamy, like the contemporary English Fabians, favored nationalization of key industries: telephones, telegraphs, railroads, and coal mines. The rest of American industry presumably would soon follow this demonstrably superior form of industrial organization.[48]

Nationalism was to be a movement led by the better sort, "those who partake most of the Spirit of the Greater Self," Bellamy called them.[49] Only the cultivated elite of this nation could understand and implement the truly moral society. "I thoroughly approve what you say as to directing your efforts more particularly to the conversion of the cultured and conservative class," Bellamy wrote to temperance leader and fellow Nationalist Frances Willard: "That was precisely the special end for which *Looking Backward* was written."[50] The movement, led by men of unquestioned moral stature, was designed to enact for the first time the moral abstractions of traditional religion: "Nationalism is applied Christianity, and as fast as men shall be filled with the real desire to apply Christianity, they are bound to become nationalists, for there is no other way."[51] Since the current mismanagers of the economic and political system were but temporary despoilers of a basically sound evolutionary process, the nationalist elite upheld the true American tradition of combining proper social change with the maintenance of institutions.

> We are the true conservative party, because we are devoted to the maintenance of republican institutions against the revolution now being effected by the money power. We propose no revolution, but that the people shall resist a revolution. We oppose those who are over-throwing the republic. . . . We are not revolutionists, but counter-revolutionists.[52]

For Bellamy and his very respectable readers, and for millions of workers and farmers as well, the great fear was annihilation by a few powerful plutocrats. Either the decent classes would immediately take the driver's seat atop the coach of evolution or base men would downgrade them into utter powerlessness. Some sort of social order was imminent; the nature of its leadership and values were the basic issues. "If the nation does not want to turn over its industries—and that means its liberties as well—to an industrial oligarchy, there is but one alternative; it must assume them itself. Plutocracy or Nationalism is the choice which, within ten years, the people of the United States will have virtually made."[53] Certain mysterious men, operating just under the surface of national life, were the source of the broad discontent which Bellamy felt. All the diverse elements that would shape the future could be understood in a unitary context; the enemy had to be identified for the holy battle to be joined.

Bellamy knew that he had to convince the working classes that they shared this mutual danger, even though his natural ties were with the middle class. Nationalist clubs were theoretically open to everyone, but they were almost always run by ministers and professional men. Bellamy expressed both anxiety about the middle-class nature of his followership and a rather gingerly flirtation with the workers when he wrote:

> Nationalism can no longer be twitted as a "kid-glove"
> movement. The workingmen are swelling its ranks very
> rapidly. A good many of them at first [felt] it was nothing
> but a fine-spun theory, but as they come to examine it
> they are bound to discover that it is the only really practi-
> cal labor party in the world.[54]

During the early 1890s, the Nationalist movement became, in
effect, the eastern branch of the Populist party. But the western
and southern Populist leaders were strange men using methods and
appeals that unnerved Bellamy. He viewed the Populist collapse
in 1896 with real relief, as it released him from an uncomfortable
partnership with men who were somehow beneath him. "While
we are left practically without a party, it is a good riddance, seeing
that the organization had fallen in bad hands," he wrote to Henry
Demarest Lloyd. Now a clear and rational declaration could be published "to explicitly declare for full nationalization of the productive and distributive machinery as our government." This document
was to be written not by the former unnatural alliance of Populists
and Nationalists but by "a sufficient number of persons of large
reputations. . . . Everything, of course, would depend on the might
of the names behind such a manifesto."[55] Although the common
man shared the dangers of men of station, Bellamy had little faith
in his ability to lead a clear battle and feared his own potential
for contaminating the true doctrine.

Bellamy knew that new doctrine as well as new class alliances
were needed to reinvigorate the seekers of the true morality of traditional American values, but he was afraid of using ideas thought
to be subversive. He rejected socialist language, putting a lid on
the threats which he felt lurked beneath the surface meanings of
such systems of analysis:

> In the radicalism of the opinions which I have expressed
> I may seem to out-socialize the socialists, yet the word
> socialist is one I never could well stomach. In the first
> place it is a foreign word in itself and equally foreign
> in all its suggestions. It smells to the average American
> of petroleum, suggests the red flag, with all manner of
> sexual novelties, and an abusive tone about God and

religion. . . . Socialist is not a good name for a party
to succeed with in America. No such party can or ought
to succeed which is not wholly and enthusiastically
American and patriotic in spirit and suggestions.[56]

By this time in his life, Bellamy was thoroughly frightened by
the unbounded chaotic passions and unsolvable contradictions that
he felt might lie underneath the surface of social change, within
the implications of doctrine, and inside the souls of men. A programmatic political movement brought on many dangers and yet
seemed far from able to capture the surging change in America
in a bounded frame of purity. Bellamy tried to locate all the
diverse, anxiety-producing problems in the hearts of a few corrupt
men and to construct, under the guidance of men of higher values,
a moral new world, within a new dimension of time, purged of
all the evil forces the few monsters stood in for in his own time.
Clean evolution to pure order was imperative; the sordidness of
many men's motives and the possibility that conflict was inherent
in all societies did not sit well with reformers who wanted
unblemished solutions. By Bellamy's time, the apparent distance
between discouraging social realities and hopes for perfection was
increasing, and utopia was receding, possibly to be reached only
through a mesmerist's trance.

8

THE DEATH OF UTOPIA AND THE CREATION OF ANTI-UTOPIA:

IGNATIUS DONNELLY

Life is a dark and wretched failure for the great mass of mankind. The many are plundered to enrich the few. . . . The rich, as a rule, despise the poor; and the poor are coming to hate the rich . . . standing armies are formed on one side; and great communistic organizations on the other; society divides itself into two hostile camps; no white flags pass from the one to the other. They wait only for the drumbeat and trumpet to summon them to armed conflict.

—Ignatius Donnelly,
Caesar's Column

It is as if one had plucked a star from its serene place of beauty and hurled it, down the air—its long train of terror and horror blazing behind it—down to blackness and ruin.

—Ignatius Donnelly,
Diary, 1868

I

In Ignatius Donnelly's eyes, when politics was emptied of all implicit moral direction, American society would surely careen out of control toward disaster. Without clear goals to justify it, the political process apparently was being captured by evil men or evil forces that were turning upon the people whom the system had been designed to serve. The culmination of this movement, if it

124

were not soon halted, would be utter social destruction, the anti-utopia of world cataclysm.

Donnelly developed this belief during a barren career as a third-party politician in rural Minnesota in the latter half of the nineteenth century. He enunciated it most clearly in his Populist writings and activities during the early 1890s, when many Americans shared his plaguing fears that the nation had gone awry and was headed toward chaos. In his personal despair as well as in his publicly expressed discontent about the society around him, Donnelly plumbed the forces of imminent breakdown which seemed to have undermined the foundations of life in the American republic. Through his political and literary creations, one can almost smell the rapidly spreading fires of disaster.

It was impossible for Donnelly to pierce the gloom and arrive at an analysis of exactly what was transpiring. He did not know whether to blame society's difficulties on the fates, who were proceeding inexorably and naturalistically among an already fallen people, or on certain men who were acting out evil designs upon a basically innocent populace but who still could be stopped. He was uncertain whether he was witness to a general process of social decay or merely to a temporary aberration imposed from without upon a sturdy society. It was unclear whether government could be opened enough to be reinvigorated with correct moral values or whether the political process was so degenerate that it would ruin all virtues that touched it. The people, who sometimes appeared eagerly corruptible, often seemed merely momentarily blinded dupes with essentially good instincts. The approaching convulsion might be cleansing or it might lead to perpetual nihilism. Donnelly's own stance toward the process and the people was uncertain: he was either a helplessly clairvoyant Cassandra or a Moses waiting for the people to hear and obey his absolutely truthful call. Even if he could build a utopian community the response of the society as a whole was impossible to predict. Perhaps the perfect community would serve as an active beacon to the impure world; perhaps it would become only a remote haven for the few visible saved, serving as a reminder of what might have been if men had only foreseen and prevented the horrendous birth of anti-utopia. Or, finally, universal fire might consume even the most abstract ideal of a distant peace.

II

Donnelly's early life conformed to much of the rags-to-riches convention, a code which he made the basis of his self-evaluation. He was born in 1831 in Philadelphia and raised by his austere and distant mother, an Irish Protestant pawnshop operator. He practiced law and wrote propaganda for the Democratic party until 1856, when he married and moved to the West to nascent Minnesota and into the emerging Republican party. He dipped into the most open and lucrative form of capitalism in the West—land speculation—hawking lots in Ninninger City, near St. Paul. "The west has been for years, still is, and for years will continue to be the El Dorado of the world," he proclaimed in 1857 in New York City. Ninninger would not grow "by chance but by combination and concentrated effort." The traditional values of ordered civilization would be imposed upon the wild new land. Donnelly did not worship the open West for its naturalness; he wanted to tame it and make it resemble Philadelphia and New York. "Imagine plains seven years since a wilderness:—now on the spot lordly mansions arise,—lighted parlours glisten and music resounds,—while refinement and luxury crowd and cluster within. Civilization seems to have flung her treasures suddenly and collectively upon the lands."[1]

The crash of 1857 halted Donnelly's swift ascent to fortune; by 1869, all the settlers of Ninninger had departed, and Donnelly's home stood alone where the town had been plotted.[2] He lived for the rest of his life upon the empty grounds of his first great plan. But he was undaunted: he entered politics. First elected lieutenant governor of Minnesota in 1859, he went to Congress in 1862, where he stayed for three terms. Donnelly differed little from other young Republican congressmen from the West. Doctrinally he was a somewhat reserved member of the radical wing of his party, but his chief interests were in land grants for railroad and industrial expansion, in river improvement bills for the Mississippi, and in legislation to encourage immigration to the West. In short, he was "almost indistinguishable from a typical Grant Era Republican," concludes Martin Ridge, Donnelly's modern political biographer.[3]

Donnelly in no manner challenged either his own assumptions

or the underlying values of the system through which he felt he was gaining a stake in life. A strong proponent of the ethic of capital accumulation, he believed that virtue followed the amassing of money and power. "Prosperity calls out the best and misfortune the worst qualities of our species," he wrote in his diary in 1867. Poverty was the outward badge of a weak inner nature, and material success proved the progressive future of a decent man in a good society. "Wealth is simply a higher civilization. The poor man stands nearest to barbarism and is shut out from the results of the cultivation of his predecessors."[4]

III

Donnelly suddenly fell from his progression to power in 1868 when he challenged the Minnesota Republican leadership and pushed for a seat in the Senate that had been scheduled for someone else. For his irregularity, he was forced out of Congress and driven from the party into political exile. Only through the ensuing personal despair did he begin to challenge his earlier values, questioning the worth of material success and political gamesmanship. He would never free himself entirely from his belief in the moral righteousness of the Algeresque conventions in which he had been trained, but he turned and fought them as best he could. Disappointment led him to new insights. As an independent politician and a maverick intellectual, he attacked the system which had expelled him; through this very personal process, he grew toward a wider awareness of what he thought was the destructiveness of American political and social institutions.

"The finest fruit matures in the shade. The noblest races in adversity."[5] In this manner, in 1875, Donnelly tried to reconcile himself to his political demise. Now proclaiming that a higher morality grew from the darker side of life, Donnelly attested both to his continued belief in the reality and worth of the success ethic and to his new sentiment that self-knowledge, which was born alone of crisis and despair, was somehow deeper and more important than the approbation of others. However, Donnelly would frequently collapse from this stoically maintained intellectual tension into hopelessness and resignation, entering into his diary his belief that he had been defeated, perhaps for all times to come. "My life has been a failure and a mistake. My hopes have so often come to naught that I cease to hope. . . . Well, well. All I can do is to face the music and take my damnable future as it comes."[6] Forced out of the seemingly natural course of public approval through wealth or office gathering, Donnelly tried to place himself against that channel and to create through dissent his own path to eminence. He was both proud and fearful of his loneliness, writing in 1889:

> I don't think my life is a "failure." I stand today a tower of strength, four square, in the world, unsustained by creed or party or faction. I have failed, it is true, to obtain that kind of success which . . . may follow fawning. I am perfectly happy and content with my fame, my beliefs, my books, my purposes, my family and my fortune.[7]

Pride notwithstanding, Donnelly's personal writings were filled with expressions of falling into powerlessness and self-destructive gloom. Breaking the rigid code of outward rules might mean plunging toward destruction, he feared. He expressed this anxiety in his diary in 1877: "Life is an ice-hill where you can only climb by sticking your toes into the crevices and hanging on for dear life with your hands. If you let go or play any antics—whiz—you are flying to the bottom of the hill."[8] He felt that being forced from public favor would open him, however morally lofty he might be, to a destruction that he was helpless to avert. Without power he could only observe, rather than control, his destiny, which others might manipulate, slowly pulverizing him. He wrote in 1881:

> Men will find it easier to go with the people than to attempt to guide them towards the right. He who does the former rides on top of the wave of public passions into harbors of ease and plunder; he who attempts the latter will find himself overwhelmed by the sea and rolled and crushed among the dirt and debris of the shore, thundered over by the breakers of public indignation.[9]

With each new literary or political project, Donnelly's hopes of regaining public recognition and self-mastery soared; with each realization that his concrete effort could not possibly attain his soul's wish, he fell anew into emptiness. Donnelly translated this almost rhythmic pattern of desire and deflation into a cyclical view of life opposed to his earlier vision of single-directioned progressivism. In 1888, he wrote of the critical rejection of one of his books: "I had hopes that the ill fortune which has pursued me for twenty years—since 1868—would have lifted and lift me; but my book is a failure, and my political prospects are dark. . . . It would seem as if my hopes rose high only to be crushed."[10] The hardest work brought only insufficient rewards; Donnelly felt he could not break out of the strangling encirclement of life and that he could not find an absolutely certain road to self-fulfillment and public applause. "I seem to travel in a circle . . . and to make no progress; and despite all my labors some one else gets the wheat of life and I have to be content with a few oats and some straw."[11]

Donnelly felt some cosmic force surely controlled this endless, shapeless repetition of ups and downs, but whether there was a single guiding cause or only mere chance in command, Donnelly felt powerless before the overwhelming processes of life. "Verily I must take note of these good and evil days and see if I can find the key to them," he wrote in 1882. "Are we indeed the plaything of good and evil fates?"[12] At his gloomiest, Donnelly felt that the outside powers were uniformly evil and destructive, not only for him but for all mankind. He was being slowly tortured by the fates and was allowed only to glimpse, not to understand, the meaning of his fall. At best, he was weakly fighting a blindly angry God, howling against the storms of impending universal chaos:

> I feel fierce and bitter, for I can see signs that are conclusive to me that all these shames and humiliations are not accidental, but that they have their times and periods, and are ruled over by external spiritual forces. I can't see through it all, nor tell where it might lead, or what compensation there may be for it all, but I expect nothing more than that my infamous misfortune will pursue me to the grave. . . . And here I am wading through mud

and fighting hurricanes and wearing my life out trying
to help mankind and save them from the flood of destruction which threatens them: and my reward is to have my
soul tortured by . . . tricks and shams.[13]

American politics, Donnelly felt, was subtly but firmly controlled by evil men employing poisonous machinations. In earlier
times, oppressive classes (southern slaveholders for example) had
made their vile causes clear and public, but now the foes of truth
veiled themselves in confusing wiles:

The secessionist was no trickster;—but a plain, blunt
man, who thought that he was right and came out into
the open to fight for his principles, and die for them if
need be. But the people are now contending with hostile
influences which shoot no guns, but insidiously sap and
mine the popular conscience; prevent law and justice, and
make free government impossible.[14]

To Donnelly, evidence of social degeneracy abounded throughout
American institutions, which were corrupted by bloated industrial-
ists, but it was difficult for him to focus upon such a pervasive
and powerful enemy and nearly impossible to engage him in open
combat. Of one belief he was certain: the total perfidy of the rich
and strong men who ran America and the primary necessity to
destroy them as the first step to purifying the nation:

As for myself I am here to fight the plutocracy; and I
have no specific measures to suggest as part of the platform, until Mammon is utterly squashed, crushed, and
driven into his hole. Then,—if I live to see the day,—I
shall . . . be prolific in [specific] suggestions. . . .
Humanity is at stake. In the awful presence let everything
else be forgotten.[15]

By no means was Donnelly devoid of programmatic political
ideas; he always made as concrete as he could the platform he
intended to replace that of the entrenched evil lords of power. The
battle against the established order, however, had to precede the

implementation of the perfected society, and this sense of conflict is central to an understanding of Donnelly. In his political career, one can trace the whole course of late nineteenth-century third-party protest activities. He was in turn a Liberal Republican, Granger, Greenbacker, Farmer's Allianceman, and finally Populist. Within each of these movements, using those programs and tactics which seemed most effective at the time, he fought the cloaked but devilish false leaders. He felt isolated from the sources of onrushing power but hoped that adherence to eternal principles would protect and succor him and the true American people. He declared in 1876:

> Let no one accuse us of vacillation or inconsistency. No party owns us. We adhere to principle and follow where it leads. We propose to make our life a protest against the slavish rule of the caucuses and rings which now afflicts this country. We are aware that this is not the pathway that leads to political honors and emoluments. We do not seek them.[16]

Donnelly felt that the sense of powerlessness which haunted him personally extended and applied to his potentialities as political leader. To oppose the forces of evil he had at hand "neither money nor newspaper, nor patronage, and it is a very unequal contest —one man against a gang of millionaires."[17] None of the traditional methods of access to influence, means with which he apparently still would have functioned comfortably, remained open to Donnelly. He was forced to rely solely on moral suasion and independent action in order to replace the force held by those who operated within the ongoing institutions. He knew that he had been chosen to show to the world the terrifying insights he had gained. Fate, by casting him down, also had revealed to him the moral way. He was certainly projecting his self-image when he had the hero of one of his novels proclaim:

> It seems to me that I have been chosen, by some extra-mundane, superhuman intelligence, out of the multitudes of mankind, and subjected to a terrible and unparalleled experience, in order that a great lesson may be taught to the world; and that it is a duty, therefore, which I

owe to the world, and which I must not shrink from or
avoid, to make known all the facts of that experience,
at whatever cost of shame or agony to myself. Blessed
is the man who can feel that God has singled him out
from among his fellows, and that the divine hand has
shaped his destiny; and yet such men usually bear on their
hearts and minds a burden of life-long woe. Those whom
God so honors he agonizes.[18]

Through cosmic insight, Donnelly felt, a truly prophetic man
could see through the gloomy cycles of individual life and collective history and lead mankind in a new and positive direction. This
unity of purpose, if it were properly demonstrated, would follow
some cleansing, culminating, worldwide catastrophe. The truly
informed mind alone would sense and broadcast the process of
destruction and resurrection: where others could not see, it could
discern a pattern of truth beneath the apparent confusion of data.
In three "scientific" works, *The Great Cryptogram* (1888), *Atlantis: The Antediluvian World* (1882), and *Ragnorak: The Age of Fire
and Gravel* (1883), Donnelly explored at length his own role as
seer.

In *The Great Cryptogram*, Donnelly tried to reveal an important
truth previously hidden by the misusages of history: Francis Bacon
wrote Shakespeare's works. The champion of truth was duty-bound
to expose especially the most deeply held misconceptions. "It must
be remembered that I am battling against the great high walls of
public prejudice and entrenched error."[19] The peculiar capitaliza-
tion of the Folio editions of Shakespeare, Donnelly argued, were
signs that Bacon planted a secret code indicating his real claim
to these plays. It only remained for Donnelly to unravel and publish
the code, thus proving Bacon's rightful place, a complex task
which he undertook with enormous energy. Donnelly believed he
had reclaimed an absolute truth through proving the literal message
of symbols which others took to be only typographical accidents.
"The operations of the minds of men are but the cunningly adjusted
parts of a great eternal spiritual design."[20]

In *Atlantis* and *Ragnorak*, Donnelly wed an extraordinary imagery of social upheaval to his revelation of underlying truth. In
Atlantis, he demonstrated the destruction of a golden age upon a

continent which was inundated by the sea. Only through such an experience of a cataclysm, Donnelly explained, could the modern observer understand the terror which permeates primitive religion. All myths welled up from a completely literal collective memory. In *Atlantis*, Donnelly lent to his images of the deluge and utopia a concrete prehistorical birth. Our origins, heretofore buried, were brought to light by Donnelly in order to explain the contemporary plight of humanity. He was "throwing new light upon all the past history of the human race, and all the great problems which now perplex the thinkers of our day."[21] In dark implications, Donnelly suggested that our civilization too might be thrown beneath the sea and that, contrarily, in a metaphorical compensation, Atlantis might rise anew. As history was cyclical, Atlantis could serve simultaneously as a warning and as an example: "These facts would seem to show that the great fires which destroyed Atlantis are still smouldering in the depths of the ocean; that the vast oscillations which carried Plato's continent beneath the sea may again bring it, with all its buried treasures, to the light."[22]

Donnelly further spelled out the moral warnings of *Atlantis* in *Ragnorak*, which concerned the destruction of a past civilization by a comet. Here, men had been living, as in *Atlantis*, in a uniformly perfect land, "for thousands of years," one "that knew no frost, no cold, no ice, no snow."[23] Then the comet hit—"the most awful convulsion and catastrophe that has ever fallen upon the globe."[24] In one sudden, unpredicted flash of fire, a civilization embodying the very best qualities of Donnelly's own was exterminated. The comet "fell upon land areas, much like our own in geographical conformation; a forest-covered, inhabitated land; a glorious land, basking in perpetual summer, in the midst of a golden age."[25] The comet was an overpowering outside force, which shattered the fragile basis of tranquility upon which an unsuspecting civilization had been built, and uncapped the seething, molten foundations of the earth, allowing them to burst upward, destroying all life. This was "an external force so mighty that it would crack the crust of the globe like an eggshell, lining its surface with great rents and seams, through which the molten interior boiled up to the light."[26] With the innocent belief of his perfection shattered, mankind was suddenly thrust out of his all-sufficient garden and forced deep into the caves of the memory of destruction. "And poor humanity! Burned, bruised, wild, stumbling, blown about like feathers in the hurricane, smitten by mighty rocks, they perish by the million; a few only reach the shelter of the caverns; and thence, glaring backward, look out over the ruins of a destroyed world.''[27] Donnelly derived a twofold prophecy from this event. The first was that history was bound to repeat on a universal scale the endless circle of birth, life, and death; and that our belief in progress and reform was only a chimera, a pretense built to prevent men from seeing that growth implied destruction, and that only disintegration fostered repurification.

> Who shall tell the age of this old earth? Who shall count the ebbs and flows of eternity? Who shall say how often this planet has been developed up to the highest forms of life, and how often all this has been obliterated in universal fire?
>
> The earth is one great tomb of life. . . . In endless series the ages stretch along—birth, life, development, destruction. And so it shall be till time is no more.
>
> Who can say that God may not bring out of the depths of space a rejuvenating comet?[28]

The second, and only apparently contradictory lesson which Donnelly drew in *Ragnorak* was that if man somehow could renew his life upon a truly moral basis, the fates could be prevented from bringing on world destruction. This was the brighter side of his vision, the emotional juxtaposition of imminent salvation to cataclysm. Insofar as he believed that mortal men, acting voluntarily, informed by their best instincts, could effectively counter natural forces with perfect solutions, Donnelly remained a utopian reformer. The otherwise inevitable flow of death could be halted if the warning prophets were heard and followed. If men were made good, the blindly angry God would gain sight and become just, and the earth would discover anew the purity and wholeness of a golden age. "Widen your heart. Put your intellect to work to so readjust the values of labor, and increase the productive capacity of Nature, that plenty and happiness, light and hope, may dwell in every heart, and the catacombs be closed forever.''[29]

As do all prophets, Donnelly feared that his warnings would be rejected by an unreformable public. Without followers, he would be forced permanently into the wilderness. Without influence he would have no role, and the world would proceed unknowingly toward the precipice. When *The Great Cryptogram* was attacked by the critics, he was distraught. The forces of Mammon were preventing him from truly reaching the people: "With wealth I could have done something for mankind; but my book is howled down by a corrupt press; I am poor and powerless:—I can only grind my teeth and cry out to heaven."[30] Only closed minds in official places greeted his enormous insights: "The small creatures were fiercely jealous to think that I had discovered something that had never occurred to their shallow brains."[31] More important than the critical refusal of his literary efforts, the people—that only conceivable vessel of redeeming values—seemed to reject the efforts for political reform that he offered to them. Perhaps they had been misguided so completely and for so long that evil morals had seeped into their very flesh and marrow. Perhaps only complete destruction through divine wrath could match their stage of degeneracy: "The people are too shallow and too corrupt to conduct a republic. It will need a God come on earth, with divine power, to save them. And are they worth saving? Will they stay saved?"[32]

Most of the time, however, Donnelly drew back from this view of a destructive climax to history. He preferred to hope that he could call on some unfathomed reservoir of virtue that still lay within all Americans, unspoiled by the swirling evils unloosed by the industrial moguls and political spoilsmen in high places. Finally he would be heard; Americans would act justly on his word, previously widening fissures of chaos would be paved over, and purified men would draw history to a utopian conclusion. The lines of battle were unmistakably drawn.

> We appeal to the American people, blind drunk with party bigotry, bloated with the lies of a dishonest press, inflamed by brass bands and stump-oratory, corrupted by money, and deluded by hollow promises; to the same American people, when it shall sit sober in its sorrows and realize that it has been the plaything and tool of tricksters and knaves, to its own undoing. Stand firm brethren! . . . Let every man resolve to do his whole duty, unawed

by clamorous majorities, unbought by the blood-money
of a triumphant Plutocracy.[33]

IV

The urge to enter a final, holy battle was widely shared in the
American crisis of the early 1890s. In his role as Populist leader
and in his anti-utopian masterpiece, *Caesar's Column*, Donnelly's
call echoed throughout the rural Midwest and South. His political
activism expressed fears as well as hopes. At times he would
organize the people into an agrarian army to save the nation; at
other times he and his followers seemed to be fighting a holding
action against a rapidly enclosing doom. Chaos seemed universal
and near, utopia distant and perhaps only for the few.

The timeless rural virtues of self-sufficiency and egalitarianism,
Donnelly had long worried, were being swamped by eastern urban
regimentation. The emerging proletariat already might be beyond
regeneration. He asked in 1878:

> What kind of people are they raising up in those eastern
> cities? Without virtue, morality, honesty, religion or man-
> hood, they are in training for an empire? It is absurd to
> suppose that such stuff can maintain a republic. The hope
> of freedom rests with the people of the great West. And
> they must look to it or bad laws will sap their prosperity
> and destroy their manhood.[34]

By 1894, the deluge seemed even more imminent, and Donnelly
urged Minnesotans to create a haven from destruction, a separation-
ist base of positive values from which to guide the rebirth of the
soon-to-be-leveled American society: "If liberty is to sink in a sea
of blood, let this state remain a peaceful oasis in the midst of tumult
and turbulence. So shall we give freedom and order a rallying point
when the storm has passed and the era of reconstruction begins."[35]

In political terms, by 1896, Donnelly was torn, as were all
Populists, between fusion with the Democratic party in order to
achieve electoral victory and a continuation of the independent
third-party course to maintain theoretical purity. Donnelly wanted
to be practical, to gain the best possible legislation in league with

the widest possible circle of allies, but he also feared being politically swamped in the process of reaching broad compromises. In 1894, he wrote, "While we will not fuse with any party, or do anything dishonorable, let us leave nothing honorable undone that will give us triumph; because triumph means the repeal of bad laws, the passage of good ones, and the lifting up of the people's burden."[36] By 1896, smelling victory, Donnelly began to favor coalition with the Democratic party. He felt that fusion would not soften the lines of electoral conflict, because the enemy was now so clear that all decent men could join in battle for the Lord. "Every man who opposes Plutocracy is our friend, our true and treasured friend, even if he does not agree with us on every public question. If he is to fight the Gold Power that is enough. Any victory, with any kind of allies, is better than the continuance of the present terrible conditions."[37] Yet even in welcoming coalition Donnelly could not quite give it his wholehearted trust and support, for he sensed that there was something diffuse and tentative in the Democrats' nomination of Bryan and in its half-swing toward the Populist position. Finally Donnelly went to the Populist convention in St. Louis, ready to accept fusion passively rather than to choose it actively. "If the Democracy adheres faithfully to their new departure there may grow up, in the course of time, one concentrated, united and triumphant party. . . . But whatever the Peoples' Party shall conclude to do at St. Louis, we shall abide by it."[38]

Fusion proved disastrous. The coalition failed to win the election, and it ruined forever the chances of creating a truly moralistic political movement by dragging populism into the ruins of contemporary partisan warfare. In 1898, he asked in bitter retrospect: "Where are you and where is the human family? Where are the promises and hopes of 1892 and 1894? Gone glimmering among the dreams that were. You cannot reconstruct a smashed egg—especially after it begins to smell. 'Fusion' is the death of reform."[39] Only through a separate, unsullied identity could populism have triumphed. In his later years, Donnelly, knowing the movement had been killed through fusion, attempted to recreate a memory of it which was unstained by opportunistic political accommodation. At least in his own retrospective vision, he tried to preserve the unique soundness and truthfulness of populism. "For we are the true reform party of the age," he insisted in 1898, "and the rest are all bogus."[40] In 1900 he ran as the Populist candidate for Vice-President, a nomination he felt was a worthless memento of old hopes. He condemned his former Democratic allies shortly before his death in 1901 in an article about the past entitled, "The Future." "Nothing but a determined purpose to cut loose from [the Democratic party] forever can bring us victory. Union with them signifies disaster. We know that now."[41]

Ironically, Donnelly's memories of his participation in the Populist party even preceding fusion must have been clouded. He had never trusted General James B. Weaver, the 1892 Populist presidential candidate and feared even more the motives of Weaver's admirers. "If attempts are not made to sell us out," he had written then, "it will be the first time in history of the world that a great movement will have escaped treachery."[42] The Minnesota party itself had deserted him in the days of its greatest promise in 1896, Donnelly felt, and had followed the false prophecies of other factional leaders. "We have been the victim of a shameful conspiracy," he had felt compelled to conclude at that time. "Every point was linked with every other."[43] Fusion without and factionalism within turned a pure movement, even in memory, quite rancid. For Donnelly, there was no cleansed political process, no reformed place free from tension and contradiction, no populace who would be rescued, no small group who could find the means to approach an isolated peace in a turbulent world.

If unchecked by a positive political movement, Donnelly long believed, the growing evils of society soon would evolve an overwhelmingly destructive, totalitarian way of life. By abnegating their responsibilities, politicians would pave the way to a future where all elements of life would be determined rather than free, where corruption would be king, operating through men emptied of will. All efforts for reform would soon be irrelevant, as men would be so warped by uncontrollable forces that they would be unable even to comprehend a virtuous position, much less to act on such a comprehension. Without the spark of moralistic reform, politics, formerly the potential method to strive for national purification, would be transformed into an evil machine reinforcing all the terrible values which had ruined it. A politics without clear moral direction would be so blindly self-serving that in the end it would destroy itself.

Donnelly created the most terrifying possible future in *Caesar's Column*, a novel written during the heat of his Populist efforts in 1892 but set in New York City in 1988. Only in fiction could he completely elucidate upon the truths of darkness and collapse which he so strongly sensed were overwhelming his world. If he could somehow show others the frightening future with all the vividness and clear certainty with which he felt it, mankind might yet be directed to hear and act to avert his prophecy. "Believing, as I do, that I read the future aright, it would be criminal in me to remain silent. . . . If God notices anything so insignificant as this poor book, I pray that he may use it as an instrumentality of good for mankind; for he knows I love his human creatures, and would help them if I had the power."[44]

Donnelly's America of 1988 was characterized by absolute rule and plunder for the plutocracy and complete misery and proletarianization for the people. "Now a single nabob owns a whole country; and a state is divided between a few great loan associations; and the men who once tilled the fields, as their owners, are driven to the cities to swell the cohorts of the miserable, or remain on the land a wretched peasantry, to contend for the means of life with vile hoards of Mongolian coolies."[45] Donnelly believed that permanent class conflict had become the central social condition and class warfare the historically inevitable culmination.

By 1988, national institutions had been corrupted for so long that negative genetic forces had been unloosed and were deteriorating the individual, warping him to fit into pernicious social arrangements. Environmental decay had ended the possibility of personal freedom. The workers, in "their incalculable multitude and their silence," were like "the resurrection of the dead." So emptied and crushed were they that they were no longer human; outside forces had turned them into machines. "They seemed . . . merely automata in the hands of some ruthless and unrelenting destiny. They lived and moved, but they were without heart or hope."[46] The ruling elite, "The Council of the Oligarchy," also had been affected by destructive evolution. Their most prominent characteristics were "incredulity, unbelief, cunning, observation, heartlessness . . . shrewdness and energy," untied to any compassion or love. They had devolved physically and phrenologically into a brutal aristocracy. "They were generally large men, with finely

developed brows—natural selection had brought the great heads to
the top of affairs.''[47] In the proletarian underground, a counterelite
had grown, which, controlled by the same social system, reflected
a similarly evil personality development. "The Brotherhood of
Destruction'' was fully as devoted to the extermination of the rich
as the Council of the Oligarchs was to absolute domination of the
masses.

> Here was the council of the Proletariat. . . . A great injus-
> tice, or series of wrongs, working through many genera-
> tions, had wrought out results that in some sense du-
> plicated each other. Brutality above had produced brutal-
> ity below; cunning there was answered by cunning here;
> cruelty in the aristocrat was mirrored by cruelty in the
> workman. High and low were alike victims—unconscious
> victims—of a system. The crimes were not theirs; it lay
> at the door of the shallow, indifferent, silly generations
> of the past.[48]

Donnelly's notorious anti-Semitism, a subject about which he
was not obsessed, must be understood in this fictional context of
evolved, systemic evil, for, as he wrote, "it was the old question
of the survival of the fittest." Jews were leaders of both the
oligarchy and the workers. Acting effectively in a brutalized system
was a species of Jewish revenge for past centuries of wrongs done
them, Donnelly felt. And in the philo-Semitism peculiar to the Jew-
hater, he concluded that in an evil setting, where all the Christian
virtues had been slain, the Jew would excel above all others. His
condemnation was rather impersonal; it was only of the position
Jews held in the social organization.

> Christianity fell upon the Jews, originally a race of
> agriculturists and shepherds, and forced them, for many
> centuries, through the most terrible ordeal of persecution
> the history of mankind bears any record of. Only the
> strong of body, the cunning of brain, the long-headed,
> the persistent, the men with capacity to live where a dog
> would starve, survived the awful trial. Like breeds like;
> and now the Christian world is paying, in tears and blood,

for the sufferings inflicted by their bigoted ancestors upon
a noble race. When the time came for liberty and fair
play the Jew was master in the contest with the Gentile,
who hated and feared him.[49]

Caesar's Column culminated in holocaust. Loosed momentarily
from their chains, the now subhuman workers destroyed every element of civilization in an uncontrollable nihilistic orgy. They had
become "omnipotent to destroy" and "powerless to create."[50] As
the end began in New York City, the troops of the oligarchy were
slaughtered by poison gas bombs dropped upon them by dirigible
pilots who had been bribed by the worker's leaders. "The dead
lie in heaps and layers in the invisible, pernicious poison."[51] Then
the mobs took over.

Like a huge flood, long dammed up, turbulent, turbid,
muddy, loaded with wrecks and debris, the gigantic mass
broke loose, full of foam and terror, and flowed in every
direction. A foul and brutal and ravenous multitude it
was, dark with dust and sweat, armed with the weapons
of civilization, but possessing only the instincts of wild
beasts.[52]

Death came to hundreds of thousands of the rich; they were shot,
stabbed, and literally torn apart by dozens of cannibalistic hands.
The hellish imagery of fires of destruction pervaded the upheaval.
"And high above the walls of fire they were thrown, and the briber
and the bribed—the villain and his instruments—all perished howling together."[53] Caesar, the leader of the Brotherhood of Destruction, "a king-devil, come fresh out of hell,"[54] forced the surviving
aristocrats to build an enormous pyramid of the bodies of the dead
nobility set in huge concrete blocks. Soon the mob turned on all
leaders and Caesar's head appeared on the tip of a pike as a mock-
ing witness to the all-encompassing death he had helped to trigger.
"The protruding tongue leered at the blazing house and the
unspeakable horrors of that assemblage, lit up, as it was, in all
its awful features by the towering conflagration."[55]

Donnelly translated the catastrophism of *Atlantis* and *Ragnorak*
into a vision of political destruction and a social anti-utopia in

Caesar's Column. Although he intended the novel to be a warning to the well placed, its most conspicuously powerful writing forced the smells of hell on earth into the reader's nostrils. Mankind had already taken the fateful turn in the path; a politics of hope, a utopian conclusion to American history, was already only a memory.

Yet even as the Western world burned beneath him, Donnelly's narrator in *Caesar's Column*, a European colonist from Africa, together with his truly enlightened New York hosts, escaped in an airship, which flew away "like a veritable Phoenix from its nest of flame."[56] The dirigible passed high above western Europe, which was also engulfed in complete destruction. Connected to the past, to the now-destroyed world only by abstract remembrances, the airship escapees settled down in a rural colony of 5,000 whites, "The Garden in the Mountains," deep in remote Ugandan heights. The single mountain pass linking this community to the rest of the world was then blocked. "[They] would completely cut off communication with the external world, making the wall so thick and strong that it would be impossible for any force that was likely to come against us to batter it down."[57] Within the colony, Donnelly's version of the Populist program of welfare legislation for a rural people was enacted. Land ownership was limited, interest abolished, money made plentiful. Public works, welfare, controls on individual gain were enacted. Donnelly projected an agrarian, humble, voluntaristic utopian community, which would stand in magnificent and undiscovered isolation in a ruined world. It was as if what Donnelly alone knew to be true would in the end become the only beacon of hopeful reality in an unbelievable world of darkness and denial.

9

UTOPIA AS MEMORY:

WILLIAM DEAN HOWELLS AND

THE WORLD OF CHANCE

There is something very curious in our relation to the divine. God is where we believe He is, and He is a daily Providence or not, as we choose. . . . We might get back to faith by taking a wider sweep and seeing God in our personal disadvantages—finding Him not only in luck but in bad luck. Chance may be a larger law, with an orbit far transcending the range of little statutes by which fire always burns, and water always finds its level.

—Mr. Kane in *The World of Chance*
by William Dean Howells

I

Although he always referred to himself as just a Buckeye, William Dean Howells never returned to the Ohio villages of his youth. He wrote nostalgically of simple rural communities, yet he had as a young man consciously rejected existence in such a locale for a cosmopolitan life in literature. This movement from country to city, from simple structure to confusing complexity, became Howells' central literary theme.

Boyhood recollections filled Howells with dread as well as pleasure. He charted this ambivalence toward his past in his autobiographical *A Boy's Town*.[1] Proximity to the beauties of nature carried with it closeness to the terrors of savagery. Howells never would feel as much a part of a group as he had with his friends during his rural Ohio youth, although he knew this social suborder had been established through physical cruelty. As soon as he left his small town, he was no longer part of the clan. When he returned for a visit, he realized that he was an outsider. After recalling quite vividly the barbarities of his friends, Howells, writing in the third person, wanted to remember only the wonderful sense of belonging: "He became more and more aware that the past was gone from him forever, and that he could not return to it. He did not forget it, but cherished its memories more fondly for that reason."[2] But he had already retold the horror which lurked just under the surface of his memory.

Howells purified this soiled image of perfect rural community in his novels and essays concerning the Shakers.[3] His esteem for their simple, kind, honest ways was abiding; he felt they had achieved, as a group, a gentle, inward quietude. This passivism always appealed to Howells.

> As I recall their plain, quaint village at Shirley, a sense of exceeding peace fills me; . . . and it seems to me that one whom the world could flatter no more, one broken in hope, or health, or fortune, could not do better than come hither and meekly ask to be taken into that quiet fold, and kept forever from his sorrows and himself.[4]

If the complex modern world, then, destroyed a man, the Shakers could keep him from himself and from the social environment which was responsible for his breakdown. This communal faith was for Howells at the same time simple moral health as opposed to worldly neuroticism and delusive escape from an overwhelming sense of oppressive reality. The community was safe because it was a special place not in or of the modern world. Whether this was a higher reality or an illusory wisp of false hope depended on Howells' temperament at the moment. The mature Howells could not remain intellectually in the Shaker fold any more than he had stayed in the hamlets of his Ohio boyhood. The community as a vantage point was not fully relevant even if the modern world proved to be disheartening. Present flux could not turn the less perplexing past into an unexamined golden age. "The new condition is always vulgar, and amidst the modern ferment we may look back upon the old stagnation and call it repose."[5] Howells knew

Shaker peace would exact his honesty as its price. He could only vacation there, never to go home again.

More positively, Howells wanted to grapple with the exasperatingly ungovernable social and economic tumult of the late nineteenth century. After well over forty years of upward mobility into the establishment of American letters, Howells, stimulated particularly by the Haymarket affair of 1886, awoke to the gigantic problems of industrializing America. In his finest novels, written during the late 1880s and early 1890s, Howells delved into a nation where progress no longer appeared inevitable, indeed, where the triumph of the forces of darkness seemed imminent.[6] He wrote, with rather complex irony, to Henry James in 1888:

> I'm not in a very good humor with "America" myself. After fifty years of optimistic content with "civilization" and its ability to come out all right in the end, I now abhor it and feel that it is coming out all wrong in the end, unless it bases itself anew on a real equality. Meantime I wear a fur-lined over-coat, and live in all the luxury my money can buy.[7]

To these nationwide problems the perfect community seemed very distant, and yet it remained a powerful memory to Howells as he tried to fathom the new. Any vision of a better world needed examination when the present was so unravelled, even if all perfect constructs carried their own distortions.

II

The World of Chance was Howells' last direct analysis of American social problems.[8] He would comment on American society as an anti-imperialist at the end of the century, as a supporter of the 1905 Niagara Movement which preceded the NAACP, and in gentle utopian romances, but never again would he approach the seething urban scene with such sharpened scalpels.[9] More than merely the last of a series of works, *The World of Chance* is a dead end. It was his demonstration of the failure of any set of national goals or of credible techniques of social action.

As *The World of Chance* opens, Percy Bysshe Shelley Ray, a

dreamy young newspaperman, with his novel, *A Modern Romeo*, in his satchel, leaves Midland on the East and West Railway bound for New York City and success. High on champagne from his farewell party, he drifts off to sleep in his Pullman berth, full of a "luxurious sense of helplessness," while "Midland slipped back into the irrevocable past."[10] With only a casual egotism as his guide, he prepares to embrace whole an utterly new environment. In New York, Ray wanders around, writing hack journalism for a living and looking with increasing vagueness for his pot of gold. More and more he can let go of his former, structured, village values, and enjoy the bohemian vicissitudes which he shares with other young writers. For all of them, the walls between long accepted propriety and newly discovered indulgence in fantasy crumble as the order of the past melts away:

> It was as if all were driving on together, no one knew why or whither; but some had embarked on the weird voyage to waste, and some to amass; their encounter formed the opportunity of both, and a sort of bewildered kindliness existed between them. Their common ignorance of what it was all for was like a bond, and they clung involuntarily together in their unwieldy multitude because of the want of meaning, and prospered on, suffered on, through vast cyclones of excitement that whirled round and round, and made a kind of pleasant drunkenness in their brains, and consoled them for never resting and never arriving.[11]

In this state of emotional and critical suspension, Ray meets, and is torn between, two men of opposing natures. The first is Mr. Kane, a self-acknowledged descendant of Cain, who is the complete cynic; the other is David Hughes, the former leader of a utopian experiment, who is now wearily disillusioned about such communities, but who remains a cosmic, innocent believer. Kane, a nonwriting writer, walks all over New York and feels as at home as he wishes and as the city permits. As he thinks nothing means anything, and therefore expects no truths, he is comfortable amidst urban chaos. Ironically, though a social activist, Hughes confines himself to his little tenement and cannot achieve any new contact with life. He could not, in this confusing late nineteenth century, relate to the complex world through the old community. In his opinion, utopian experiment had receded to a place of anachronistic, segregated insignificance; it no longer could instruct the world. Hughes concludes that "the community saved itself from chance by shutting out the rest of the world. It was selfish too. The Family must include the whole world."[12]

Ray draws no conclusions on his own from these opposing outlooks. He has no sense of philosophy by which to judge experience nor does he feel any compelling need to establish his own point of view. Interested, at any rate, only in tactics for self-advancement, he contents himself with a fitful admiration for both men.

Events concerning Ray's unpublished novel do push him toward personal and social insight. By sheer accident, the first publisher to whom he shows *A Modern Romeo* had once played a role in an amateur production of *Romeo and Juliet* and he befriends the unknown young writer. Later, eager to take an artistic plunge, the publisher accepts the book out of friendship. Ignored for weeks by the critics, the novel suddenly becomes successful through an extremely laudatory notice written by a reviewer who had taken the book home by accident and had watched it fall open to a passage on hypnotism just when that subject was running through his mind.[13]

The cumulative nature of all these lucky coincidences, added to a dawning awareness of the chance manner by which he meets and loses friends, finally have an impact on Ray. He is bemused and benumbed by the unreasonableness of the string of events in his life. His successes and failures have no relation to his own efforts. Nothing makes sense in the way he had formerly conceived of reason and sequence and goals. Finally, Ray returns to Midland for a visit. Suspended, spaceless and timeless in his rumbling Pullman berth, he releases his mind from all rationality and drifts:

> He began to wonder if life had not all been a chance with him. Nothing, not even the success of his book, in the light he now looked at it in, was the result of reasoned cause. That success had happened; it had not followed. . . . He had found the same caprice, the same rule of

mere casualty, in the world which we suppose to be ordered by law—the world of thinking, the world of feeling.[14]

Flux springs Ray, as it had the cynic Kane, from any belief in universal determinism. Yet unlike Kane, Ray can still, even as the old order dies, value the quality of human experience in itself. Curiously, he is now freed to create new sets of meaningful symbols, and like Hughes, if he can find a well of stoicism to counter his enormous loneliness, he might now be able to search for a new community. Or perhaps he will meander, relishing life, toward Nowhere.

NOTES

INTRODUCTION

1. Fred Somkin, *Unquiet Eagle: Memory and Desire in the Idea of American Freedom, 1815-1860* (Ithaca, N.Y., 1967), 72.

2. Arthur E. Bestor, Jr., "Patent-Office Models of the Good Society," *American Historical Review* 58 (April 1953): 514.

3. Ibid., 506.

4. The narrowing of moral reform thought in the 1850s is discussed by John Higham, in his lecture, "From Boundlessness to Consolidation: The Transformation of American Culture, 1848-1860" (Ann Arbor, Michigan, 1969), and by John L. Thomas, "Anti-Slavery and Utopia," in Martin Duberman, ed., *The Anti-Slavery Vanguard* (Princeton, 1965), 240-269. The Civil War as the precipitating element in the transformation of reform thought is emphasized by George M. Fredrickson in *The Inner Civil War: Northern Intellectuals and the Crisis of the Union* (New York, 1965).

5. Robert H. Wiebe, *The Search for Order: 1877-1920* (New York, 1967), 133-163. Wiebe entitles his chapter that discusses this transformation "Revolution in Values."

6. A brilliant portrayal and analysis of one modern utopian community is Tom Wolfe, *The Electric Kool-Aid Acid Test* (New York, 1968).

CHAPTER 1

1. [Josiah Warren], "Explanation of the Design and Arrangements of the Cooperative Magazine" [Cincinnati, 1827], 2.

2. Albert Brisbane, *A Concise Exposition of the Doctrines of Association,* 2d ed. (New York, 1843), 7.

3. Albert Brisbane, *Social Destiny of Man* (Philadelphia, 1840), vii.

4. Brisbane, *Concise Exposition*, 3.

5. Redelia Brisbane, *Albert Brisbane: A Mental Biography* (Boston, 1893), 171.

6. Ibid., 190-191.

7. Ibid., 190.

8. "Brisbane to Jules Lechevalier, June 1832" in Hubert Bourgin, *Fourier* (Paris, 1905), 437, n. 3.

9. Brisbane, *Albert Brisbane*, 184.

10. Brisbane to Charles Fourier, November 20, 1836, in Bourgin, *Fourier*, 474-475, n. 4. See also Brisbane to Fourier, August 1, 1836, in Bourgin, 474, n. 1.

11. William Bailie, *Josiah Warren* (Boston, 1906), 5.

12. Warren, *True Civilization*, 4th ed. (Cliftondale, Mass., 1869), vi.

13. Ibid.

14. Ibid., 25.

15. Ibid., ix.

16. Ibid., 19.

17. Ibid., 24.

18. Warren, *Manifesto* [New Harmony, Ind., November 27, 1841], 1.

19. Warren, *Written Music Remodeled* (Boston, 1860), 3.

20. Brisbane, *Social Destiny of Man*, 480.

21. Warren to Stephen Pearl Andrews, April 17, 1851, Houghton Library, Harvard University, Cambridge, Mass.

22. Brisbane, *Albert Brisbane*, 245.

23. Morris Hillquit, *History of Socialism in the United States* (New York, 1903), 29-131, and G. D. H. Cole, *A History of Socialist Thought* (London, 1963), I, 62-74, are two clear expositions of Fourier's thought. For a fuller discussion, see Nicholas V. Riasanovsky, *The Teachings of Charles Fourier* (Berkeley, Cal., 1969). A useful selection from Fourier's prolix writings is Jonathan Beecher and Richard Bienvenu, eds., *The Utopian Vision of Charles Fourier* (Boston, 1971). Also see *Ouvres Complètes de Charles Fourier* (Paris, 1966-1968), 12 vols.

24. Brisbane, *Concise Exposition*, 51.

25. Brisbane took out six patents for his tubes between 1869 and 1884. He also worked on improved ovens. *Albert Brisbane Manuscripts*, Illinois Historical Survey, University of Illinois Library, Urbana, Ill., entries for April 9, 1867; May 29, 1884; April 1888. For Warren's inventions, see his *Manifesto*; Warren to William Maclure, October 5, 1839, *Josiah Warren Manuscripts*, New Harmony Workingmen's Institute Library, New Harmony, Ind. See also Ewing C. Baskette, ed., *Six Letters of Josiah Warren Concerning Stereotype Printing* (Springfield, Ill., 1951).

26. Warren, *Manifesto*, 8.

27. *Boston Investigator,* April 11, 1849 (typescript copy of the original in the University of Michigan Library, Ann Arbor, Mich.).

28. Warren, *Notebook,* July 21, 1842, Warren Manuscripts.

29. Brisbane, "Association," *New York Tribune,* July 21, 1842; see also Brisbane, *Concise Exposition,* 3.

30. Warren, *True Civilization,* 99.

31. Brisbane, "Association," *New York Tribune,* June 22, 1843. Even before his conversion to Fourierism, Brisbane had dismissed the idea of using party politics for reform. "There is no discussion of principles there. It is only a strife between individuals." Brisbane, "Diary of Travels to Paris and Berlin," January 4, 1832, Syracuse University Library, Syracuse, N.Y. Warren also frequently denounced politics and government. See for example his *True Civilization, an Immediate Necessity* (Boston, 1863), 16-17, 33.

32. Brisbane, *Social Destiny of Man,* 348.

33. Ibid., 132; Brisbane, "Association," *New York Tribune,* May 23, 1842.

34. Brisbane, *Social Destiny of Man,* 244.

35. Warren, *The Emancipation of Labor* (Boston, 1864), 6.

36. Quoted in Bailie, *Warren,* 54-55.

37. Josiah Warren, "Letter on Equitable Commerce," New Harmony, Ind., February 1844, 1-2.

38. Warren, *Practical Applications of the Elementary Principles of True Civilization to Everyday Life* (Princeton, Mass., 1873); Josiah Warren to Stephen Pearl Andrews, April 17, 1851, copy in Houghton Library; James J. Martin, *Men Against the State* (De Kalb, Ill., 1953), 11-107; Bailie, *Warren,* passim; Raymond L. Hawkins, *Positivism in the United States* (Cambridge, Mass., 1938), 104-124; William Pare, "Trialsville and Modern Times," *Chamber's Edinburgh Journal* 18 (December 18, 1852): 395-397; Moncure Conway, "Modern Times," *The Fortnightly Review* 6 (July 1, 1865): 421-434.

39. Brisbane to George Ripley, December 9, 1845, in Octavius B. Frothingham, *George Ripley* (Boston, 1882), 184.

40. Brisbane, "Letter from Mr. Brisbane," *The Harbinger* 4 (May 22, 1847): 376.

41. Brisbane, "Letter from Mr. Brisbane, Paris, June 13, 1844," *The Phalanx* 1 (July 13, 1844): 205.

42. Brisbane, *Albert Brisbane,* passim; Brisbane, "Association," *New York Tribune,* January 17, May 2, 23, 27, August 11, 30, September 9, 1843; Victor Considerant, *The Great West* (New York, 1854), 6, 26, and *European Colonization in Texas* (New York, 1855), 3; Garrett R. Carpenter, *Silkville: A Kansas Attempt in the History of Fourierist Utopianism, 1869-1892* (Emporia, Kans., 1954), 14; Brisbane to Elizah P. Grant,

November 1869, and "Plan of the Transitional Organization of Industry, January 1868," Brisbane Manuscripts; Albert Brisbane—E. P. Grant Correspondence, *E. P. Grant Manuscripts*, University of Chicago Library. The fullest description of many of the American Fourierist communities is in John Humphrey Noyes, *History of American Socialisms* (Oneida, N. Y., 1870), 181-563.

43. Brisbane to Redelia Brisbane, October 28, 1875, Brisbane Manuscripts. In the same correspondence, see his letter of July 12, 1884, where he wrote in part, "Can I expiate my past mistakes, follies, ideal errors, want of practical views and ideas? I think not unless I write something of eternal value to the race. . . ." Also on this point see Brisbane, *Albert Brisbane*, 250-251.

44. Brisbane to Redelia Brisbane, April 7, 1875, Brisbane Manuscripts.

45. Brisbane, *General Introduction to Social Sciences* (New York, 1876), iv.

46. Brisbane to Redelia Brisbane [circa July 1884], Brisbane Manuscripts.

47. Brisbane, "Plan of the Transitional Organization of Industry," 11, 12, 15.

48. Brisbane to His Son, Arthur, January 13, 1887, Brisbane Manuscripts.

49. Warren, Letter to E. H. Haywood, Princeton, Mass., July 1873, in Bailie, *Warren*, 128.

50. *The Word* 2 (September 1873): 5; ibid., 2 (March 1874): 3; *Woodhull and Claflin's Weekly*, numbers 55-68 (June 3-September 23, 1871). The followers were William B. Greene in the first place and Stephen Pearl Andrews in the second.

51. Warren, *True Civilization, an Immediate Necessity*, 107.

52. Warren to Stephen Pearl Andrews, June 10, 1852, copy in Houghton Library. One example where Warren names specific plotters is in Warren, *Periodical Letters* 1 (April 1858): 121-126.

CHAPTER 2

1. The Early Diaries of Isaac T. Hecker, Entry for May 16, 1843, Hecker Manuscripts, Archives of the Paulist Fathers, New York City.

2. John Van Der Zee Sears, *My Friends at Brook Farm* (New York, 1912), 72.

3. Ibid., 72-73.

4. "George William Curtis to John S. Dwight, August 18, 1843," in George W. Cooke, ed., *Early Letters of George William Curtis to John S. Dwight* (New York, 1898), 108.

5. Curtis tells of this nicknaming in a letter written in 1890 to Walter Elliott, Hecker's first biographer: *Life of Father Hecker* (New York, 1891), 55. The story, "Earnest the Seeker," by William Channing, had appeared in the *Dial* (July, October, 1840): 48-58, 233-242. It was a tale of a young man's unconsummated aesthetic flirtation with the Catholic church.

6. Curtis to Dwight, June 29, 1846, in Cooke, *Early Letters,* 253-254.

7. Hecker, Early Diaries, February 1843.

8. Ibid., August 13, 1843.

9. Hecker to His Family, December 28, 1842, Hecker Manuscripts.

10. Ibid., February 22, 1843.

11. Hecker, Early Diaries, June 24, 1843.

12. Hecker to His Family, December 26, 1842, Hecker Manuscripts.

13. Hecker, Early Diaries, February 3, 1843.

14. Hecker to His Family, December 28, 1842, Hecker Manuscripts; Hecker, Early Diaries, May 4, 1843.

15. Hecker, Early Diaries, January 11, 1843.

16. Hecker to His Family, December 26, 1842, Hecker Manuscripts.

17. Ibid., December 27, 1842.

18. Ibid., May 16, 1843.

19. Hecker, Early Diaries, May 31, 1843.

20. Ibid., May 11, 1843. Ora Sedgwick understood these terms in her relationship with Isaac, whom she found strange, yet attractive. They had a correspondence in the following years which she described as being on "high spiritual themes." "A Girl of Sixteen at Brook Farm," *Atlantic Monthly* 85 (March 1900): 402.

21. Margaret Fuller could well have been the spiritual side. See Zoltan Haraszti, *The Idyll of Brook Farm* (Boston, 1937), 20. John S. Dwight was a rejected admirer of Almira; see ibid., 19-22.

22. Hecker, Early Diaries, April 18, 1843. Hecker later tried to obliterate Almira's name, but never fully succeeded, perhaps because he did not want to cross her memory fully out of his life. Cf. Vincent F. Holden, *The Early Years of Isaac T. Hecker, 1819-1844,* "Studies in American Church History," 29 (Washington, D. C., 1939), 135-136.

23. Hecker, Early Diaries, October 17, 1843.

24. Ibid., August 13, 1843.

25. Ibid., March 30, 1844.

26. Ibid., August 14, 1844. Significantly, it is at this point that Isaac does not feel compelled to obliterate Almira's name in the diary passage.

27. Ibid., July 23, 1843. Much of the preceding discussion of Hecker's identity crisis and his search for personal ideology has been informed by Erik Erikson, *Young Man Luther* (New York, 1958).

28. Ibid., October 17, 1843.

29. Ibid., June 26, 1843.

30. Ibid., July 31, 1843.

31. Ibid., June 27, 1843.

32. Hecker to His Family, July 23, 1843, Hecker Manuscripts.

33. Hecker, Early Diaries, July 17, 1843.

34. Ibid., July 25, 1843.

35. See for example, ibid., March 4, 1844.

36. The proposed trip was the subject for an interesting exchange of letters: E. H. Russell, ed., "A Bit of Unpublished Correspondence between Henry Thoreau and Isaac Hecker," *Atlantic Monthly* 90 (September 1902): 370-376.

37. Hecker to Orestes Brownson, June 4, 1844, in Holden, *Early Years,* 221-222.

38. Hecker, Early Diaries, May 23, 1844.

39. Ibid., June 13, 1844.

40. Ibid., December 18, 1844.

41. Ibid.

42. Ibid., October 26, 1844.

43. Memorandum written at Clapham, England, October 24, 1848, in Elliott, *Life,* 225, 227.

44. Joseph McSorley, *Father Hecker and His Friends* (St. Louis, 1952), 15-40.

45. The story of the founding of the Paulists is told in exhaustive detail in Vincent F. Holden, *The Yankee Paul: Isaac Thomas Hecker* (Milwaukee, 1958), 205-413.

46. Hecker to Richard Simpson, September 12, 1862, in Abbott Gasquet, ed., "Some Letters of Isaac T. Hecker," *Catholic World* 86 (June 1906): 362.

47. Isaac T. Hecker, *Questions of the Soul,* 6th ed. (New York, 1869), 275-276.

48. Ibid., 124.

49. Elliott, *Life,* 292.

50. Hecker, *Questions of the Soul,* 293.

51. Ibid., 58.

52. Elliott, *Life*, 293.

53. Cf. Louis F. McKernan, "Father Hecker and the Press," *Catholic World* 186 (February 1958): 326-332.

54. Hecker to Simpson, January 27, 1863, *Catholic World* 86 (May 1906): 235.

55. Elliott, *Life,* 296.

56. Ibid., 294.

57. Ibid., 296.

58. Ibid., 295.

59. James Parton, "Our Roman Catholic Brethren," *Atlantic Monthly* 21 (May 1868): 566.

60. Elliott, *Life*, 371.

61. Ibid., 414 (a Hecker letter of early 1886).

62. Ibid., 413.

63. Ibid., 381.

64. After his death, ironically, conflict appeared over his legacy after a translation of Elliott's *Life of Hecker* appeared in France in 1897. He was used as ammunition by both sides in the battle between liberals and traditionalists within the French church. In 1899, Leo XIII condemned "Americanism"—revisionist, anti-authoritarian tendencies of some of the clergy. Generally this was a period of reaction in the church, and though Leo's condemnation was vague, the Paulists, in reaction to it, lost much of their missionary edge. Adrian Dansette, *Religious History of Modern France*, II (Freiburg, West Germany, 1961), 138-149; John B. Sheerin, "The Paulist Apostolate," *Commonweal* 69 (December 26, 1958): 334-336.

65. Orestes A. Brownson, *The Convert or Leaves from My Experience* (New York, 1877), 200.

66. Ibid.

67. Brownson to Hecker, June 6, 1844, in Holden, *The Yankee Paul*, 91.

68. In England, John Henry Newman moved into a similar, static vision of Catholicism in the years 1843-1847. With his conversion, he secluded himself and, at least in his public stance, went beyond doubt and movement. "From the time that I became a Catholic, of course, I have no further history of my religious opinions to narrate. In saying this, I do not mean to say that my mind has been idle, or that I have given up thinking on theological subjects; but that I have had no changes to record, and have had no anxiety of heart whatever." Newman, *Apologia Pro Vita Sua* (New York, 1950), 237.

69. Orestes A. Brownson, "Sparks on Episcopacy," *Brownson's Quarterly Review* 1 (July 1844), quoted in Arthur M. Schlesinger, Jr., *Orestes A. Brownson* (Boston, 1939), 181.

70. Orestes A. Brownson, *The Spirit Rapper: An Autobiography* (Detroit, 1884), 270.

71. Hecker, "Doctor Brownson and the Workingman's Party Fifty Years Ago," *Catholic World* 45 (May 1887): 207.

72. Hecker, "Doctor Brownson and Catholicity," *Catholic World* 46 (November 1887): 233.

73. Hecker, "Doctor Brownson and Bishop Fitzpatrick," *Catholic World* 45 (April 1887): 7.

156 	NOTES, PP. 43-51

CHAPTER 3

1. John Humphrey Noyes, "The Progressive Nature of Regeneration," in George W. Noyes, ed., *Religious Experience of John Humphrey Noyes* (New York, 1923), 383.

2. Noyes, *Home-Talks,* ed. Alfred Barron and George Noyes Miller (Oneida, N. Y., 1875), 25.

3. Noyes, "Home Talk," *The Oneida Circular* 2 (November 17, 1852): 3.

4. Noyes' conversion took place during the height of the Great Revival in Vermont. Cf. David M. Ludlum, *Social Ferment in Vermont: 1791-1850* (New York, 1939), 56.

5. Noyes, "Extracts from Diary, July 1, 1832," in Noyes, *Religious Experience,* 42.

6. Noyes, "Extracts from Diary, August 5, 1832," 51.

7. Noyes, "Confession of Religious Experience [circa January 1834]," in Noyes, *Religious Experience,* 104.

8. Ibid., February 20, 1834, 110.

9. Noyes, "Extracts from Diary [circa March 1, 1834]," 121.

10. Noyes, "Extracts from Diary, May-June 1834," 137, 139.

11. Ibid., 143.

12. "Noyes to his sister, Elizabeth Noyes, November 12, 1834," in Noyes, *Religious Experience,* 172-175.

13. "Mrs. Polly Noyes' Recollections," in George W. Noyes, ed., *John Humphrey Noyes: The Putney Community* (Oneida, 1931), 30.

14. "Statement of Mrs. Polly Noyes, March 1839," in Noyes, *Putney,* 33.

15. "Pride of Motherhood: Paper by Noyes Probably Written Late in 1845," in Noyes, *Putney,* 94-96.

16. "Notes by Mrs. Polly Noyes," January 21, 1841, in Noyes, *Putney,* 93.

17. *Daily Journal of Oneida Community* 3 (June 12, 1867): 588-589.

18. Noyes, *The Berean* (Putney, Vt., 1847), 243. This is the most compact source for Noyes' theological positions. It is a collection of pieces written from his salvation until 1847.

19. Ibid., 144, 201, 217.

20. Noyes, "First Principles, Summer 1842," in Noyes, *Putney,* 54.

21. Noyes, *Bible Communism* (Brooklyn, N. Y., 1853), 42.

22. Noyes, *History of American Socialisms* (Philadelphia, 1870), 149, 151, 198.

23. [Noyes], *The Oneida Community* (Wallingford, Conn., 1865), 20.

24. Pierrepont Noyes, *My Father's House: An Oneida Boyhood* (New York, 1937), 79.

25. Noyes, *Bible Communism,* 37.

26. Noyes, "My First Act in Sexual Freedom," (*n.d.*), in Noyes, *Putney,* 201-202.

27. Noyes to Harriet H. Skinner, August 1, 1846, in Noyes, *Putney,* 202.

28. Cf. Hubbard Eastman, *Noyesism Unveiled* (Brattleboro, Vt., 1849).

29. Noyes, *Bible Communism,* 40.

30. Ibid., 31.

31. Noyes, *Home-Talks,* 122.

32. Noyes, *Bible Communism,* 53.

33. Ibid., 35.

34. [Noyes], *Handbook of the Oneida Community* (Oneida, 1871), 50-51.

35. Noyes, *Male Continence* (Oneida, 1872), 9-10.

36. Noyes, *Dixon and His Copyists* (Wallingford, Conn., 1871), 35.

37. [Noyes], *Third Annual Report of Oneida Community* (Oneida, 1851), 21-22.

38. [Noyes], *Mutual Criticism* (Oneida, 1876), 94.

39. Pierrepont Noyes, *My Father's House,* 18.

40. "Statement of G. W. Hamilton," *Daily Journal of Oneida Community* 1 (March 12, 1866): 191.

41. Corinna Ackley Noyes, *The Days of My Youth* (Kenwood, N. Y., 1960), 50.

42. [Noyes], *Third Annual Report,* 16.

43. Noyes to G. W. Robinson [1846], in Noyes, *Putney,* 193.

44. *First Annual Report of Oneida Community* (Oneida, 1849), 20.

45. *The Oneida Circular* N. S. 7 (April 4, 1870): 20.

46. *The Oneida Circular* N. S. 3 (April 23, 1866): 41.

47. "Statement of J. H. Noyes," *Daily Journal of Oneida Community* 1 (February 17, 1866): 116-117. On this same fear see Noyes' comments in *The Oneida Circular* N. S. 3 (November 26, 1866): 289-290.

48. A convenient summary of Oneida industrialism is Walter Edmonds, *The First Hundred Years: 1848-1948* (Oneida, 1948). Designs and uses for the traps are described in Sewell Newhouse, *The Trapper's Guide,* ed. John Humphrey Noyes, 2d ed. (Oneida, 1867).

49. [Noyes], *Handbook of Oneida Community* (Oneida, 1875), 21.

50. Ibid.

51. Robert A. Parker, *A Yankee Saint: John Humphrey Noyes and the Oneida Community* (New York, 1935), 261.

52. Noyes, *Home-Talks,* 25.

53. Noyes, *Essay on Scientific Propagation* (Oneida, 1875), 17. It is interesting to note that there was a tradition of near-incest, marriage between first cousins, in the Noyes family, Parker, *A Yankee Saint,* 60.

54. Noyes, *Essay on Scientific Propagation,* 17.

55. Parker, *A Yankee Saint,* 257.

56. Ibid.

57. Pierrepont Noyes, *My Father's House,* 10; Parker, *A Yankee Saint,* 259.

58. Parker, *A Yankee Saint,* 263.

59. Ibid., 282; Pierrepont Noyes, *My Father's House,* 158.

60. The best description of Noyes' last years is in Parker, *A Yankee Saint,* 292-304.

CHAPTER 4

1. Horace Mann, "The Necessity of Education in a Republican Government," in his *Lectures on Education* (Boston, 1845), 142; Mary P. Mann, *Life and Works of Horace Mann,* 2d ed. (Boston, 1891), II, 168.

2. Mann to James K. Mills, November 29, 1843, Horace Mann Manuscripts, Massachusetts Historical Society.

3. Mann, "Necessity of Education," *Lectures on Education,* 157; Mann, *Life and Works,* II, 183.

4. Mann, "Necessity of Education," *Lectures on Education,* 161; Mann, *Life and Works,* II, 187.

5. Mann, *Third Annual Report of the* [Massachusetts] *Board of Education, Together with the Third Annual Report of the Secretary of the Board* (Boston, 1839), in Mann, *Life and Works,* III, 10.

6. Mann, *Twelfth Annual Report* (1848), in Mann, *Life and Works,* IV, 251-252.

7. Mann to His Family, June 29, 1814, Mann Manuscripts. The best discussion of the young Horace Mann is in Jonathan C. Messerli, *Horace Mann: A Biography* (New York, 1972).

8. Mann to His Family, September 25, 1816, Mann Manuscripts.

9. Mann to James K. Mills, May 4, 1844, Mann Manuscripts.

10. Mann to Mrs. Josiah Quincy, Jr. (*n.d.*), Horace Mann Letters, Boston Public Library. By permission of Boston Public Library.

11. Mann to His Family, November 22, 1817, Mann Manuscripts. See also in the same collection his letter to his family of October 7, 1817.

12. Mann, *Third Annual Report,* in Mann, *Life and Works,* III, 27-28. Mann makes a similar argument in his lecture, *A Few Thoughts for Young Men* (Boston, 1850), 54.

13. The best discussion of this relationship is in Messerli, *Horace Mann,* 141-162.

14. Mann to Mary Peabody, August 26, 1833, Mann Manuscripts.

15. Mann, Journal, 1837-1843, June 15, 1837, Mann Manuscripts.

16. Ibid., April 21, 1839.

17. Mary Peabody to Mann, August 1836, Mann Manuscripts.

18. Mann, Journal, March 26, 1843, Mann Manuscripts, emphasis added.

19. Mann to His Sister, Lydia B. Mann, July 1836, Mann Manuscripts.

20. Mann to Austin Craig, January 6, 1856, Mann Manuscripts. There is a similar self-analysis in a long letter, undated, to an unnamed recipient in Mann, *Life and Works,* I, 10-16.

21. Mann to Austin Craig, June 16, 1854, in W. S. Harwood, *Life and Letters of Austin Craig* (New York, 1908), 174-175.

22. "My feelings of sympathy with you on the manifold perplexities of your position demand from me friendly words (and sometimes upward-looking ones), but I must not permit them to blind me to the fact that I feel no call of duty to come to you." Austin Craig to Mann, August 17, 1857, in Harwood, *Life and Letters,* 208. Craig did go to Antioch for a brief time shortly after this letter was written.

23. Craig's motives for leaving Antioch are unclear. Ironically, he became the second president of the college (from 1864 to 1868), a post in which he was miserably unhappy.

24. Mann to Charles Sumner, March 10, 1856, Mann Manuscripts.

25. Theodore Parker to Samuel Gridley Howe, August 26, 1859, in George A. Hubbell, *Horace Mann* (Philadelphia, 1910), 248-249.

26. "Association of the Masters of the Boston Public Schools," *Remarks on the Seventh Annual Report of the Honorable Horace Mann* (Boston, 1844); Mann, *Reply to the Remarks of Thirty-One Boston Schoolmasters* (Boston, 1844); "Association of the Boston Masters," *Rejoinder to the Reply* (Boston, 1845); Mann, *Answer to the Rejoinder* (Boston, 1845). For a second public controversy, see Matthew Hale Smith, *The Bible, the Rod, and Religion in Common Schools* (Boston, 1847); Mann, *Sequel to the So-Called Correspondence between the Rev. M. H. Smith and Horace Mann* (Boston, 1847); M. H. Smith, *Reply to the Sequel* (Boston, 1847).

27. *Remarks on the Seventh Annual Report,* 128, 136, 139.

28. Mann, *Reply to the Remarks,* 45, 48, 61, 76, 144, 158.

29. Ibid., 90, 135.

30. Mann to Henry Barnard, March 21, 1840, Henry Barnard Collection, New York University (photostatic copy in the Horace Mann School Library, Riverdale, N. Y.).

31. Mann, "The Editor's Address to the Public," *Common School Journal* 5 (January 2, 1843): 6.

32. Mann, "Go Forth and Teach: An Oration Delivered before the Authorities of Boston, July 4, 1842," reprinted by the Committee on the

Horace Mann Centennial, National Education Association (Washington, D.C., 1937), 16-17.

33. Merle Curti, *The Social Ideas of American Educators* (New York, 1935), 123. A useful monograph on phrenology is John D. Davies, *Phrenology: Fad and Science* (New Haven, 1955). The basic tome of phrenology, and one which deeply influenced Mann, was written by his friend, George Combe, *The Constitution of Man* (Edinburgh, 1828).

34. Mann to Bayard Taylor, January 15, 1855, Bayard Taylor Collection, Cornell University Library (photostatic copy in the Horace Mann School Library).

35. Mann to Henry Barnard, May 2, 1840, Barnard Collection, New York (Photostatic copy in the Horace Mann School Library).

36. Mann, "Baccalaureate Address Delivered at Antioch College, 1857," in Mann, *Life and Works*, V, 496-497.

37. Mann, "Necessity of Education," in his *Lectures on Education*, 139; Mann, *Life and Works*, II, 165.

38. Mann, "Prospectus," *Common School Journal* 1 (November 1839): 7.

CHAPTER 5

1. Margaret Fuller, *Women in the Nineteenth Century* (1844), in Arthur B. Fuller, ed., *Margaret Fuller's Works* (Boston, 1860), II, 109. See also Margaret Fuller to unnamed correspondent, October 10, 1840, in R. W. Emerson, W. H. Channing, and J. F. Clarke, eds., *Memoirs of Margaret Fuller Ossoli* (Boston, 1860), II, 44-47.

2. Fuller, Journal [circa 1841], in Emerson et al., *Memoirs*, II, 73.

3. Fuller to William H. Channing, December 13, 1840, Fuller Manuscripts, Boston Public Library (hereafter BPL). By permission of BPL.

4. Fuller to William H. Channing, December 22, 1840, in Emerson et al., *Memoirs*, II, 57.

5. Journal, n.d., in Emerson et al., *Memoirs*, II, 74.

6. Fuller, "Swedenborg and His Disciples," *New York Tribune*, July 7, 1845.

7. Emerson et al., *Memoirs*, I, 133.

8. Journal, n.d., in Emerson et al., *Memoirs*, II, 73.

9. Fuller to unnamed correspondent, 1840, in Emerson et al., *Memoirs*, II, 29.

10. Fuller to William H. Channing, May 7, 1847, in Emerson et al., *Memoirs*, II, 209.

11. Fuller to Marcus and Rebecca Spring, December 12, 1849, MSS

Letters, IX, Fuller Manuscripts, Houghton Library, Harvard University (hereafter HL). The Fuller Manuscripts at Houghton include bound volumes of MSS Letters and bound editions of Margaret Fuller MSS, entitled "Works of Margaret Fuller Ossoli," prepared by her brother, Richard F. Fuller. This edition will hereafter be referred to as MSS Works.

12. Fuller, Journal fragment, March 10, 1849, Fuller Manuscripts, BPL. By permission of BPL.

13. Fuller, "Unfinished Sketch of Youth" (1840), in Emerson et al., *Memoirs*, I, 15.

14. Fuller to Her Father, February 19, 1825, MSS Letters, IX, Fuller Manuscripts, HL.

15. Journal, May 1840, in Emerson et al., *Memoirs*, I, 291-292.

16. "Unfinished Sketch of Youth," in Emerson et al., *Memoirs*, I, 24.

17. Fuller to William H. Channing, August 1843, in Thomas Wentworth Higginson, *Margaret Fuller Ossoli* (Boston, 1884), 311.

18. Journal fragment, 1839, MSS Works, V (1), 27, Fuller Manuscripts, HL.

19. Perry Miller, *Margaret Fuller: American Romantic* (Garden City, N.Y., 1963), 52. Throughout this study, Miller focuses on Margaret Fuller as a counter to Emerson both in philosophy and in lifestyle.

20. Ralph Waldo Emerson to Margaret Fuller, October 24, 1840, in Ralph L. Rusk, ed., *The Letters of Ralph Waldo Emerson* (New York, 1939), II, 353.

21. Fuller to Ralph Waldo Emerson, October 1841, in Rusk, *Letters of Emerson*, II, 456-457, n. 334.

22. Fuller to Ralph Waldo Emerson, July 1844, in Rusk, *Letters of Emerson*, III, 252, n. 63.

23. Fuller, "M'Kenney's *Memoirs*," *New York Tribune*, July 8, 1846.

24. Fuller, "Groton and Providence," March 1834, MSS Works, III, 367, Fuller Manuscripts, HL.

25. Fuller to unnamed correspondent, n.d., in Emerson et al., *Memoirs*, I, 99.

26. Fuller to J. F. Clarke, May 4, 1830, in Emerson et al., *Memoirs*, I, 70.

27. Fuller to William H. Channing, February 21, 1841, in Higginson, *Margaret Fuller Ossoli*, 112.

28. Emerson et al., *Memoirs*, I, 297.

29. Journal fragment [circa 1840], MSS Works, I, 581, Fuller Manuscripts, HL.

30. Fuller to William H. Channing, March 22, 1840, in Higginson, *Margaret Fuller Ossoli*, 309.

31. Fuller to Ralph Waldo Emerson, December 20, 1847, in Emerson

et al., *Memoirs*, II, 224-225. Fuller's whole European experience is carefully and sympathetically narrated in Joseph Jay Deiss, *The Roman Years of Margaret Fuller* (New York, 1969).

32. Fuller to Her Sister, Mrs. E. K. Channing, June 19, 1849, in Fuller, *Margaret Fuller's Works*, IV, 437.

33. Fuller to Richard F. Fuller, July 8, 1849, MSS Works, II, 881, Fuller Manuscripts, HL.

34. Emerson et al., *Memoirs*, II, 312.

35. Ibid., 327.

36. Fuller to William Storey, May 10, 1850, MSS Letters, IX, Fuller Manuscripts, HL.

37. Emerson et al., *Memoirs*, II, 312.

38. Fuller to Richard F. Fuller, January 8, 1850, MSS Letters, IX, Fuller Manuscripts, HL.

39. Journal fragment, February 6, 1850, Fuller Manuscripts, BPL.

40. Fuller to unnamed correspondent, April 16, 1850, in Fuller, *Margaret Fuller's Works*, II, 386.

41. Interesting descriptions of the shipwreck are in Emerson et al., *Memoirs*, II, 341-352, in Higginson, *Margaret Fuller Ossoli*, 276-280, and in Deiss, *Roman Years*, 311-313.

42. Earlier, in June 1849, she had joined Ossoli at an artillery post which she thought would be unmercifully shelled and gave a packet of papers to an American friend in case of her death. The post was not attacked. See Lewis Cass, Jr., to Mrs. E. K. Channing, May 10, 1851, in Fuller, *Margaret Fuller's Works*, II, 389-393.

CHAPTER 6

1. George William Curtis, "The American Political Doctrine of Liberty: An Oration Delivered before the O.B.K. Society of Harvard University, July 12, 1862," in Charles Eliot Norton, ed., *Orations and Addresses of George William Curtis* (New York, 1894), I, 112-113.

2. Curtis, "Constitutional Opposition," *Harper's Weekly* 8 (February 20, 1864): 114.

3. Curtis to Charles Eliot Norton, March 11, 1861, Curtis Manuscripts, Houghton Library, Harvard University, Cambridge, Mass.

4. Curtis, "The Easy Chair," *Harper's Monthly* 23 (August 1861): 411.

5. Curtis, "April, 1865," *From the Easy Chair, Third Series* (New York, 1894): 91. George M. Fredrickson discusses the impact of the war on northern intellectuals as a whole in *The Inner Civil War* (Cambridge, Mass., 1965).

6. Curtis, "The Easy Chair," *Harper's Monthly* 64 (March 1882): 618.

7. Curtis to John S. Dwight, March 3, 1844, in George W. Cooke, ed., *Early Letters of George William Curtis to John S. Dwight* (New York, 1898), 157-158.

8. Curtis to Dwight, April 8, 1844, in Cooke, *Early Letters*, 164.

9. Curtis to Dwight, March 3, 1844, in Cooke, *Early Letters*, 154.

10. Curtis to Dwight, April 22, 1845, in Cooke, *Early Letters*, 207.

11. Curtis to Isaac T. Hecker, October 8, 1843, Hecker Manuscripts, Archives of the Paulist Fathers, New York City.

12. Curtis to Dwight, June 6, 1846, in Cooke, *Early Letters*, 247.

13. Curtis, "Destiny," in Cooke, *Early Letters*, 251.

14. This visit to Egypt and Syria was made in 1849-1850, following three years of travel in Europe. From his observations, he wrote *Nile Notes of a Howadji* (New York, 1851) and *The Howadji in Syria* (New York, 1852).

15. Curtis, *Nile Notes of a Howadji*, 22.

16. Ibid., 35.

17. Ibid., 74.

18. Ibid., 91, 92.

19. Ibid., 134.

20. Ibid., 137. As opposed to Curtis' romantic view of this dancing, Gustave Flaubert saw the same girls fourteen months later and, realist that he was, took them sexually. Cf. Lewis P. Shanks, "Terpsichore, Apollo and Mrs. Grundy," *Bookman* 67 (June 1928): 409-410.

21. Curtis, *The Howadji in Syria*, 240-241.

22. Ibid., 12.

23. Ibid., 62.

24. Curtis, "The Easy Chair," *Harper's Monthly* 14 (May 1857): 846.

25. Ibid., *Harper's Monthly* 19 (October 1859): 705, 706.

26. Curtis to his wife, February 24, 1860, in Gordon Milne, *George William Curtis and the Genteel Tradition* (Bloomington, Ind., 1956), 106.

27. Curtis, "The Spoils System and the Progress of Civil-Service Reform: An Address Delivered before the American Social Science Association, at its Meeting in Saratoga, New York, September 8, 1881," in Norton, *Orations*, II, 196.

28. Curtis, "The Progress of Reform: An Oration Delivered at the Second Annual Meeting of the National Civil-Service Reform League, held at Newport, Rhode Island, August 1, 1883," in Norton, *Orations*, II, 297-298.

29. Curtis, "Civil-Service Reform: An Address Delivered before the American Social Science Association, at its Meeting in New York City, in October, 1869," in Norton, *Orations*, II, 4.

30. Ibid., in Norton, *Orations*, II, 27-28.

31. Curtis, "The Easy Chair," *Harper's Monthly* 21 (August 1860): 411.

32. Ibid.

33. Curtis, "The Right of Suffrage, A Speech Made in the Constitutional Convention of the State of New York, July 19, 1867," in Norton, *Orations*, I, 209.

34. Curtis, "Political Infidelity: A Lecture, March, 1864," in Norton, *Orations*, I, 147.

35. Curtis, "Machine Politics and the Remedy, An Address to Independent Republicans, Delivered in Chickering Hall, New York, May 20, 1880," in Norton, *Orations*, II, 153.

36. Curtis, "The Public Duty of Educated Men: An Oration Delivered at the Commencement of Union College, Schenectady, New York, June 27, 1877," in Norton, *Orations*, I, 273.

37. Curtis, "The Leadership of Educated Men: An Address Delivered before the Alumni of Brown University, at Providence, Rhode Island, June 20, 1882," in Norton, *Orations*, I, 333.

38. Ibid., 327, 331, 332.

39. Curtis, "Charles Sumner: A Eulogy Delivered before the Legislature of Massachusetts, in the Music Hall, Boston, June 9, 1874," in Norton, *Orations*, III, 229-230.

40. Curtis, "The Leadership of Educated Men," in Norton, *Orations*, I, 335.

41. Curtis, "The Easy Chair," *Harper's Monthly* 37 (June 1868): 130.

42. Curtis to Norton, September 30, 1877, Curtis Manuscripts. In a similar mood, Curtis had cast down a glance from his summer house on the campaign for Grant's reelection in 1872. "But what a nasty campaign it is! We here among the hills read peacefully every evening of the great battle that resounds below. I hope that you have kept cool in this volcanic season." Curtis to Charles A. Dana, September 2, 1872, Charles A. Dana Manuscripts, Massachusetts Historical Society, Boston, Mass.

43. Curtis to Norton, October 13, 1869, Curtis Manuscripts.

44. Quoted in Ari Hoogenboom, *Outlawing the Spoils: A History of the Civil Service Reform Movement* (Urbana, Ill., 1961), 159-160.

45. Chauncey M. Depew, *My Memory of Eighty Years* (New York, 1924), 80.

46. Quoted in Edward Cary, *George William Curtis* (Boston, 1894), 286.

47. Curtis to an unnamed correspondent, June 10, 1884, in Cary, *George William Curtis*, 289.

48. Curtis, "The Society of the Army of the Potomac: An Oration Delivered at the Nineteenth Annual Reunion of the Army of the Potomac,

held at Gettysburg, Pennsylvania, July 3, 1888,'' in Norton, *Orations*, III, 79.

49. Curtis' most balanced editorial on strikes was "The Telegraph Strike," *Harper's Weekly* 27 (August 4, 1883): 482.

50. Curtis, "The Chicago Police and the Anarchists," *Harper's Weekly* 30 (May 15, 1886): 306. The following year, when the outraged William Dean Howells requested Curtis to join with other prominent men of letters in appealing the convictions and sentences of the anarchists, Curtis angrily refused him, and declared that the judges had acted with total correctness. Curtis to William Dean Howells, September 23, 1887, Curtis Manuscripts.

51. Curtis to John J. Pinkerton, May 14, 1892, quoted in Hoogenboom, *Outlawing the Spoils*, 266.

CHAPTER 7

1. Edward Bellamy, "Looking Forward," *The Nationalist* 2 (December 1889): 4.

2. Bellamy, "Declaration of Principles," (1888), in Bellamy, *Edward Bellamy Speaks Again* (Kansas City, 1937), 31-32.

3. Laurence Gronlund, *The Co-operative Commonwealth* (Cambridge, Mass., 1965), 89. See also his explicitly Nationalist work, *Our Destiny* (Boston, 1891).

4. Bellamy, "Progress of Nationalism in the United States," *North American Review* 154 (June 1892): 743.

5. Bellamy, "Concerning the Founding of Nationalist Colonies," *The New Nation* 3 (September 23, 1893): 434. See also his piece, "The Colony Idea," *The New Nation* 2 (January 16, 1892): 36.

6. Bellamy, "Story Fragment," Bellamy Manuscripts, Houghton Library, Harvard University, Cambridge, Mass., Binder 1, Notebook C, 4. In another story, one of his characters wrote, "I constantly see myself through the reversed telescope, a little fellow standing afar off, and aching with curiosity." Edward Bellamy, Journal, Bellamy Manuscripts, Binder 1, Journal 3, 69.

7. Bellamy, "Plots for Stories," Bellamy Manuscripts, Binder 2, Notebook 1, 29.

8. Bellamy, Hawaiian Island Notebooks, Bellamy Manuscripts, Binder 2, 12.

9. Bellamy, Journal, Bellamy Manuscripts, Binder 1, Journal 1 (December 1871), 7.

10. Ibid., Journal 2 [1874], 32.

11. Ibid., Journal 1 (July 1875), 33.

12. Ibid., Journal 3, 75.

166   NOTES, PP. 109-120

13. Bellamy, "Eliot Carson," Bellamy Manuscripts, Binder 2, 21.
14. Ibid., 13.
15. Ibid., 22.
16. Ibid., 33.
17. Bellamy, Journal, Bellamy Manuscripts, Binder 1, Journal 3, 110.
18. Ibid., 119.
19. Bellamy, "Extra-Hazardous," *Appleton's Journal*, N.S. III (November 1877): 436-441.
20. Bellamy, "Almost a Suicide," Bellamy Manuscripts, Binder 3, 14.
21. Bellamy, "The Religion of Solidarity" (1874), in Arthur E. Morgan, ed., *The Philosophy of Edward Bellamy* (New York, 1945), 13.
22. Ibid., 20.
23. Bellamy, "Blindman's World" [188?], in Bellamy, *Blindman's World and Other Stories* (Boston, 1898), 24.
24. Ibid., 29.
25. Bellamy, "To Whom This May Come" [188?], in Bellamy, *Blindman's World*, 408.
26. Bellamy, *Dr. Heidenhoff's Process* (New York, 1880).
27. Bellamy, *Miss Ludington's Sister* (Boston, 1884).
28. Bellamy, "How I Came to Write *Looking Backward*," *The Nationalist* 1 (May 1889): 1.
29. Bellamy to John L. Thomas, July 29, 1891, Bellamy Manuscripts.
30. Bellamy, *Looking Backward, 2000-1887* (Cambridge, Mass., 1967), 97.
31. Ibid., 122.
32. Ibid., 127.
33. Ibid., 126.
34. Ibid., 127.
35. Bellamy, *Equality* (New York, 1897), 340.
36. Bellamy, *Looking Backward*, 178.
37. Ibid., 253; see also his comments in ibid., 304-305.
38. Ibid., 216.
39. Ibid., 230.
40. Ibid., 270.
41. Ibid., 226.
42. Ibid., 175.
43. Bellamy, *Equality*, 364.
44. Bellamy, *Looking Backward*, 141.
45. Ibid., 142.
46. Bellamy to Mason Green, January 27, 1894, in Mason Green, "Edward Bellamy" (1925), a biography in manuscript form in the Bellamy Manuscripts.
47. Bellamy, "Progress of Nationalism," 746, 747.

48. Bellamy's political program for his own day was most clearly enunciated in "First Steps Toward Nationalism," *The Forum* 10 (October 1890): 174-184.

49. Bellamy, *Equality*, 153.

50. Bellamy to Frances Willard [1889], in Arthur E. Morgan, *Edward Bellamy* (New York, 1944), 249.

51. Bellamy, "The Churches and Nationalism," *The New Nation* 1 (December 5, 1891): 710.

52. Bellamy, "Nationalism—Principles, Purposes: Address of Edward Bellamy at Tremont Temple, Boston, on the Nationalist Club Anniversary, December 19, 1889," in Bellamy, *Edward Bellamy Speaks Again*, 59.

53. Bellamy, "Plutocracy or Nationalism—Which?: Address of Edward Bellamy at Tremont Temple, Boston, May 31, 1889," in Bellamy, *Edward Bellamy Speaks Again*, 42.

54. Bellamy, *Talks on Nationalism* (Chicago, 1938), 90.

55. Bellamy to Henry Demarest Lloyd, December 5, 1896, Henry Demarest Lloyd Manuscripts, State Historical Society of Wisconsin, Madison, Wis.

56. Bellamy to William Dean Howells, June 17, 1888, Bellamy Manuscripts.

CHAPTER 8

1. Ignatius Donnelly, "Minnesota: Address Delivered at the Broadway House, New York, March 27, 1857" (New York, 1857), 5, 10, 12.

2. Dudley S. Brainard, "Ninninger, A Boom Town of the Fifties," *Minnesota History* 13 (June 1932): 127-151.

3. Martin Ridge, *Ignatius Donnelly: The Portrait of a Politician* (Chicago, 1962), 124.

4. Donnelly, Diary, October 28, 1867, in Theodore Nydahl, ed., "The Diary of Ignatius Donnelly, 1856-1884" (Ph.D. diss., University of Minnesota, 1942), I, 332; ibid., "Memoranda for 1867," in Nydahl, "Diary," I, 310; ibid., "Memoranda for 1870," in Nydahl, "Diary," I, 401.

5. Donnelly, Diary, "Memoranda for 1875," in Nydahl, "Diary," I, 615.

6. Ibid., November 3, 1880, in Nydahl, "Diary," II, 854.

7. Ignatius Donnelly to Reverend Martin Mahoney, January 1, 1889, Letterbooks of Ignatius Donnelly LXXV, 300, microfilm roll 152, copy of the original in the Donnelly Manuscripts, Minnesota Historical Society.

8. Donnelly, Diary, "Memoranda for 1877," in Nydahl, "Diary," I, 660.

9. Ibid., "Memoranda for 1881," in Nydahl, "Diary," II, 918-919.

10. Donnelly, Diary, July 18, 1888, microfilm roll 47, Donnelly Manuscripts.

11. Ibid., December 9, 1885, microfilm roll 46, Donnelly Manuscripts.

12. Ibid., March 26, 1882, in Nydahl, "Diary," II, 928.

13. Ibid., May 17, 1892, microfilm roll 48, Donnelly Manuscripts.

14. (Minneapolis and St. Paul) *Representative* 1 (April 19, 1893): 1.

15. Ibid. (December 27, 1893): 1.

16. (St. Paul) *Anti-Monopolist* 3 (July 13, 1876): 1.

17. (St. Paul) *Pioneer Press* (April 19, 1885) quoted in Ridge, *Ignatius Donnelly*, 223

18. Donnelly, *Doctor Huguet* (Chicago, 1891), 7-8.

19. Donnelly, *The Great Cryptogram* (Chicago, 1888), vi.

20. Ibid., 515. Also see his last book, *The Cipher in the Plays, and on the Tombstone* (Minneapolis, 1899). Donnelly's fascination in hidden truth to be revealed through codes apparently began in 1864, while he sat in Congress, when he used that means to sell government secrets, gold and tobacco prices, to a speculator. Cf. Ridge, *Ignatius Donnelly*, 91-92. Donnelly's cryptographic method contained so many possible permutations that in fact it was no system at all. He could have found whatever message he willed. For a clear and fascinating discussion by professional cryptologists, see William F. and Elizabeth S. Friedman, *The Shakespearean Ciphers Examined* (Cambridge, Mass., 1957), 27-50.

21. Donnelly, *Atlantis: The Antediluvian World* (New York, 1882), 480.

22. Ibid., 44.

23. Donnelly, *Ragnorak: The Age of Fire and Gravel* (New York, 1883), 45.

24. Ibid., 51.

25. Ibid., 57.

26. Ibid., 64.

27. Ibid., 108.

28. Ibid., 436, 439.

29. Ibid., 441.

30. Donnelly, *Diary* [circa July 1888], microfilm roll 47, Donnelly Manuscripts.

31. Ibid., February 19, 1890, microfilm roll 47, Donnelly Manuscripts.

32. Ibid., November 6, 1896, microfilm roll 48, Donnelly Manuscripts.

33. *Representative* 2 (November 7, 1894): 1.

34. *Anti-Monopolist* 4 (April 4, 1878): 1.

35. *Representative* 2 (July 11, 1894): 1.

36. Ibid., 2 (June 13, 1894): 1.

37. Ibid., 3 (February 26, 1896): 2.

38. Ibid., 4 (July 13, 1896): 2.

39. Ibid., 5 (April 13, 1898): 2.

40. Ibid., 5 (June 22, 1898): 2.

41. Ibid., 8 (November 8, 1900): 2.

42. Donnelly to Jerry Simpson, May 15, 1892, Letterbooks, LXXIV, 434-435, microfilm roll 152, Donnelly Manuscripts.

43. *Representative* 4 (July 29, 1896): 2.

44. Donnelly, *Caesar's Column* (Cambridge, Mass., 1960), 5.

45. Ibid., 97.

46. Ibid., 38.

47. Ibid., 119.

48. Ibid., 149.

49. Ibid., 32.

50. Ibid., 258.

51. Ibid., 255.

52. Ibid., 256.

53. Ibid., 270.

54. Ibid., 272.

55. Ibid., 290.

56. Ibid.

57. Ibid., 300.

CHAPTER 9

1. William Dean Howells, *A Boy's Town* (New York, 1890).

2. Ibid., 240.

3. Shakers and Shaker communities are in the center of four of Howells' novels: *The Undiscovered Country* (New York, 1880); *The Day of Their Wedding* (New York, 1896); *A Parting and A Meeting* (New York, 1896); *The Vacation of the Kelwyns: An Idyll of the Middle Eighteen-Seventies* (New York, 1920). In addition, see Howells' essay on Shirley, a Shaker community, in *Three Villages* (Boston, 1884), 69-113.

4. Howells, *Three Villages*, 74-75.

5. Ibid., 101.

6. This grouping and evaluation of Howells' novels, generally agreed upon by his critics, is best presented in Edwin H. Cady, *The Realist at War: The Mature Years, 1885-1920, of William Dean Howells* (Syracuse, 1958).

7. Howells to Henry James, October 10, 1888, in Mildred Howells, ed., *Life in Letters of William Dean Howells* (Garden City, N.Y., 1928), I, 417.

8. Howells, *The World of Chance* (New York, 1893).

9. For Howells' softer utopian commentaries, see his works *A Traveler*

from Altruria (New York, 1894), and *Through the Eye of the Needle* (New York, 1907), which was a rewriting of essays composed in 1895. Also see Clara and Rudolf Kirk, eds., *Letters of an Altrurian Traveler* (Gainesville, Fla., 1961).

10. Howells, *The World of Chance*, 6.
11. Ibid., 214.
12. Ibid., 184.
13. Ibid., 54-65, 312, 346-353.
14. Ibid., 374.

SELECTIVE BIBLIOGRAPHICAL ESSAY

General Works on American Utopianism

The best starting place for a study on utopianism in America is Arthur E. Bestor, Jr.'s brilliant article, "Patent-Office Models of the Good Society," *American Historical Review* 58 (April 1953): 505-526. I share many of Bestor's assumptions about the openness of ante-bellum American society and the nature of utopian communitarianism. In addition, Bestor's monograph, *Backwoods Utopia: The Sectarian and Owenite Phases of Communitarian Socialism, 1663-1829* (Philadelphia, 1950), which should be read in conjunction with John F. C. Harrison, *The New Moral World: Robert Owen and the Owenites* (New York, 1968), and Bestor's Ph.D. dissertation "American Phalanxes" (Yale University, 1938), are central studies of utopian communitarianism in the United States.

I found many works to be persuasive while I was formulating this book, but here I list only those I found indispensable. Some of Bestor's arguments are extended and others reevaluated by Fred Somkin in *Unquiet Eagle: Memory and Desire in the Idea of American Freedom, 1815-1860* (Ithaca, N. Y., 1967). Somkin's study assesses ante-bellum American society as a more ambivalent period than does Bestor, in which hopes for creation of a new man in the new world were tempered by anxieties over loss of control of the national direction. John L. Thomas argues that the period of the greatest spread of abolitionism during the political crisis of the 1850s was also the time when reformers, under pressure, lost their broader cultural program of utopianism; see his "Anti-Slavery and

Utopia," in Martin Duberman, ed., *The Anti-Slavery Vanguard* (Princeton, 1965), 240-269. In a somewhat similar manner, John Higham argues that the 1850s saw the beginning of the end of open-ended social experimentation, in his lecture, "From Boundlessness to Consolidation: The Transformation of American Culture, 1848-1860" (Ann Arbor, 1969). The experience of the Civil War, I have argued, relying to a great extent on the theses developed by George M. Fredrickson in *The Inner Civil War: Northern Intellectuals and the Crisis of the Union* (Cambridge, Mass., 1965), made national loyalty a test which further eroded the earlier natural plausibility of the utopian communitarian approach. Of the many fine studies of later nineteenth-century society, I found both Richard Hofstadter, *The Age of Reform* (New York, 1955), and Robert H. Wiebe, *The Search for Order* (New York, 1967), to be at the same time intellectually disciplined and emotionally persuasive books. Wiebe's reformers are somehow freer than Hofstadter's, and their struggle to shape a complex national society, though never without enormous inner tension, in Wiebe's portrayal, was nevertheless more conscious and human than the reactionism of Hofstadter's disinherited.

American utopian communities have received frequent and often repetitious treatment. The broadest general study of ante-bellum reform, Alice Felt Tyler's *Freedom's Ferment: Phases of American Social History from the Colonial Period to the Outbreak of the Civil War* (1944, New York, 1962), is full of bibliographical suggestions for utopianism and allied social movements. The best survey of American communities remains John Humphrey Noyes, *History of American Socialisms* (1870; reprint, New York, 1961). Noyes took most of his information from A. J. MacDonald, who had visited most of the communities he then wrote about. MacDonald's manuscripts are now deposited in the Yale University Library, New Haven, Conn. Three other older discussions of communities remain standard: Charles Nordhoff, *The Communistic Societies of the United States* (1875; reprint, New York, 1965); William A. Hinds, *American Communities and Co-Operative Societies* (1875; rev. ed., Chicago, 1908); and Morris Hillquit, *History of Socialism in the United States* (1903; reprint, New York, 1965). Several more recent studies are less useful. These include Gilbert Seldes, *The Stammering Century* (1928; reprint, New York,

1965); Lewis Mumford, *The Story of Utopia* (New York, 1923); Francis T. P. Russell, *Touring Utopia* (New York, 1932); Victor F. Calverton, *Where Angels Feared to Tread* (Indianapolis, 1941); Arthur E. Morgan, *Nowhere Was Somewhere* (Chapel Hill, N. C., 1946); Vernon L. Parrington, Jr., *American Dreams: A Study of American Utopias* (1947; reprint, New York, 1964); Mark Holloway, *Heavens on Earth* (New York, 1951); Charles Madison, *Critics and Crusaders: A Century of Protest*, 2d ed. (New York, 1957); and Everett Webber, *Escape to Utopia* (New York, 1959). Rosabeth Moss Kanter, *Commitment and Community: Communes and Utopias in Sociological Perspective* (Cambridge, Mass., 1972), came to my attention too recently for use here.

Because of the overemphasis American intellectual historians generally have awarded to the transcendentalists, Brook Farm, the transcendentalist utopian effort, has been the most studied single community. Three monographs on the subject are quite good: Charles Crowe, *George Ripley: Transcendentalist and Utopian Socialist* (Athens, Ga., 1967), studies the leader of Brook Farm. Edith R. Curtis, *A Season in Utopia: The Story of Brook Farm* (New York, 1961), and Lindsay Swift, *Brook Farm* (New York, 1908), are studies of the community as a whole. Two editions of Brook Farm documents are very well done: Henry W. Sams, ed., *Autobiography of Brook Farm* (Englewood Cliffs, N.J., 1958), and Zoltan Haraszti, *The Idyll of Brook Farm* (Boston, 1937). Of the many Brook Farm memoirs, I found the following most useful: Georgiana Bruce Kirby, *Years of My Experience* (New York, 1887); Amelia E. Russell, *Home Life at Brook Farm* (Boston, 1900); John Van Der Zee Sears, *My Friends at Brook Farm* (New York, 1912); Ora G. Sedgwick, "A Girl of Sixteen at Brook Farm," *Atlantic Monthly* 85 (March 1900): 394-404.

Among the many works correlative to the ones I used most directly, several were especially stimulating. Marguerite Young, *Angel in the Forest* (1948; reprint, New York, 1966), is a fine novelist's meditation on the history of New Harmony. Clara E. Sears, *Bronson Alcott's Fruitlands* (Boston, 1915), and Odell Shepard, *Peddler's Progress: The Life of Bronson Alcott* (Boston, 1937), consider Alcott's utopian experimentation. A. J. G. Perkins and Theresa Wolfson, *Frances Wright: Free Enquirer* (New York, 1939), and William A. Waterman, *Frances Wright* (New York,

1924), are the starting places for the discussion of an early feminist and communitarian leader. Adin Ballou, *Autobiography* (Lowell, Mass., 1896), and Philip S. Padleford, "Adin Ballou and the Hopedale Community," (Ph.D. dissertation, Yale University, 1942), discuss an important pacifist leader of a utopian experiment. Albert Shaw, *Icaria* (New York, 1884), and Jules Prudhommeaux, *Icarie et Son Fondateur Etienne Cabet* (Paris, 1907), discuss a French community in America, while Carl Wittke, *The Utopian Communist: A Biography of Wilhelm Weitling* (Baton Rouge, La., 1950), is a pioneering study of pre-Marxist, German-American socialism. I found Paul K. Conkin's study of the Hutterites in *Two Paths to Utopia* (Lincoln, Neb., 1964), and Edward D. Andrew's *The People Called Shakers* (New York, 1953), to be the most insightful discussions of Protestant sectarian communal organizations. Two useful monographs are Robert V. Hines, *California's Utopian Colonies* (San Marino, Cal., 1953), and William H. and Jane H. Pease, *Black Utopia: Negro Communal Experiments in America* (Madison, Wis., 1963).

I have made no attempt to discuss utopianism as an abstract idea or to place this study in a general, western European intellectual setting. The clearest history of utopian theories is Joyce O. Hertzler, *The History of Utopian Thought* (New York, 1923). Many useful essays are contained in *Daedalus* 40 (Spring 1965), an issue devoted to studies on utopia, and in Sylvia L. Thrupp, ed., *Millennial Dreams in Action: Comparative Studies in Society and History*, Supplement II (The Hague, Netherlands, 1962). Glenn Negley and J. Max Patrick, *The Quest for Utopia* (1952; reprint, Garden City, N.Y., 1962), is a well-chosen anthology. Arthur L. Morton, *The English Utopia* (London, 1952), and W. H. G. Armytage, *Heavens Below: Utopian Experiments in England, 1560-1960* (London, 1961), are useful introductions to utopianism in that country. Frank E. Manuel, *French Utopias* (New York, 1966), is a good collection for France. Three wide-ranging essays on European utopianism are especially valuable: Ernest Lee Tuvenson, *Millennium and Utopia: A Study in the Background of the Idea of Progress* (Berkeley, Cal., 1949); Karl Mannheim, *Ideology and Utopia* (New York, 1936); and Norman Cohn, *The Pursuit of the Millennium* (London, 1957). The latter two studies concern the real explosiveness of attempts to implement utopian ideas in already highly structured societies.

Finally, several essays point up the current resurgence of utopian hopes. Herbert Marcuse's works, especially *Eros and Civilization* (New York, 1955), and Norman O. Brown, *Life Against Death* (Middletown, Conn., 1959), and his *Love's Body* (New York, 1966), yearn toward men made complete. Tom Wolfe, *The Electric Kool-Aid Acid Test* (New York, 1968), deals with a West Coast utopian community focused around LSD, while Richard H. Blum, *Utopiates* (New York, 1964), much less thoroughly looks at the same phenomenon in the East. B. F. Skinner, in his behavioralist paradise, *Walden Two* (New York, 1948), portrays the socially conditioned man as the culminating product of a stimulus-response utopia; it is this man whom the young utopians now want to remake in quite the opposite manner.

Albert Brisbane and Charles Fourier

The Albert Brisbane Manuscripts, strong especially for Brisbane's later years, are located in the Illinois Historical Survey, Urbana, Ill. Brisbane's European travel diaries, written in 1830-1832, are in the Syracuse University Library, Syracuse, N. Y. As an old man Brisbane dictated his memoirs to his young wife. The consequent distortions are both useful for analysis of his spirit as he aged and dangerous in terms of accuracy of memory: Redelia Brisbane, *Albert Brisbane: A Mental Biography* (Boston, 1893). This book should be read in conjunction with Arthur E. Bestor's careful and bibliographically suggestive article, "Albert Brisbane—Propagandist for Socialism in the 1840's," *New York History* 28 (April 1947): 128-158. The most important publications written by Brisbane are his *Social Destiny of Man* (Philadelphia, 1840), and *A Concise Explanation of the Doctrines of Association* (New York, 1843). Brisbane restated himself decades later in *General Introduction to Social Sciences* (New York, 1876). In addition, he translated and edited two volumes of Charles Fourier's works: *The Theory of Universal Unity* (New York, [1857]), and *Theory of Social Organization* (New York, 1876). To reach the masses, Brisbane wrote a great deal for newspapers and journals. His column appeared from one to four times a week in the *New York Tribune*, from March 1, 1842, to September 9, 1843. Among his magazine articles are: "Fourierism and the Socialists," *Dial* 3 (July 1842): 86-89; columns in *The Phalanx*, October 5, November 4, December 5, 1843; May 18, July 13, 30, 1844; and articles in the *Harbinger*, June 27, July 4, 25, August 15, 1846; February 27, April 14, May 22, 1847. As Brisbane had only a limited number of ideas, these pieces are extremely repetitious in tone and content.

Fourier, Brisbane's master, also repeated himself endlessly. A convenient collection of his central ideas is Jonathan Beecher and Richard Bienvenu, *The Utopian Vision of Charles Fourier* (Boston, 1971). Hugh Doherty translated one of Fourier's lengthier works and added a still useful introduction in *The Passions of the Human Soul* (London, 1901), 2 vols. John S. Dwight and Parke Godwin, as well as Brisbane, popularized Fourier in America: Dwight, *Lectures on Association* (Boston, 1844); Godwin, *Association, or A Concise Exploration of the Practical Parts of Fourier's Social Science* (New York, 1843); *Popular View of the Doctrines of Charles Fourier* (New York, 1844); *Democracy, Constructive and Pacific* (New York, 1884.) An excellent recent study is Nicholas V. Riasanovsky, *The Teachings of Charles Fourier* (Berkeley, Calif., 1969). It should be read in conjunction with Hubert Bourgin, *Fourier: Contribution à L'Etude du Socialism Français* (Paris, 1905). The basic volumes of Fourier are *Ouvres Complètes de Charles Fourier* (Paris, 1966-1968), 12 vols.

Several aspects of Brisbane's career are discussed in Victor Considerant, *European Colonization in Texas* (New York, 1855), and his *The Great West* (New York, 1854), and Garett R. Carpenter, *Silkville: A Kansas Attempt in the History of Fourierist Utopianism, 1869-1892* (Emporia, Kan., 1954). An important letter by Brisbane is reprinted in Frothingham, *George Ripley* (Boston, 1882), 181-185.

Josiah Warren

The best starting place for Josiah Warren is James J. Martin, *Men Against the State* (De Kalb, Ill., 1953), 11-107. This heavily annotated study of Warren is full of suggestions for further reading. In conjunction with the Martin study, William Bailie, *Josiah Warren* (Boston, 1906), and Eunice M. Shuster, *Native American Anarchism* (Northampton, Mass., 1932), are of central importance. Only scattered Warren manuscripts are extant, a fate typical for reformers who spent most of their lives in the West. The most important collections are in the New Harmony Workingmen's Institute Library, New Harmony, Ind., and in the Labadie Collection, University of Michigan Library, Ann Arbor, Mich. Houghton Library, Harvard University, Cambridge, Mass., has two series of letters from Warren to his chief disciple, Stephen Pearl Andrews; and Ewing Baskette edited "Six Letters of Josiah Warren Concerning Stereotype Printing" (Springfield, Ill., 1951).

Warren had two deceptive writing habits—pamphleteering and putting the same book out under different titles. His most important book, which went through many editions, is *True Civilization*, 4th ed. (Cliftondale, Mass., 1869). Three books detailing his grand analysis are: *Practical Details of Equitable Commerce* (New York, 1854); *True Civilization an Immediate Necessity, and the Last Ground of Hope for Mankind* (1863; reprint, New York, 1967), and *Practical Applications of the Elementary Principles of True Civilization to the Minute Details of Everyday Life* (Princeton, Mass., 1873). His works on music include: *A New System of Notation of Music* (New Harmony, 1843), and *Written Music Remodeled and Invested with the Simplicity of An Exact Science* (Boston, 1860). Among his many pamphlets are: *To the Friends of the Social System* (Cincinnati, 1827); *Manifesto* (1841; reprint, Berkeley Heights, N. J., 1952); *Letter on Equitable Commerce* (New Harmony, 1844); *Periodical Letters on True Civilization* (1854-1858); *Modern Government and Its True Mission* (March 1862); *The Emancipation of Labor* (Boston, 1864); *The Quarterly Letter* (Cliftondale, 1867); *Response to the Call of the National Labor Union* (Boston, 1871); *Letter to E. H. Haywood* (Princeton, Mass., 1873). Warren edited the short-lived *Peaceful Revolution* (1833, 1848), and contributed to *Woodhull and Claflin's Weekly* no. 55-68 (June 3-September 23, 1871), and to *The Word*, July 1872, May, September 1873, March 1874.

Additional secondary material on Warren is in Raymond L. Hawkins, *Positivism in the United States, 1853-1861* (Cambridge, Mass., 1938); William Pare, "Trialsville and Modern Times," *Chamber's Edinburgh Journal* 18 (December 18, 1852): 395-397; and Moncure Conway, "Modern Times," *The Fortnightly Review* 6 (July 1, 1865): 421-434, and Conway, *Autobiography* (Boston, 1904), I: 264-268.

Stephen Pearl Andrews demonstrated his discipleship to Warren in *The Science of Society* (Boston, 1851, 1888), but moved much closer to the system-making of Comte and Brisbane in *The Basic Outline of Universology* (New York, 1872). Also see a recent study by Madeleine B. Stern, *Pantarch: A Biography of Stephen Pearl Andrews* (Austin, Tex., 1968).

Isaac T. Hecker

Isaac T. Hecker's early letters and diaries provide a historian's dream: truly introspective and honest self-analysis written during a period of great psychological stress. Along with many more manuscripts, these documents are located in the Archives of the Paulist Fathers, New York City. Much of this material is reprinted in Vincent F. Holden, *The Early Years of Isaac T. Hecker, 1819-1844*, "Studies in American Church History," 29 (Washington, D.C., 1939). Holden has also written *The Yankee Paul: Isaac T. Hecker* (Milwaukee, 1958). Walter Elliott, *The Life of Father Hecker* (New York, 1891), is detailed and quite fair-minded. It should be read in conjunction with Elliott's "Personal Reminiscenses," *Catholic World* 101 (April 1915): 89-98. Joseph McSorley, *Father Hecker and His Friends* (St. Louis, 1952), is less interesting. Hecker himself wrote three books that are often revealing: *Questions of the Soul*, 6th ed. (New York, 1869); *Aspirations of Nature* (New York, 1857); *The Church and the Age*, 2d ed. (New York, 1896). Of Hecker's periodical articles, a series of five on Orestes Brownson are especially important for the parallels and differences Hecker felt Brownson's life contained in comparison to his own: *Catholic*

World 45 (April, May, July 1887): 1-7, 200-208, 466-472; 46 (October, November 1887): 1-11, 222-235. Hecker's review, "The Transcendental Movement in New England," *Catholic World* 23 (July 1876), does not denounce his former friends. Collections of Hecker letters are available in two journal articles: E. H. Russell, ed., "A Bit of Unpublished Correspondence between Henry Thoreau and Isaac Hecker," *Atlantic Monthly* 90 (September 1902): 370-376, and Abbot Gasquet, "Some Letters of Father Hecker," *Catholic World* 86 (May, June, July 1906): 233-245, 356-365, 456-465.

Orestes Brownson's books, *The Spirit-Rapper: An Autobiography* (1854; reprint, Detroit, 1884), and *The Convert, or Leaves from My Experience* (1857; reprint, New York, 1877), analyze his view of reform and conversion. The standard modern study of Brownson is Arthur M. Schlesinger, Jr., *Orestes A. Brownson: A Pilgrim's Progress* (Boston, 1939). Carl F. Krummel, "Catholicism, Americanism, Democracy and Orestes Brownson," *American Quarterly* 6 (Spring 1954): 19-31, stresses, as I have, Brownson's rigid orthodoxy during all his years as a Catholic. Another unusual and somewhat parallel conversion to the Roman Catholic church is recollected in John Henry Cardinal Newman, *Apologia Pro Vita Sua* (1864; reprint, New York, 1950).

L'Abbé Dufresne, "Personal Recollections of Father Hecker," *Catholic World* 67 (June 1898): 324-340, is the memoir of a priest who knew Hecker, while James Parton, "Our Roman Catholic Brethren," *Atlantic Monthly* 21 (April, May 1868): 432-451, 556-574, based to a large extent on an interview with Hecker, is a fascinating and sympathetic attempt by an American Protestant to come to grips with the presence of Catholicism in the United States. Several modern articles focusing on the impact of Hecker and the Paulists should be mentioned: James M. Gillis, "Father Hecker and His Friends," *Catholic World* 176 (January 1953): 246-251; Robert T. Handy, "Father Hecker, A Bridge between Catholic and Protestant Thought," *Catholic World* 202 (December 1965): 158-164; Louis F. McKernan, "Father Hecker and the Press," *Catholic World* 186 (February 1958): 326-332; Walter F. Ong, "Man Between Two Worlds," *Catholic World* 186 (May 1958): 86-94; Wilfred Parsons, "Brownson, Hecker and Hewit," *Catholic World* 153 (July 1941): 396-408; John B. Sheerin, "The Second Paulist

Century," *Catholic World* 186 (January 1958): 241-245, and his "The Paulist Apostate," *Commonweal* 69 (December 26, 1958): 334-346; Lawrence Williams, "Thoreau and Roman Catholicism," *Catholic Historical Review* 42 (July 1958): 157-172; Michael Williams, "Views and Reviews," *Commonweal* 28 (June 17, 1938): 212. Finally, on the controversy in Europe over Hecker and "Americanism," a useful summary is Adrien Dansette, *Religious History of Modern France* (Paris, 1948; Freiburg, West Germany, 1961), 138-149.

John Humphrey Noyes and the Oneida Community

The John Humphrey Noyes manuscripts, located in the Mansion House, the still-surviving central structure of the Oneida Community, are not open to the public. They were most recently used, it appears, by Robert A. Parker in his often perceptive study, *A Yankee Saint: John Humphrey Noyes and the Oneida Community* (New York, 1935). Maren Lockwood Carden's recent book, *Oneida: Utopian Community to Modern Corporation* (Baltimore, 1969), deals less with Noyes than with Oneida as a changing community. Also see her article based primarily on her Oneida research, "The Experimental Utopia in America," *Daedalus* 94 (Spring 1965): 401-418. The two best sources on Noyes, which emphasize his early years, are editions of his letters and journals, prepared by his son George: *Religious Experience of John Humphrey Noyes* (New York, 1923), and *John Humphrey Noyes: The Putney Community* (Oneida, 1931). George Noyes seems to have been faithful to his father's spirit if not always to his writing style.

As well as writing *History of American Socialisms* (1870; reprint, New York, 1961), Noyes penned many pamphlets and periodical articles. His chief essays on social and sexual management are: *Male Continence* (Oneida, 1872); *Essay on Scientific Propagation* (Oneida, 1875), and *Mutual Criticism* (Oneida, 1875). Four compilations of Noyes' periodical pieces are especially useful: *The Way of Holiness* (Putney, Vt., 1838) and *The Berean* (Putney, 1847) reprint the central theses of his theological development in the formative period, 1834-1846; *Bible Communism* (Brooklyn, N.Y., 1853), describes social practices at Oneida; *Home-Talks*, ed. Alfred Barron and George Noyes Miller, (Oneida, 1875), is a collection of Noyes' ideas from a later period, taken in shorthand from fireside chats. The three *Annual Reports* of Oneida (1849-1851), and four *Handbooks* of the community (1865, 1867, 1871, 1875), written mainly by Noyes, are the representation of his efforts as he wanted the world to learn of them. A more explicit self-defense is his *Dixon and His Copyists* (Oneida, 1874). Noyes also wrote for and edited religious periodicals: *The Perfectionist* (New Haven, 1834-1836); *The Witness* (Ithaca, N.Y., 1837-1843); *The Perfectionist* (Putney, 1843-1846); *Spiritual Magazine* (Putney, Oneida, 1846-1850); *Free Church Circular* (Oneida, 1850-1851); *The Circular* (Brooklyn, Oneida, 1851-1876); and *The American Socialist* (Oneida, 1876-1879). For a short time, the community published a tiny but fascinating newspaper, *The Daily* (Oneida, 1866-1868).

In addition to the Parker and Lockwood works, Leonard Bernstein presents a clear exposition of some of Noyes' religious ideas in "The Ideas of John Humphrey Noyes, Perfectionist," *American Quarterly* 5 (Summer 1953): 157-165. Ernest R. Sandeen has written a provocative psychoanalytic essay, "John Humphrey Noyes as the New Adam," *Church History* 40 (March 1971): 82-90. Mulford Q. Sibley has an interesting discussion, "Oneida's Challenge to American Culture," in Joseph J. Kwait, ed., *Studies in American Culture* (Minneapolis, 1960), 41-62. Walter D. Edmonds, *The First Hundred Years: 1849-1948* (Oneida, 1948), is a useful sketch of Oneida as a business community. Whitney R. Cross' excellent book, *The Burned-Over District* (Ithaca, 1953), places Noyes in the wider religious framework of western New York during the first half of the nineteenth century, while David M. Ludlum discusses Noyes in a different place and manner in *Social Ferment in Vermont: 1791-1850* (New York, 1939). Two Oneida ladies wrote chatty and informative reminiscences about daily life at the community: Harriet V. Worden, *Old Mansion House Memories* (articles from *The Circular*, 1870-1871; reprint, Oneida, 1950), and Corinna Ackley Noyes, *The Days of My Youth* (Oneida, 1960). An impressively searching and honest account of Noyes' impact on the emotional life of at least one of his children is delivered by Pierrepont Burt Noyes in *My Father's House: An Oneida Boy-hood* (New York, 1937). Of the many works contemporaneous with Noyes, the most helpful are Allen Estlake, *The Oneida Community* (London, 1900), a defense of Noyes; William Hepworth Dixon, *New America* (London, 1867), 2 vols., and his *Spiritual Wives* (London, 1868), 2 vols.; and Hubbard Eastman, *Noyesism Unveiled* (Brattleboro, Vt., 1849), which contains vicious attacks. Noyes' strong relationships with two contemporaries is documented in Wendell and Francis Garrison, *William Lloyd Garrison* (New York, 1885), II, 144-152, 207, and in Charles C. Sellers, *Theophilus, the Battle-Axe* (Philadelphia, 1930), a study of Theophilus Gates. Finally, there is an ordinary account of Oneida, but one decorated by beautiful illustrations, in *Frank Leslie's Illustrated Magazine* 30 (April 2, 9, 16, 1870): 38-41, 49, 54-57, 70-71, 76.

Horace Mann

The enormous literature by and about Horace Mann is carefully catalogued in Clyde King, *Horace Mann, 1796-1859: A Bibliography* (Dobbs Ferry, N.Y., 1966). King locates many scattered Mann manuscripts; the chief collection—and the one I used most extensively—is in the Massachusetts Historical Society, Boston, Mass. The central written sources by Mann are his twelve *Annual Reports of the Secretary of the Board of Education of Massachusetts* (Boston, 1837-1848), available both in the [Massachusetts] *Common School Journal* for those years, and in Mary Peabody Mann, *The Life and Letters of Horace Mann* (Boston, 1891), 5 vols. This biography also reprints Mann's collected *Lectures on Education* (Boston, 1845), as well as several of his speeches delivered at Antioch College late in his career. Most of Mann's addresses and pamphlets against slavery, composed while he served in Congress, were reprinted in *Slavery: Letters and Speeches* (Boston, 1851). I found two speeches in addition to these collections to be especially useful: "Go Forth and Teach: An Oration Delivered before the Authorities of the City of Boston, July 4, 1842" (reprinted by the Commission on the Horace Mann Centennial, National Education Association, Washington, D.C., 1937), and "A Few Thoughts for A Young Man" (Boston, 1850). A great deal of Mann's righteous indignation comes forth in two pamphlet wars with the upholders of traditional authority: Boston School Masters, *Remarks on the Seventh Annual Report of the Honorable Horace Mann, Secretary of the Massachusetts Board of Education* (Boston, 1844); Mann, *Reply to the Remarks of Thirty-One Boston School-Masters* (Boston, 1844); Boston School Masters, *Rejoinder to the Reply of Honorable Horace Mann* (Boston, 1845); Mann, *Answer to the Rejoinder of Twenty-Nine Boston School-Masters* (Boston, 1845); also Reverend M. H. Smith, *The Ark of God on a New Cart* (Boston, 1847); Mann, *Sequel to the So-Called Correspondence between the Rev. M. H. Smith and Horace Mann* (Boston, 1847); Smith, *Reply to the Sequel of Honorable Horace Mann* (Boston, 1847).

Jonathan C. Messerli has written the first scholarly modern biography of Mann, *Horace Mann: A Biography* (New York, 1972). The best of the rest of the Mann biographies is George A. Hubbell, *Horace Mann: Educator, Patriot and Reformer* (Philadelphia, 1910). Also see Louise Hall Thorp, *Until Victory: Horace Mann and Mary Peabody* (Boston, 1953); E. I. F. Williams, *Horace Mann: Educational Statesman* (New York, 1939); and B. A. Hinsdale, *Horace Mann and the Common School Revival* (New York, 1898). Merle Curti wrote a sympathetic but deeply probing essay on Mann in *The Social Ideas of American Educators* (New York, 1935), 101-138. Howard Mumford Jones' "Horace Mann's Crusade," in Daniel Aaron, ed., *America in Crisis* (New York, 1952), 91-107, is facile and insensitive. A recent study by Michael B. Katz, *The Irony of Early School Reform* (Cambridge, Mass., 1968), attacks middle-class moral reformers like Mann for their imposition of values through rigid, centralized institutions upon the lower classes.

Several books and articles are helpful in their discussions on particular phases of Mann's career. Raymond B. Culver, *Horace Mann and Religion in the Massachusetts Public Schools* (New Haven, 1929), and Neil G. McCloskey, *Public Schools and Moral Education* (New York, 1938), treat Mann's often tortuous secularism. Don M. Wolfe, "The Plastic Mind: Tocqueville and Horace Mann," *Western Humanities Review* 11 (Summer 1957): 233-249, in my opinion, greatly overdoes Mann's escape from a sense of sin in his moralistic writings. Joy E. Morgan, *Horace Mann at*

Antioch (Washington, D.C., 1938); and Hubbell, *Horace Mann in Ohio* (New York, 1900), discuss Mann in his last calling as college president, while W. S. Harwood, *Life and Letters of Austin Craig* (New York, 1908), documents Mann's difficult relationship with the young Rev. Craig whom he wanted to woo to Ohio. For the use Mann and others made of phrenology, see John D. Davies, *Phrenology: Fad and Science* (New Haven, 1955). The views of Mann's teacher in these scientific matters, George Combe, are most clearly presented in his *The Constitution of Man* (Edinburgh, 1828), and in his *Lectures on Popular Education* (Boston, 1839). Finally, interesting analogies could be drawn between Mann and another group of conservative intellectuals discussed in Wilson Smith, *Professors and Public Ethics: Studies of Northern Moral Philosophers before the Civil War* (Ithaca, 1956).

Margaret Fuller

The blue-penciling of Margaret Fuller's manuscripts was carried out in the name of propriety by Emerson, William Henry Channing, John F. Clarke, and Margaret's brothers, Arthur and Richard. The shells of her manuscript writings are in Houghton Library, Harvard University, and the Boston Public Library. Her long correspondence with Emerson runs through several volumes of Ralph L. Rusk's edition of *The Letters of Ralph Waldo Emerson* (New York, 1939), 6 vols. An unsuccessful romance is preserved in Julia Ward Howe, ed., *Love-Letters of Margaret Fuller, 1845-1846* (New York, 1903). The heavily blue-penciled but nevertheless indispensable *Memoirs of Margaret Fuller Ossoli* (Boston, 1852, 1875), 2 vols., were edited by Emerson, Channing, and Clarke. Arthur Fuller edited her collected *Works* (Boston, 1860), 4 vols., which include *Art, Literature and the Drama*; *Women in the Nineteenth Century*; *At Home and Abroad*; *Life Without and Life Within*. Margaret Fuller, *Summer on the Lakes* (Boston, 1844), is a rambling account of a trip on the Great Lakes, interspersed with book reviews and philosophical discourses. Fuller's contributions to the *Dial* (1840-1844), her columns in the *New York Tribune* (1844-1846), and other periodical article references are listed as an appendix to Mason Wade's excellent collection, *The Writings of Margaret Fuller* (New York, 1941), 595-600.

In many ways, Thomas Wentworth Higginson's *Margaret Fuller Ossoli* (Boston, 1884), remains the most perceptive biography. A very brief, but well-done biography by Arthur W. Brown, *Margaret Fuller* (New York, 1964), is the best modern study on her, while Mason Wade, *Margaret Fuller: Whetstone of Genius* (New York, 1940), is interesting although sometimes too reserved. Joseph Jay Deiss has uncovered much new material and presents it with vigor and some sentimentality in *The Roman Years of Margaret Fuller: A Biography* (New York, 1969). Perry Miller's edition of Fuller's writing, *Margaret Fuller: American Romantic* (Garden City, N.Y., 1963), is an excellent collection, with a typically insightful running commentary by Miller, who apparently turned to the emotional Fuller with enormous relief after having studied the thin-lipped Emerson for too long at one time. Katharine Anthony, *Margaret Fuller: A Psychological Biography* (New York, 1920), in its day a pioneering application of psychology to history, now seems a little uneven in the quality of its insights.

George William Curtis

George William Curtis wrote and wrote and wrote. His genteel column, "The Easy Chair," appeared in *Harper's Monthly* from 1854 until 1892, and his political editorials graced *Harper's Weekly* between 1863 and 1892. *Harper's* issued three quite representative collections of "Easy Chair" pieces in 1893 and 1894 and also reprinted some of his literary essays in *Literary and Social Essays* (New York, 1894) and *Ars Recte Vivendi* (New York, 1898). Curtis also talked and talked and talked—he was one of the most sought-after orators of his day. His closest friend, Charles Eliot Norton, edited Curtis' *Orations and Addresses* (New York, 1894), 3 vols. This edition is the best single source for Curtis' arguments for civil service reform. Curtis' contemplative voyaging of the early 1850s produced *Nile Notes of a Howadji* (New York, 1851); *The Howadji in Syria* (New York, 1852), and *Lotus-Eating: A Summer Book* (New York, 1852). Lewis P. Shanks brilliantly discusses these books in "Terpsichore, Apollo, and Mrs. Grundy," *Bookman* 67 (June 1928): 409-410. Curtis' *Potiphar Papers* (New York, 1853) and *Prue and I* (New York, 1856) were the most gentle of satires on manners, while his novel *Trumps* (New York, 1861), on the same questions, was his only exploration of a literary form that he found personally uncongenial.

The largest collection of Curtis manuscripts is in the Houghton Library, Harvard University. It consists of short, polished, and generally uninteresting letters, half of which were exchanged with Charles Eliot Norton in the best Brahmin manner of quiet effusions of mutual praise. There is a particularly interesting correspondence, one which demonstrates his considerable political acumen, between Curtis and President Hayes, in the Rutherford B. Hayes Memorial Library, Fremont, Ohio. Gordon Milne, in his careful and inclusive study, *George William Curtis and the Genteel Tradition* (Bloomington, Ind., 1956), contains a full bibliography of Curtis manuscripts, dozens of additional listings of periodical articles by Curtis, and a great number of secondary references. Milne is stronger on Curtis' literary position; his politics is discussed at greater length by an associate and admirer of Curtis, Edward Cary, *George William Curtis* (Boston, 1894). Ari Hoogenboom places Curtis the reformer in a wider context in his valuable study, *Outlawing the Spoils: A History of the Civil Service Reform Movement, 1865-1883* (Urbana, Ill., 1961). John M. Tomsich deals with Curtis as a literary figure in *A Genteel Endeavor: American Culture in the Gilded Age* (Stanford, Calif., 1971). George W. Cooke, *Early Letters of George William Curtis to John S. Dwight, Brook Farm and Concord* (New York, 1898), is a series of musings by a young, self-styled Emersonian individualist, about to vaporize into thinnest air.

For Curtis' early years, see Florence B. Lennon, "The Influence of Brook Farm on George William Curtis, 1842-1872" (Master's thesis, University of Colorado, 1947). Caroline Ticknor edited "Some Early Letters of George William Curtis," *Atlantic Monthly* 114 (September 1914): 363-376. Lyon N. Richardson and Curtis W. Garrison present much of the Curtis-Hayes material in "Notes and Documents: George William Curtis, Rutherford B. Hayes and Civil Service Reform," *Mississippi Valley Historical Review* 32 (September 1945): 235-250.

Edward Bellamy

The most accessible Bellamy manuscripts, lovingly edited by Arthur E. Morgan, are in the Houghton Library, Harvard University. Of particular importance to me were several of Bellamy's typescripts of unpublished stories. In addition, some important manuscripts remain in family hands in Springfield, Massachusetts. I found one very revealing letter from Bellamy in the Henry Demarest Lloyd Manuscripts, State Historical Society of Wisconsin, Madison, Wisconsin. Sylvia E. Bowman, in her detailed study, *The Year 2000: A Critical Biography of Edward Bellamy* (New York, 1958), appends a very lengthy and generally accurate bibliography. The other modern biography is Arthur E. Morgan, *Edward Bellamy* (New York, 1944). Morgan also edited some early Bellamy manuscripts in *The Philosophy of Edward Bellamy* (New York, 1945), while Sylvia E. Bowman edited a collection of articles concerning Bellamy's impact on other nations, *Edward Bellamy Abroad* (New York, 1962).

Four of Bellamy's novels were of central importance to me: *Dr. Heidenhoff's Process* (New York, 1880); *Miss Ludington's Sister* (Boston, 1884); *Looking Backward, 2000-1887* (1888; reprint, 1967), and *Equality* (New York, 1897). In addition to a posthumous collection of his short stories, *The Blindman's World and Other Stories* (Boston, 1898), I found "Extra-Hazardous," *Appleton's Journal* 3 (November 1877): 436-441, to be of major interest. During the years of his greatest fame, Bellamy wrote for *The Nationalist* and *The New Nation*, publications of the Nationalist movement (see the lists in Bowman, *The Year 2000*, 347-375). Several of these pieces and others as well are collected in *Edward Bellamy Speaks Again!* (Kansas City, Mo., 1937), and in *Talks on Nationalism* (Chicago, 1938).

Bellamy's contemporary, Laurence Gronlund, anticipated much of the Nationalist program in *The Co-Operative Commonwealth* (1883; reprint, 1965), and contributed to the Nationalist movement explicitly in *Our Destiny* (Boston, 1891). English critic William Morris countered what he considered to be Bellamy's "cockney paradise" in his extraordinary, bucolic utopian romance, *News from Nowhere* (1890; in his *Collected Works*, XVI, London, 1912),

13-211, and in his review, "Looking Backward," *Commonweal* 5 (June 22, 1889): 184-195.

Of the many modern commentaries on Bellamy, Daniel Aaron's *Men of Good Hope* (New York, 1951), 92-132, is the most sympathetic and the fairest. He discusses Bellamy as an enormously hopeful but by no means simple "village utopian." John L. Thomas provides a lengthy and interesting discussion of Bellamy in his introduction to the 1967 reprint of *Looking Backward*. Thomas is currently completing a study of the utopian thought of Bellamy, Henry Demerest Lloyd, and Henry George. David Bleich feels that Bellamy was something of a precursor of the liberationism of Herbert Marcuse in his "Eros and Bellamy," *American Quarterly* 16 (Fall 1964): 445-459. I have maintained that Bellamy turned away from this position. Additional discussions of Bellamy include: George D. Becker, "Edward Bellamy's Utopia, American Plan," *Antioch Review* 14 (June 1954): 181-194; Louis Filler, "Edward Bellamy and the Spiritual Unrest," *American Journal of Economics and Sociology* 8 (April 1949): 239-249; John Hope Franklin, "Edward Bellamy and Nationalism," *New England Quarterly* 11 (December 1938): 739-772; Elizabeth Sadler, "One Book's Influence," *New England Quarterly* 17 (December 1944): 530-555; two articles by Joseph Schiffman, "Edward Bellamy's Altruistic Man," *American Quarterly* 6 (Fall 1954): 195-202, and "Edward Bellamy's Religious Thought," *Publications of the Modern Language Association* 68 (September 1953): 716-732; and two pieces by Robert L. Shurter, "The Literary Works of Edward Bellamy," *American Literature* 5 (November 1933): 229-234, and "The Writing of Looking Backward," *South Atlantic Quarterly* 38 (July 1939): 255-261.

Ignatius Donnelly

Martin Ridge's carefully researched political biography, *Ignatius Donnelly: The Portrait of a Politician* (Chicago, 1962), contains an excellent bibliography. The Donnelly Manuscripts, located in the Minnesota Historical Society, St. Paul, Minnesota, are ponderous in scope. His Diaries (1856-1901) are extremely revealing, and his letterpress Letterbooks are strong for his years as Alliance and

Populist organizer. The Diaries for the years 1856 to 1884 are available in a well-edited two-volume Ph.D. dissertation by Theodore Nydahl, "The Diary of Ignatius Donnelly" (Minneapolis, 1943). Donnelly edited two weekly newspapers, the (St. Paul) *Anti-Monopolist*, 1874-1878, and the (St. Paul-Minneapolis) *Representative*, 1893-1901. In his editorials in these journals, especially during his Populist years, Donnelly spelled out most fully his political philosophy.

Donnelly wrote eight books: *The American People's Money* (Chicago, 1895), a pot-boiler arguing for cheap money; *Atlantis: The Antediluvian World* (New York, 1882); *Caesar's Column* (1890; reprint, 1960); *The Cipher* (Minneapolis, 1899); *Doctor Huguet* (Chicago, 1891), a relatively liberal novel on race relations; *The Golden Bottle* (St. Paul, 1892), a thinly fictionalized Populist tract; *The Great Cryptogram* (Chicago, 1888); and *Ragnorak: The Age of Fire and Gravel* (New York, 1883). Of Donnelly's many pamphlets, I found his propaganda pieces, *Statement of the Basis of Organization of the City of Ninninger* (Ninninger City, 1856), and *Minnesota: Address Delivered at the Broadway-House, New York City, March 27, 1857* (New York, 1857), to be wonderfully florid. Many of his congressional speeches were reprinted as pamphlets, as is still the custom (cf. Ridge, *Ignatius Donnelly*, 409-410).

Several periodical articles are of special use. The rise and fall of Donnelly, the real estate boomer, is recorded in Dudley S. Brainard, "Ninninger, A Boom Town of the Fifties," *Minnesota History* 13 (June 1932): 127-151. Three pieces by John D. Hicks place Donnelly in a wider Populist setting: "The Origins and Early History of the Farmer's Alliance in Minnesota," *Mississippi Valley Historical Review* 9 (December 1922): 203-226; "The People's Party in Minnesota," *Minnesota Historical Bulletin* 10 (November 1924): 531-556; "The Political Career of Ignatius Donnelly," *Mississippi Valley Historical Review* 8 (September-June 1921): 80-132. Oscar Handlin, "American Views of the Jews at the Opening of the Twentieth Century," *Publications of the Jewish American Historical Society* 40 (June 1951): 323-344, and John Higham, "Anti-Semitism in the Gilded Age: A Reinterpretation," *Mississippi Valley Historical Review* 43 (March 1957): 559-578, are the best starting points for the perhaps overdone discussion of Populist anti-

Semitism. William F. and Elizabeth S. Friedman, *The Shakespearean Ciphers Examined* (Cambridge, Mass., 1957), is a sound analysis by professional cryptologists of those critics who have attempted to discredit Shakespeare's authorship by revealing another writer's coded hand in plays attributed to Shakespeare. Alexander Saxon quite intelligently compares *Looking Backward* to *Caesar's Column*, in "Caesar's Column: The Dialogue of Utopia and Catastrophe," *American Quarterly* 19 (Summer 1967): 224-238.

John D. Hicks' book, *The Populist Revolt* (Minneapolis, 1931), though no longer fashionable, started the modern discussion of populism, and in many ways it remains the most detailed study. Hofstadter's *The Age of Reform* was the most powerful book in the American historiography of the 1950s because of its intellectual sophistication and its reflection of an American need for consensus. His use of social psychology led him to attack more than to sympathize, while Norman Pollack, *The Populist Response to Industrial America* (Cambridge, Mass., 1962), and Walter T. K. Nugent, *The Tolerant Populists* (Chicago, 1963), are useful correctives to Hofstadter but perhaps argue a little too hard for the consistency and rationality of a group of men who had to struggle very strenuously to formulate a meaningful position in an extremely hostile world. When historians feel that rationalism is the stake, they can proceed to reductionism in any number of directions. C. Vann Woodward, *Tom Watson: Agrarian Rebel* (New York, 1938), is a model biography, always critical but also always compassionate. Watson's life paralleled that of Donnelly in many ways, and because of the heightened insight of Woodward's book, the analogy might gain special meaning for the reader.

William Dean Howells

In addition to writing *The World of Chance* (New York, 1893), William Dean Howells confronted the idea of utopia in *A Traveler from Altruria* (New York, 1894) and in a series of articles in *Cosmopolitan* magazine written from 1892 to 1894, reprinted in part in *Through the Eye of the Needle* (New York, 1907), and in Clara and Rudolf Kirk, eds., *Letters of an Altrurian Traveler* (Gainesville, Fla., 1961). Howells wrote four novels concerning Shaker communities, which raised many of the issues discussed here: *The Undiscovered Country* (New York, 1880); *The Day of Their Wedding* (New York, 1896); *A Parting and a Meeting* (New York, 1896); and *The Vacation of the Kelwyns* (New York, 1920). *New Leaf Mills* (New York, 1913) was a semiautobiographical account of an attempt by Howells' father to recapture the spirit of rural community in a small economic experiment with a mill. *A Hazard of New Fortunes* (New York, 1890), Howells' most intense and complex work, is filled with the sense of personal doubt and social dislocation which later informed *The World of Chance*. Three memoirs reflect Howells' mature reflections on lost youth, lost community, lost Eden: *Three Villages* (Boston, 1884); *A Boy's Town* (New York, 1890), and *Years of My Youth* (New York, 1916).

Of the enormous quantity of Howells criticism and biography, I found most useful Kenneth S. Lynn, *William Dean Howells: An American Life* (New York, 1971); Mildred Howells, *Life in Letters of William Dean Howells* (Garden City, N.Y., 1928), 2 vols., and Edwin H. Cady's two-volume biography, *The Road to Realism*, and *The Realist at War* (Syracuse, N.Y., 1956, 1958). A good short study is Clara Kirk and Rudolf Kirk, *William Dean Howells* (New York, 1962). Robert L. Hough, *The Quiet Rebel: William Dean Howells as Social Commentator* (Lincoln, Nebraska, 1959), is a very literal reading of Howells' motives, while George C. Carrington, Jr., portrays, with considerable insight, if with too much intellectual structure, the anxieties and doubts that anguished Howells, in *The Immense Complex Drama: The World and Art of William Dean Howells* (Columbus, Ohio, 1966). This theme of double-mindedness is developed, in another form, concerning Howells' attitudes toward women, in William Wasserstrom, "William Dean Howells' The Indelible Stain," *New England Quarterly* 32 (December, 1959): 486-495. The importance to Howells of the memory of the village is emphasized by Benjamin A. Sokoloff, "William Dean Howells and the Ohio Village: A Study in Environment and Art," *American Quarterly* 11 (Spring 1959): 58-75.

INDEX

xix, 7, 79, 106
See also New communities

Warren, Josiah, 4-19 *passim,*
   43
absolute truth, 5
equitable commerce, 8, 9
first principle, 7
individualism, 8
inventions of, 10
music and mathematics, 9
Owen, influence of, 7
political views, 12

theories, failure of, 18
time stores, 15
utopian communities
   idea of, 8, 11, 12, 14, 15
   participation in, 15
view of science and God, 9
Weaver, James B., 138
Weld, Theodore, 45
Willard, Frances, 120
Workingman's party, 21

Yale Theological Seminary,
   44, 45